SNAFU

SNAFU

GREAT AMERICAN MILITARY DISASTERS

GEOFFREY REGAN

AVON BOOKS ◆ NEW YORK

SNAFU: GREAT AMERICAN MILITARY DISASTERS is an original publication
of Avon Books. This work has never before appeared in book form.

AVON BOOKS
A division of
The Hearst Corporation
1350 Avenue of the Americas
New York, New York 10019

Copyright © 1993 by Geoffrey Regan
Cover Art by Dan Troiani, *Retreat By Recoil*; Illustration by Christopher Erkmann
Maps by Gillian Regan
Published by arrangement with the author
Library of Congress Catalog Card Number: 93–24828
ISBN: 0-380-76755-4

Library of Congress Cataloging in Publication Data:
  Regan, Geoffrey.
Snafu : great American military disasters / Geoffrey Regan.
    p. cm.
1. United States—History, Military.   2. Disasters—United States—
History. I. Title.
E181.R35 1994   92-24828
355'.00973—dc20   CIP

First Avon Books Trade Printing: November 1993

AVON TRADEMARK REG. U.S. PAT. OFF. AND IN OTHER COUNTRIES, MARCA REGISTRADA,
HECHO EN U.S.A.

Printed in the U.S.A.

OPM 10 9 8 7 6 5 4 3 2 1

To Janine

Contents

Introduction

IN AN INCREASINGLY COMPLEX WORLD PROFESSIONAL INCOMPE-
tence is a matter of concern not only to those who suffer
from it—and who can place his hand on his heart and say
that he has never experienced the frustration that comes
from a spiraling in standards—but also to the competent
members of a profession whose concern is to maintain its
reputation. It is hardly in the interests of lawyers, politicians or doctors, or indeed the members of a hundred different callings, to shelter those who are not properly
qualified for their job, or whose performance brings the
reputation of the profession under scrutiny. Professional
associations are jealous in defense of standards of behavior that may have been built up over generations, perhaps
centuries. Even as well established a calling as medicine
was once considered the preserve of charlatans and moun-
tebanks. So it seems perfectly reasonable to me to subject
the military profession to the same kind of scrutiny that
others have been compelled to impose upon themselves.
It may be argued, of course, that the difficulties inherent
in the military profession impose stresses of an entirely
different kind to those in other occupations. Few doctors
or accountants literally put their lives on the line during
their professional practices. Nevertheless, if the pressures
of high command are likely to make such remarkable demands on an individual then it is clearly incumbent on
those making senior appointments to ensure that they
weed out those who are incapable of filling them before
they can do any serious damage.

My aim in writing this book is a relatively simple one,

namely to illustrate a problem that undeniably exists and has existed since men became civilized enough to inflict war on each other. The British military psychologist Norman Dixon was, I believe, the first person to subject this field of study to his own discipline of experimental psychology in his brilliant book, *On the Psychology of Military Incompetence*. Dixon's concern was to identify a distinct personality type that is prone to reach incorrect decisions under the stressful conditions of military service. However, in order to identify this "authoritarian personality"—of which there are few better examples than American general Douglas MacArthur—he needed to "play down the other factors in order to focus more clearly upon possible psychological determinants" in the events that surround military disasters. He chose to subject military incompetence to certain laws. In his view "good commanders remain pretty much the same. Likewise bad commanders have much in common with each other." It is at this point that military history and psychology diverge. As a military historian I am not much concerned with general theories of history, rather with the individual features that make each occasion unique. The psychologist, on the other hand, examines the causes of military disasters to identify factors that contribute to them, in order to establish general laws.

As a historian rather than a psychologist or soldier, I have chosen to present the subjects in their entirety, with a full range of factors, one or more of which were involved in causing the military disaster. Thus, the inability of a tetchy Admiral Vernon to work with a less able and over-promoted General Wentworth goes far to explain the British debacle at Cartagena. The selection of the brave but unbalanced John Burgoyne to lead the British advance from Canada in 1777 was less damaging to the British cause than the fact that the incompetent Lord George Germain in London had muddled the plans so badly that neither Burgoyne nor the British commander-in-chief General Howe knew precisely what was expected of them. And poor gouty Arthur St. Clair had every reason to feel short-changed by the Washington administration that failed to equip his expedition properly and sent him to fight the Indians with a bunch of cowardly militiamen who were as likely to plunder their own supplies as they were to give a good account of themselves against the redskins.

The psychologist, of course, would find his explanation of some of my disasters by subjecting the generals to the couch. The feeble and timorous William Hull might make a suitable case for treatment. But he was out of his depth against the arch-professional General Brock and, like St. Clair, he found it impossible to get much out of the militia that made up much of his force. Hull had not looked for high command and certainly qualifies as a victim rather than a villain in our rogues' gallery. Would Norman Dixon have found much to psychoanalyze in Lieutenant General John Whitelocke, the grim and uncouth officer sent to command the British expedition to Buenos Aires in 1806? Whitelocke cuts an unlovable figure during the whole episode but again is merely a victim of a British government that had taken leave of its senses. The task Whitelocke was set was impossible from the first and his failure certain. What might interest Dixon, however, is the particular way in which he failed. And what of the American commander Stephen Kearney, who, having just achieved one of the epic marches of American history, lost control of himself and his men and undertook a battle as if to stretch his legs or to keep his men from getting bored? His failure was an extraordinary one, quite unnecessary and perfectly ridiculous in the context of the Mexican War.

The Civil War marks a watershed in American history as it does in this book. The tone of the subject is darker. There is less that is bizarre, more that is grim—and tragic. The blunders, when they occur, are very bloody ones. At Chickamauga Rosecrans and Bragg, like too unwilling wrestlers, lumber about looking for an opening. So ponderous are the movements that it comes like a shaft of lightning against a stormy sky when Rosecrans makes his fatal mistake and Longstreet exploits it, cutting the Union Army in half. Perhaps Freud would have been able to account for Rosecrans's moment of madness?

My choice of Gettysburg and Cold Harbor was conditioned by the need to resist the easy pickings presented by a series of blunderers who led the Army of the Potomac to unnecessary disasters. Ambrose Burnside presents a figure comparable to that of General Redvers Buller in Britain and Marshal Achille Bazaine in France. Each had enjoyed success at lower levels of command but each was incapable of the highest office and failed totally to come to terms with the task of commander-in-chief of an army. Burnside's blunders at Fredericksburg, the Crater and elsewhere make grim reading and yet it is difficult to blame him for mistakes that could have been predicted by a more rigorous selection panel. Ulysses S. Grant and Robert E. Lee, on the other hand, stand high in most military historians' list of great commanders. They need no apologists and so their reputations are immune from the sniping of writers like myself. Each of them is fully capable of standing before the Court of History and admitting his grievous faults in battle: Grant's loss of patience at Cold Harbor, and Lee's flight from reality at Gettysburg. Their mistakes led to two of the bloodiest episodes of the entire Civil War— and Lee's, quite possibly, to a turning point in the entire military struggle. Unlike Hull and Burnside, such great commanders cannot accuse those who appointed them. Their failures were their own, proving that in the stress of battle the line between success and failure can be a very thin one even for the greatest commander.

After the Civil War the Spanish-American War of 1898 has, with apologies to those for whom any war is bloody and unforgivable, an Alice in Wonderland flavor. The destruction of the Spanish fleet at Manila by Admiral Dewey introduces us to an incompetent commander with a heart, a man willing to accept the shame and disgrace of defeat rather than inflict death and suffering on his men. Unlike Burnside, Admiral Montojo was not prepared to make mere gestures with the lives of those he commanded. He duly anchored his ships where the Americans could sink them in shallow water, hoping his men could paddle ashore rather than drown.

It may be asked why I have selected no examples from the First World War. After all, the United States—though late into the field—tried to make up for lost time by squandering the lives of her troops with the same gay abandon shown by her British and French allies in 1916. The truth, though, is that it was not until 1918 that large numbers of American troops reached France, by which time the increased professionalism of the combatants saved the Americans—who often fought in conjunction with the French—from making memorable mistakes of their own.

The same cannot be said of the Second World War. American isolationism after 1918 seemed to have its most potent effect on military science. Thus, in contrast with the tremendous advances in tank and aircraft development made in Fascist Germany and Japan—and to a lesser extent in France—America like Britain looked on the 1914–18 struggle as the war that had "ended war." They were wrong and they were going to have to pay for it. The American baptism of fire in North Africa—at Sidi Bou Zid and Kasserine—was a particularly harsh one. Green troops and overripe commanders, most of First World War vintage, were pitched into battle against elite German fighting men with the best equipment and skilled commanders. If the Americans can be accused of anything it surely must be the unprofessionalism, particularly at highest levels, that had failed to prepare their men for modern combat. Yet it was a lesson the Americans quickly learned. A starker and altogether grimmer affair was that of Operation Tiger in 1944, where a thousand lives were lost through a chapter of accidents, each of which seemed insignificant in itself yet taken together subjected American soldiers to a cruel martyrdom in the cold, dark waters of the sea off Devon in England. And because the preparations for D day were so advanced the truth of this blunder was concealed not just until the end of the war but for more than thirty years afterwards.

The folly of "Bull" Halsey at Leyte Gulf was too important to omit from any study of incompetence. Halsey was a great, fighting admiral but his failure to appreciate the wider purpose of the truly oceanic fighting at Leyte was frankly unforgivable. It was leadership of a B western kind that might have enabled the Japanese to inflict a stinging defeat on the Americans even at so late a stage in the war. Had the Japanese admirals—notably Kurita—not made even greater errors of judgment Halsey might have been punished most severely.

Since the Second World War the United States has taken on the mantle of Defender of the Free World, a role that has involved her in numerous difficult and unfulfilling missions. We have moved from the battlefield to the politician's office and yet errors have not grown less. In the person of Douglas MacArthur the Americans had a commander who had grown beyond the point of criticism. His messianic personality—clearly masking a complex of inner doubts—made him almost impossible to be restrained by even presidential power. An aged and paranoiac Titan, whose best days were far behind him, was a poor choice to fight the first great struggle of the Cold War. If MacArthur failed in Korea it was because he should never have been there in the first place and Truman acted only just in time to remove him. In a nuclear age it was dangerous to leave such toys in the hands of men in their dotage.

Like great battles performed offstage in Shakespeare's plays, the wars of the past were distant affairs, reported days afterwards and sanitized before reaching the public by being filtered through the various levels of command. Vietnam changed all that. It was the first television war and it is astonishing that the American service chiefs failed to see television as the great propaganda weapon it undoubtedly was. The war was being fought in the "hearts and minds" of ordinary Americans and yet—during the Tet offensive—the Communists were able to carry their message, even if it was only the simple one that they were not beaten, straight into the homes of the American voter. It was a blunder that changed the progress of a war as clearly as a disaster on the battlefield. Nor had President Carter learned this lesson when, after Operation Impossible to rescue the Iranian hostages had failed, he allowed Ayatollah Khomeini and his fanatical followers to ram home to the American people the full humiliation they had suffered. Never was defeat more real for a beaten people than the sight of their burned and dead warriors being picked over and desecrated *in their own front rooms.*

My final selection had to be the second Gulf War (as opposed to the first Iran/Iraq conflict)—the unnecessary war, as it is now being widely called. The final conflict was the outcome of failed American policy, and if ever there was an example of a president shooting himself in the foot, it was George Bush with Saddam Hussein, the leader he had encouraged as a counterweight to the fundamentalist regime in Iran. Hindsight might make us bold in condemning Bush's failure to complete the overthrow of the dictator and, because in democratic countries the voice of the people prevails, it is Bush and not Saddam Hussein who has gone.

In conclusion I would like to stress that it has never been my intention to snipe at reputations or belittle the achievements of brave men. As a historian I have striven to illustrate the facts of military incompetence and to show that failure within the profession of arms stems from a very wide range of factors. In a sense the wonder should be that incompetence has not been more widespread. This book has concerned itself with those cases where the difficulties inherent in the tasks were too great for the participants to solve. The consequences were terrible in terms of human suffering, and for that reason—if for no other—they deserve to be studied and their lessons pondered.

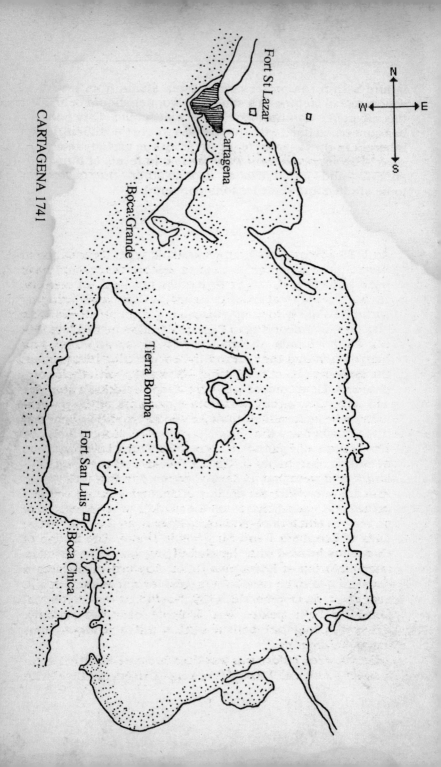

CARTAGENA 1741

Fort St Lazar

Cartagena

Boca Grande

Tierra Bomba

Fort San Luis

Boca Chica

N
W — E
S

The Siege of Cartagena, 1741

In 1739 A BRITISH SEA CAPTAIN NAMED ROBERT JENKINS FOUND himself at the center of a cause célèbre that would have been farcical had its consequences not been so serious. He was asked to attend the House of Commons, bringing with him a nasty-looking object—his mummified ear—in a glass bottle. According to Captain Jenkins he had lost this ear at the hands of Spanish privateers, who first half hanged him and then cut off the ear, bidding him present the bleeding object to his king—George II—with their compliments. How much truth there was in Jenkins's story we will never know, but in Britain opponents of the government were determined to make the most of this opportunity to embarrass the "peace party" of Sir Robert Walpole. The actions of Spanish privateers had long been the bane of British merchants in the Caribbean and the South Atlantic, and were just as deeply resented in Britain's American colonies. With the decline of Spanish power it seemed incumbent upon Britain—as the world's preeminent naval power—to teach the Spaniards a lesson, as they had in the days of Elizabeth I and Sir Francis Drake. The House of Commons buzzed with the kind of jingoism more usual in later Victorian or Edwardian times. The ordeal of Captain Jenkins was to be used as a pretext for war against Spain, and when, on October 19, 1739, hostilities were declared, London's bells pealed out. Walpole observed ruefully, "They may ring their bells now, they will be wringing their hands before long."

Only a week before war was declared a new British commander—Admiral Edward Vernon—arrived in the Carib-

bean to replace Commodore Brown. His instructions were
clear: "to commit all hostilities he could against the Spaniards, protect Jamaica, and assist the colonists of Georgia
and South Carolina if they were attacked." To this end, he
attacked Porto Bello in November and succeeded in destroying its defenses. It was a victory of sorts but in a
Britain anxious for success its importance was exaggerated. Vernon became the hero of the hour, and his words
on Caribbean strategy were set in bronze. It was Vernon's
view that a blow against Cartagena, a port city on the Caribbean coast of Colombia, would weaken Spain's influence
and trade, and there were many influential men, on both
sides of the Atlantic, who were prepared to take Vernon at
his word. When Vernon reconnoitred Cartagena and declared, "I think I know now as much of the avenues to their
harbors as they do themselves," it was tantamount to a
divine instruction that Cartagena should become the target
for Britain's next attack. A combined operation was
planned for nine thousand troops—supplied by both Britain and her American colonies—to cooperate with Vernon's fleet in the capture of Cartagena. But Vernon had
severe reservations about the role allocated to the army.

In Vernon's view Spain's trade could be destroyed only
if Britain commanded the seas. By forcing Spain to open
her harbors to British traders and by depriving her of Pe-
ruvian bullion she would be forced to make peace or else
face bankruptcy. There really was no need for an army of
occupation, which might waste away in the dreadful climate of the Caribbean. For Vernon the army was almost
irrelevant. It was his fleet that was vital, and his conduct
during the subsequent siege of Cartagena must be seen in
terms of his desire to minimize damage to his ships. For
a start, Vernon's fleet was very short of seamen and the
arrival of twenty-two more undermanned ships from Britain, with sickly crews, would swiftly exhaust the local supply of seamen. Vernon knew that a Franco-Spanish fleet of
thirty ships was in the Caribbean and so he could never
afford to relax. In the event of an attack on Cartagena, Vernon suspected that France might come to Spain's aid by a
swift descent on Jamaica. And it was the fear of being overwhelmed at sea that dominated Vernon's thinking throughout 1740 and 1741.

During the spring of 1740 recruiting for the expedition

was carried out on both sides of the Atlantic, and by April
1 British soldiers were assembling on the Isle of Wight,
there to be drilled by Brigadier General Wentworth. The
army commander was to be Lord Cathcart, an able orga-
nizer who was to find his every effort thwarted by the incompetence of the War Office. The main problem was that
Britain had enjoyed a quarter century of peace, and because the idea of a standing army had been anathema to
her politicians, Britain's military machine was not just
rusty but positively decrepit. The quality of recruits was
risible, Cathcart commenting, "They may be useful a year
hence, but at present they have not strength to handle their
arms." The aim had been to raise six new regiments of
marines, but the opportunity to introduce new blood had
been missed and the new units were produced by trans-
ferring half the men of nine existing regiments and a third
from another. To compound the farce one of the regiments
thus denuded was subsequently ordered to sail to the West
Indies on active service. Cathcart was worried from the
start that what new blood he did have would be unable to
endure the rigors of the climate in the Caribbean, which
had always been a graveyard for European soldiers.

News from across the Atlantic did not improve matters.
It was reported that the deputy governor of Virginia, Colonel Spotswood, who was to have been second-in-command
to Cathcart, had died. In view of Wentworth's skills as a
drill master, amply demonstrated by his work on the Isle
of Wight, Cathcart pressed for him to be appointed to Spotswood's place. A worse decision could hardly have been
made, as events were to show. Adept and confident at taking orders, Wentworth lacked the skills necessary to give
them effectively. He had not led a major military force before and was to demonstrate the dangers of promoting a
man beyond his ability.

By July 1740 Cathcart was content that his troops were
as prepared as they were ever going to be and informed the
Admiralty that he would shortly be ready to sail. Unfortunately, the problem of manpower was not confined to the
army alone, and the army commander now learned that the
fleet would not be ready for some weeks, due to a shortage
of sailors. Although by mid August the six thousand British
troops were ready aboard the transports they were kept in
port by contrary winds. The soldiers, cooped up for six

weeks in the crowded transports, consumed much of the food intended for the voyage and many developed scurvy, even though fresh fruit and vegetables were available a "stone's throw away" on land. Sixty men died of scurvy. Even though at last the winds became favorable the fleet did not set sail. News of a French fleet sailing westward made it essential to reinforce the naval escort. More ships were assembled for an escort but it was soon found that although there were ships in plenty there were not enough sailors to man them. There was no alternative but for the now-fuming Cathcart to remedy the deficiency and turn over two of his line regiments—the 34th and 36th—as well as six hundred of his new marines, to act as sailors for the duration of the voyage. This set an unfortunate precedent for the whole operation.

It had originally been intended to keep the destination of the fleet secret. Cathcart certainly believed this was still so and was astonished when one of his secret orders was reported to him as being the small talk of the coffee houses in Portsmouth. The national newspapers published details of the fleet's destination as well as a full account of the troops being sent and the strength of the fleet. Any Spanish spy would have found himself redundant.

It was not until November that the fleet eventually set sail—four months after the troops had first gone aboard their transports. Flying the flag of Admiral Sir Challenor Ogle, the armada sailed to the Caribbean, to rendezvous at Jamaica with Admiral Vernon's squadron. The first ship arrived at Prince Rupert's Bay on December 12 and the rest within the following few days. During the voyage 484 men died of smallpox, scurvy, typhus and dysentery, including General Cathcart himself, whose poor condition was exacerbated by too liberal a dosage of Epsom salts. The death of Cathcart was a blow from which the expedition never recovered. His deputy, Brigadier General Wentworth—as we have already seen—was not up to the task and consequently allowed the naval commanders, notably the dominant Vernon, to intrude in matters of military jurisdiction.

At Jamaica Wentworth first met the American troops, under the command of Colonel Gooch. Like the recruiting officers in Britain, the Americans had filled their ranks with poor quality material—men physically and mentally unsuited to the rigors of campaigning in harsh conditions, ready to run away at the first opportunity or mutiny if the chance arose. It was not a promising prospect for Anglo-American cooperation, especially when Colonel Gooch found out that the British authorities were refusing to pay and provision his men. The result was that the American soldiers were forced to "live off the country"—no easy task in Jamaica at that time. Nor were the Americans any more resistant to the scurvy, dysentery and yellow fever that had already begun to reduce the British ranks. By the beginning of 1741, Wentworth's combined command of nine thousand Anglo-American troops had lost over six hundred dead and fifteen hundred sick.

Vernon's combined fleet was now held up by fear of French intentions. With a strong French fleet in Caribbean waters under the Marquis d'Antin, the British dare not begin an attack on Cartagena that would leave Jamaica open to counterattack. Fortunately for Vernon, the local mosquito was impartial in European mercantile struggles, and struck at French sailors as willingly as at their Anglo-Saxon counterparts. The marquis, Vernon was soon pleased to hear, was forced to return to France, his fleet decimated by yellow "jack." This cleared Vernon for immediate action and he pressed Wentworth to prepare an assault on Cartagena, which he assured the general was an easy target. Wentworth was merely putty in the admiral's hands. Aware of his own inadequacies and his fortuitous promotion, Wentworth was only too eager to please his distinguished colleague. Unlike Vernon, Wentworth had no experience of warfare in the Caribbean and like so many British officers of that period he had had no command experience. His own lack of self-confidence and his total dependence on the navy led him to subordinate himself to Vernon. This was unfortunate, because ashore Wentworth was supposed to be in sole command. And for the important decisions of the expedition a General Council of War was to be called, which would consist of two senior land officers, two senior sea officers and Governor Trelawny of Jamaica, if he were available. At such councils a decision could be reached by a simple majority, though either Vernon or Wentworth needed to be a part of the majority vote. However, from the start Vernon viewed himself as the president of the council, a position to which he had no right. Wentworth's deference to Vernon encouraged him to allocate 37 percent of his entire military force to the navy to make up manpower deficiencies. Wentworth assumed that these men would be returned when needed but this was easier said than done—and as events were to show, Vernon was loath to release his new sailors. Thus instead of a combined operation Vernon behaved as commander-in-chief and acted as if the army were there to serve the needs of the fleet and not vice versa.

On March 4, the British fleet arrived off Cartagena and prepared to assault the city. Much of Vernon's confidence in his ability to take the city rested on the fact that it had been successfully besieged four times in the past: in 1560, 1565, 1586 and—most recently—in 1697, by the French. However, after this last disaster, a Spanish engineer, Juan de Herrera y Sotomayor, had been employed to strengthen the city's defenses. The Spanish viceroy, Sebastian d'Eslava, had 2,095 regular soldiers and 1,500 militia at his disposal for the defense of the city, but his main hopes rested on the heavily gunned fortresses that ringed Cartagena, where the veteran Spanish officer Don Blas de Lezo held command. Far from being helpless, Cartagena was now a tough nut to crack and Vernon's tendency to underestimate Spanish morale was a fatal flaw in the leadership of the operation.

First it was necessary for Vernon's ships to break into the great harbor in order to land Wentworth's troops. The only entrance, known as the Boca Chica, was lined with a series of strong forts that would have to be destroyed by the guns of the fleet or else captured by a marine landing before the ships could pass through the Boca Chica, over the boom and past the ships that the Spaniards had scuttled to block the channel.

On March 9 Admiral Ogle, with the *Princess Amelia*, the *Norfolk*, the *Russell* and the *Shrewsbury*, began the bombardment of the two smaller outer forts, St. Jago and San Felipe, easily battering them into submission. This was followed the next day by a full landing on Tierra Bomba by all Wentworth's troops, with the exception of the 34th and 36th regiments, who were needed by Vernon, and the Americans, whom nobody trusted to behave themselves.

Tierra Bomba commanded the Boca Chica channel, facing one remaining fortress, known as Fort San Luis. Although this was the strongest fort he had faced so far, there

was little in the Spanish castle that should have worried
Wentworth. Yet Vernon and Ogle were forced to watch from
their ships in amazement as the general began to dig in on
the island, employing double and triple sentries everywhere as if he expected to be assaulted from the rear. Two
days passed and nothing was attempted. Vernon now wrote
a peremptory letter to Wentworth of a kind that is rarely—
if ever—sent by one commander to another. Addressing
Wentworth as if he were a particularly obtuse infant, Vernon suggested that he should "push forward part of [his]
force against Fort San Luis," that he should "put the rest
of [his] men under canvas"; further, that he should "hasten
[his] engineers to the siege of the fort" and that he should
use just a few men as sentries instead of his whole army.
That Wentworth did not explode on the receipt of such a
patronizing script says a lot for him. In fact, he knew something Vernon did not know and would scarcely have believed anyway. The army had set out with just one specialist
engineer officer competent to conduct a siege—Jonas
Moore—and he had not yet arrived at Cartagena. The other
engineers, as Wentworth knew only too well, had been selected from the new recruits and did not know their business. Nor were his artillerymen real gunners. They had also
been selected from the raw recruits and had set up their
battery in direct line with the British camp, with the result
that every shot the Spaniards returned either hit them or
fell amongst the soldiers' tents, killing and wounding a
hundred men on the first day. Wentworth was ashamed to
admit these deficiencies to Vernon, yet soon he would need
both naval engineers and naval gunners to do the work
that the army could not do for itself.

On March 15 Jonas Moore finally arrived. He at once
surveyed Fort San Luis and concluded that he would need
a minimum of sixteen hundred men to construct a siege
battery. In the hostile climate and with the need to clear
heavily wooded ground, this large force of laborers would
be essential. When Vernon heard this he was furious but
had to accept the report of an expert. While he waited for
the army to capture this "paltry fort" his ships had to lay
out at sea—at the mercy of the winds and with some of
them losing their anchor cables, which were cut by the
rocky seabed.

Wentworth continued to press Vernon to release more

of his soldiers, notably Cavendish and Bland's regulars.
Vernon responded by sending two hundred Americans
ashore but telling Wentworth that he would spare no more
until the fleet was safely in the lagoon. While the soldiers
labored long and hard to build their siege battery, Vernon
launched an independent raid by sailors and marines
against the Albanicos battery, which had been troubling
Wentworth's men in their work. It was a great success,
though it encouraged Vernon to discount the fighting qualities of the Spanish troops. The truth was that the battery
had been sparsely defended and that, with a stout wall in
front of them, the Spaniards could be relied on to give a
good account of themselves.

On March 21 Vernon summoned a naval council of war
to discuss the army's lack of progress. Frustrated beyond
patience, Vernon decided to assault Fort San Luis with four
men-of-war, not even informing Wentworth of his decision
to attack. But news then reached him that Wentworth's
battery was ready: twenty twenty-four-pounder cannon.
Even the naval engineers at the site were satisfied. The
bombardment began but—contrary to expectation—the
Spaniards did not surrender. And worse was to follow:
Wentworth's only reliable engineer—Jonas Moore—was
killed alongside his guns.

Vernon was beside himself with anger, berating Wentworth for not taking the fort. As he pointed out, the rainy
season was imminent, which would put a stop to operations. Vernon now ordered four of his battleships to attack
Fort San Luis. What happened next was the clearest indication of the fact that ships cannot silence forts—a lesson
that, it would appear, needs to be learned in every fresh
generation. After a heavy bombardment the fort remained
almost unscathed—though Vernon claimed it had been silenced—while the *Boyne* and the *Hampton Court* were
badly damaged and the *Prince Frederick* was disabled by
enemy fire. In the words of Tobias Smollett, author of the
novel *Roderick Random*, who was present:

> Having cannonaded the fort during the space of four
> hours, we were all ordered to slip our cables and sheer
> off; but next day the engagement was renewed and con-
> tinued from the morning till the afternoon when the
> enemy's fire from Boca Chica slackened and towards

evening was quite silenced. A breach being made on
the other side by our land battery, large enough to
admit a middle sized baboon, provided he could find
means to climb up to it—our general proposed to give
the assault that very night and actually ordered a detachment on that duty. Providence stood our friend
upon this occasion, and put it into the hearts of the
Spaniards to abandon the fort, which might have been
maintained by resolute men till the day of Judgement.[1]

Wentworth informed Vernon that no reasonable breach
had been made in the walls of the fort, but the admiral
insisted that the enemy would run if the fort were attacked.
Vernon was right. Wentworth braced himself to act only to
find that as his men poured up to the walls the Spaniards
retreated without firing a shot. Soon the Union flag was flying
from the flagpole. One unsavory incident—the shooting of
a young British drummer who had been sent to demand a
parley—intensified the bitterness of the fighting. At last
the Boca Chica channel was open to the British, but at
what cost: 130 battle casualties and 850 dead and sick from
disease!
Wentworth's troops reembarked for the short journey
around the harbor to Cartagena. One final fort stood between them and their goal—Fort St. Lazar—and a council
of war was called to discuss this problem. Wentworth had
asked for five thousand men to be landed for the attack on
St. Lazar but Vernon told him that fifteen hundred was all
he needed and that disembarking more would simply waste
time. Hardly reassured, Wentworth advanced toward the
fort, brushing aside light Spanish opposition. So feeble was
the Spanish resistance at this stage that a prompt assault
on the fort followed by an advance on the city would almost
certainly have given Wentworth both prizes at once. But
Wentworth was cautious, fearing that all was too easy and
expecting to face further ruses and ambushes. Again the
admirals fumed aboard their ships as Wentworth missed
a golden opportunity. Instead he set up camp several miles
from the fort and called on Vernon to send him the rest of
his men. The admiral agreed but with a bad grace, replying,
"Delay is your worst enemy.... We hope that you will be
master of St. Lazar tomorrow." Wentworth did not agree
and summoned his officers to a council of war that con-

cluded that the fort could not be taken by assault, for its
walls were too high. It would have to be besieged. He therefore asked Vernon if the fleet could carry out a bombardment
for him. Vernon, believing that his ships had carried the
brunt of the fighting so far and that the army had done
nothing, replied by condemning Wentworth for not following up his chance the day before. Shaken by the admiral's
letter, Wentworth now made a complete U-turn and decided
on an assault against the unbreached fort. The imminence
of the rainy season, and the fact that through some administrative blunder no tents or tools had been landed with
the men, convinced him that he had better get something
done quickly. Sleeping in the open, without tents, more
and more of his men were succumbing to illness. Yet even
a short bombardment from a nearby hill called La Popa
would have rendered the fort uninhabitable. The most am-
ateurish of artillerymen could have seen that Fort St. Lazar
was fatally compromised by the hill, but Wentworth continued to miss the obvious. With his only qualified engineer
dead and without tools from the fleet, no siege battery was
possible. Faced with no alternative but an immediate assault on the fort, Wentworth decided on a night attack,
assaulting the north and south walls of the fort simultaneously. As often happens with night attacks, particularly
if the commander is weak and the troops inexperienced,
everything went wrong.

The main party of some one thousand men under Colonel
Wynyard were guided toward the weak southern wall of Fort
St. Lazar—where there was no ditch—by two Spanish deserters. Meanwhile, another column of British troops, commanded by Colonel Grant and, curiously, accompanied by
Wentworth himself—though not in a command capacity—
were to feint an attack on the hornwork to the north of the
fort. Both columns began their advance at three A.M. and
Wynyard's men immediately encountered problems. In the
darkness they missed their way and found the ground far
steeper than they had been led to expect, so much so that
they were forced to advance on hands and knees. They were
in fact clambering up the steep eastern slope of the hill,
which was protected by three lines of trenches. The British
grenadiers led the assault but, as they called for the scaling
ladders to mount the walls, it was found that the Americans
who were carrying them had been placed at the rear of the

column. In the darkness a search was made for the Americans, and it was soon discovered that they had taken to
their heels and—what was worse—had taken the ladders
with them. The grenadiers were just thirty yards from the
walls when suddenly the Spaniards opened a devastating
fire on them from point-blank range. There was no alternative now but for the men to rush the walls, regardless of
casualties, but who was there to lead them? Wynyard
seems to have been paralyzed. He and his officers, quite
unaccustomed to being in action, behaved as if they were
on the parade ground, advancing slowly in perfect order
and trying to fire volleys. In the murderous hail of fire the
redcoats simply stood, reloaded, and fired as if they were
on the practice range. No officer showed any urgency and
the men fell in hundreds as the Spaniards poured grape-
shot and musket fire into their thinning ranks. The grenadiers, showing a coolness under fire that was both
admirable and ridiculous, threw their grenades into the fort
only to discover that fewer than one in three of them actually exploded—through faulty design their casings were
too thick. There was no alternative but for Brigadier General Guise, who was supervising the whole operation, to
recall Wynyard's column.

Colonel Grant's column on the north face fared little better, particularly because the colonel was one of the first
men to fall. To fire their volleys the British infantry lined
up like skittles in an alley and the Spanish cannon cut
swathes through them. The call for British artillery support
fell on deaf ears because the cannons had inconveniently
been left far behind the assaulting columns. For over an
hour, on both sides of the fort, the British redcoats obeyed
orders, laying down their lives in a hopeless cause. Without
leadership the men went through their drills like clock-
work soldiers. As day broke, the guns of Cartagena joined
the fight and poured shot into the British lines, now hopelessly exposed. But the redcoats refused to give way and
stood their ground until Spanish infantry issued from the
city to try to cut off the remnants of Grant's command.
Only now did Wentworth order his men to withdraw, having
suffered nearly 50 percent casualties, with the officers providing tempting targets for Spanish sharpshooters. The
mortally injured Grant's last words were recorded as: "The

general ought to hang the guides and the king ought to
hang the general."

Admiral Vernon was adamant that Wentworth was incompetent and had mismanaged the whole affair. Why had
he chosen to accompany the feint attack—and in a junior
capacity at that? Why had the vital scaling ladders been
placed in the care of the unreliable American troops and
why had there been no artillery support for the British
attackers? And yet if Wentworth were to blame for the failure to take Fort St. Lazar it was probably because he
launched the attack without first securing a breach. For
this decision we know that the real culprit was Vernon
himself.

The next day Wentworth called a council of war. Apart
from battle casualties, which were heavy enough, yellow
fever was now taking a heavy toll daily. By April 10 effective
British strength had shrunk to less than thirty-two
hundred men. The best of the old-line regiments had been
killed or wounded in the fighting and the survivors included twelve hundred Americans, who could not be
trusted with any duty at all. Wentworth told Vernon that
unless he agreed to release sailors and engineers to construct a battery to attack Fort St. Lazar the expedition was
effectively over. Vernon tried to persuade the general to
renew his assaults on the fort but without success. The
rain fell heavily on April 11—a clear indication that time
had run out and the wet season was upon them.

Breakdown between army and navy was now complete.
Wentworth no longer trusted Vernon, and the admiral was
convinced that Wentworth was an incompetent fool. On
April 14 another council of war was held at which Wentworth declared that his effective force was just 3,517, no
longer enough to bear the burdens of the operation. Unless
Vernon would commit his sailors to help, the operation
would have to be cancelled. It was more a question now of
allocating guilt for the fiasco and in this Vernon was the
master. He was able to color his reports in such a way that
Wentworth's every move became suspect. Even after it had
been decided to abandon the siege and the troops were
reembarked, Vernon could not resist having the last word—
an explosive one—by sending in a ship to bombard the city.
At least it could not be said that the navy had abandoned
the fight. But adverse winds meant that the transports,

filled with wounded and sick men, had to remain off the coast of Cartagena for a further ten days. When planning the expedition Lord Cathcart had provided hospital ships and surgeons, but he had not imagined losses of the kind that had been suffered. There were shortages all around. Tobias Smollett was an assistant surgeon with the expedition, and he describes in graphic detail the suffering of the men in these dreadful days. In spite of the torrid weather water was short and the food unspeakably bad:

> We had languished five weeks on the allowance of a purser's quart *per diem* for each man, in the torrid zone, where the sun was vertical, and the expense of bodily fluid so great, that a gallon of liquor could scarcely supply the waste of twenty-four hours; especially as our provision consisted of putrid salt beef, to which the sailors gave the name of Irish horse; salt pork of New England, which, though neither fish nor flesh, savoured of both; bread from the same country, every biscuit whereof, like a piece of clock-work, moved by its own internal impulse, occasioned by the myriads of insects that dwelt within it; and butter served out by the gill, that tasted like train-oil thickened with salt.[2]

Relations were now so bad between Wentworth and Vernon that the army commander would not deign to ask the admiral for further help, and so hundreds of soldiers suffered while surgeons aboard the men-of-war smoked their pipes and carved mementos of the voyage. The sailors were generally horrified at the treatment the army doled out to its own men. When a soldier died, instead of wrapping his body in a shroud and weighting his heels before dropping him into the sea, as was naval practice, his colleagues simply heaved him over the side, to be eaten by sharks or pecked at by flocks of seabirds. The air around the fleet—still because of the lack of wind—became poisonous with the smell of disease and putrefaction. By the time the fleet sailed away from Cartagena there were just seventeen hundred men fit for action out of the original force of nine thousand, and of the men who had sailed from England under Cathcart over 90 percent had died on the expedition.

All that was left was to apportion the blame. As the fleet

bore away the mournful remnants of the expedition, Wentworth and Vernon continued their war of words, which had replaced the struggle against the enemy. In the words of Smollett:

> The Demon of Discord, with her sooty wings, had breathed her influence upon our counsels; and it might be said of these great men as of Caesar and Pompey, the one could not brook a superior, and the other was impatient of an equal; so that, between the pride of one, and insolence of another, the enterprise miscarried, according to the proverb, "Between two stools, the backside falls to the ground."[3]

In his dispatches to London, Vernon—a man of many words—praised the work of the navy throughout the operation. His men had captured forts and struck the Spaniards a heavy blow. On the other hand, his silence on the work of the army spoke volumes. In Wentworth's dispatches all was pessimism: he blamed everyone but the man who had most deserved his criticism—Admiral Vernon. On arrival at Portsmouth, by a curious mischance Wentworth's letters to the government were misplaced and delayed, while Vernon's missives arrived with all haste. It was Vernon's view of the campaign that became the accepted one and Wentworth's merely the apology of an unsuccessful and incompetent officer, promoted beyond his ability.

The Campaign of Saratoga, 1777

AT THE BATTLE OF MINDEN IN 1759 THERE OCCURRED THE MOST celebrated example of cowardice in British military history. Lord George Sackville, the commander the British cavalry in the allied army of Prince Ferdinand of Brunswick, was ordered by the prince to pursue the retreating French and put them to rout. Instead of instantly leading his squadrons into the attack, Sackville stayed where he was, claiming that he did not understand the prince's order. The order was presented to him twice more, by different aides, but Sackville declared that he would not accept the order unless it was from the prince himself. When his second-in-command, the Marquis of Granby, tried to lead the attack, Sackville stopped him and the French subsequently escaped. When news of the fiasco reached England, King George II ordered Sackville to be court-martialed on a charge of cowardice and drummed out of the army. The king further decreed that Sackville should never be allowed to serve his king and country again in any official capacity. Sackville's fall was "prodigious," according to his contemporary, Horace Walpole, but the king was mistaken if he thought that Lord George's career was ended. With the accession of King George III in 1760 much of the opprobrium surrounding the name of Sackville disappeared and through his numerous friends George began to repair his network of political connections that were so vital to high office in eighteenth-century England. As a member of Lord North's faction, Sackville—who had assumed the name of Germain to benefit from a bequest—rose to become colo-

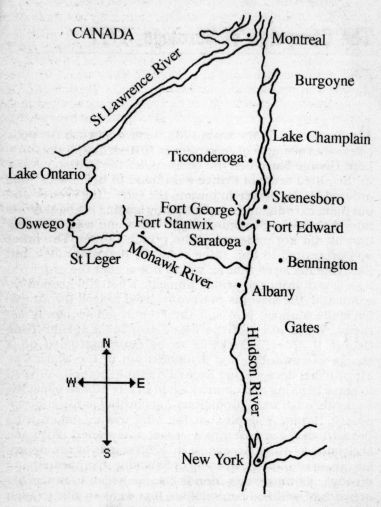

THE SARATOGA CAMPAIGN 1777

nial secretary in 1775, charged with the suppression of the revolt by the American colonies.

By the winter of 1776 the British still retained the advantage in the war, although their leisurely and indecisive approach to campaigning meant that they were not able to exploit the advantages they won in formal engagements. The rebels, far more mobile and with a good knowledge of the countryside, were able to melt away when the need arose and reassemble elsewhere. For the British and German troops—accustomed to fighting long campaigns in Europe—logistics were a considerable problem. Every British army needed to be supported by long baggage trains, as well as numerous remounts for the cavalry and oxen for hauling the heavy guns. This vulnerable "tail" to every army meant that lightning strikes, of the kind George Washington had used to win an unexpected victory at Trenton at Christmas 1776, were not an option open to British commanders. The tactics of American frontiersmen, fighting in loose order and relying on individual initiative, reduced the advantage the British possessed in discipline and steadiness under fire.

Moreover, the British were at an even greater disadvantage in having two men running the war, often in conflict with each other. The commander-in-chief, Sir William Howe, in America, and the colonial secretary, Lord George Germain, in London, had not been on good terms with each other since a combined army/navy fiasco at Saint-Malo in 1758. Each felt the other had showed the greater incompetence that day on the coast of France, and it was a national tragedy that the two of them should have been in positions that enabled them to wreak revenge on each other and on their country. They were separated by three thousand miles of sea—with letters and dispatches taking upwards of a month to arrive at their destination. With their respective roles so ill defined, the slowness of communications deprived them of the chance to quickly coordinate their actions, even had they wished to do so. A further problem was that neither would be completely open with a man he did not trust. The result was that, once Sir John Burgoyne joined the discussions, it was possible for Germain and Howe to work through Burgoyne rather than directly with one another. And if Burgoyne—as turned out to be the case—had firm views of his own and ambitions to match them, then the opportunity for misunderstanding was multiplied. In the final analysis the British disaster at Saratoga was the product of three minds operating in disharmony.

In the fall of 1776, Sir Guy Carleton had advanced from Canada down the Richelieu River and Lake Champlain to attack Fort Ticonderoga, but had failed to capture it by the time severe winter conditions set in. But Carleton's second-in-command, Lieutenant General John Burgoyne, did not lose faith that the Canadian route was the best way of breaking the resistance of the colonists. Traveling to London in the winter of 1776, Burgoyne took his plan to Lord George Germain, the colonial secretary, hoping to be appointed to lead a new expedition from Canada in the spring of 1777.

Burgoyne recommended an extension of Carleton's plan of 1776, employing a route south from Montreal to New York using lake and river where possible and reducing the distance it was necessary to march overland to a mere twenty miles. He envisaged leading the army to Albany in person, whereupon he would be joined by a force under Sir William Howe marching north from New York. In this way the rebellious colonies would be split asunder, with New England—heartland of the revolt—being cut off from the southern and central colonies. This was a bold suggestion but seemed eminently reasonable in view of Britain's resources, notably in water transport. Ironically, just two years before, the Continental Congress at Philadelphia had actually received a warning that if the British gained control of the Hudson River they might easily split "the eastern and southern confederates, divide our strength, and enfeeble every effort for our common preservation and security." Clearly Burgoyne had hit on the rebels' weak point. All he needed was to win over Germain and Howe to his proposals. But this was easier said than done.

It seemed at first that everyone on the British side— including Germain and Howe—was in agreement that Burgoyne's plan was an excellent one. But just saying so was not enough. They failed to appreciate that the plan was a complex one that depended on close cooperation among all the participants. And this would be difficult within the context of a divided command—in London and America— separated by three thousand miles of ocean. A further problem was the nature of Burgoyne's own personality. He was not a career soldier, content to serve his king and country and take his rewards in the shape of ribbons, medals and public applause. Applause—certainly—and flattery were pleasant to his ears, but he was not to be bought for ribbons. Burgoyne was an ambitious man—a glory hunter—and although a good soldier, he was very much a man of his times. Ambition drove him hard: Horace Walpole dubbed him "Julius Caesar Burgonius." He had already bought himself a seat in Parliament as a way of furthering his military career. He was a *bon viveur*—a playwright—and a frequenter of high society. He was renowned as a gambler and it was said he was willing to stake anything on a throw of the dice. He had always been popular with King George III, and in 1772 managed to use his connections to secure a promotion to the rank of major general. Although he had seen service on the battlefields of Europe in his youth, his later promotions were earned more at court or in the boudoir.

While Burgoyne was in London in December 1776, the king entertained him at court and listened attentively to his plans for the campaign. King George was impressed as always with this suave officer and became convinced—through Burgoyne's outrageous flattery—that here indeed was the man destined to restore Britain's position in the Americas. So encouraged was Burgoyne that when he met some of his cronies at Brook's Club in Pall Mall on Christmas Day he wagered with the politician Charles James Fox: "Within the year I shall return from America victorious." Fox was amused by his arrogant friend but shrewdly bet against him, replying that a year hence he expected to see him back in London as a prisoner on parole. The wager—fifty guineas, by today's standard quite a large bet of more than five thousand dollars—was recorded in the club's book and later collected by Fox once news of Saratoga had reached London.

The problem for Burgoyne was that while he was successfully winning over the king, Lord Germain had not yet been convinced and Sir William Howe—in America—still had his doubts about the northern campaign. On October 9, 1776, Howe had written to Germain agreeing that it was important to "open up communication with Canada" by moving up the Hudson River. In this way he had hoped to carry the war into the heartland of the rebellion: New England. But Howe was by no means as committed to this plan as was Burgoyne, and on November 30 he wrote again to Germain asking for reinforcements. According to Howe fifteen thousand men would be needed to hold New York and advance on Albany, while twelve thousand attacked Boston and a further ten thousand threatened the rebel capital of Philadelphia. Furthermore, it is in this letter that Howe makes it clear for the first time that he regards the operation against Philadelphia as of prime importance and hopes to carry it out once the Hudson River campaign has been completed. Everything depended on the British government's finding fifteen thousand reinforcements, either from Germany or Russia, as mercenaries. When Germain received this letter—exactly one month later—he was alarmed to hear that Howe needed so many extra men. Men were money, and he replied on January 14: "When I first read your requisition for a reinforcement of fifteen thousand rank and file, I must own to you that I was really greatly alarmed, because I could not see the least chance of my being able to supply you with the Hanoverians or even the Russians in time." But then Germain began to juggle figures in an attempt to cut down Howe's demands. By including sick men, prisoners and deserters—and by claiming that these were still part of the effective strength of Howe's army—he reduced the commander-in-chief's figure of fifteen thousand men to just seventy-eight hundred. A request for this many replacements, he said, he would be prepared to present to the king.

Yet even before he received Germain's reply, with its specious argument, Howe had already changed his own mind. Suspecting that he was asking too much he decided to simplify his plans for 1777. Aware that Burgoyne and a Canadian army could not possibly reach Albany until September at the earliest, Howe concluded that if he were to wait for Burgoyne his own troops would have to remain inactive throughout most of the campaigning season. He therefore recommended a radical alteration to Burgoyne's original plan. To avoid demanding too many reinforcements, Howe told Germain, it might be wiser for him to strike at Philadelphia—hotbed of the revolution—which he could do with just the troops currently at his disposal. As he told Germain, "By this change, the offensive plan towards Boston must be deferred until the proper reinforcements arrive from Europe, that there may be a corps to act defensively on the lower part of the Hudson River, to cover Jersey on that side, as well as to facilitate, in some degree, the approach of the army from Canada."

Howe had changed the whole thrust of Burgoyne's plan. Far from a two-pronged advance on Albany, designed to split the rebellious colonies asunder, Howe was now suggesting that the northern army should operate almost entirely alone, supported from New York by perhaps a defensive demonstration on the lower Hudson River. The main thrust from Howe's army would instead be against Philadelphia, with Burgoyne's operation as a kind of sideshow to the main attraction: Howe's conquest of the rebel capital. The plaudits would be his and not Burgoyne's. As far as the commander-in-chief was concerned the junction at Albany would not now take place. The British government could insist that he advance from New York to support Burgoyne only by sending him the reinforcements he had requested. And if, by some chance, Howe was able to complete the Philadelphia campaign before the fall he was prepared to consider the possibility of helping Burgoyne. But it was a big if.

This important dispatch of December 20 from Howe was held up and Germain only received it on February 23, by which time its contents struck him as even more disturbing. For much of January he and Burgoyne had been working on the "grand strategy"—the advance to Albany from Canada—and now it seemed that Howe was not going to agree to it. Before Germain could reply, another letter arrived from Howe, dated January 20, which developed his Philadelphia idea further. Germain responded to both Howe's letters in a dispatch on March 9. The problem was that Germain now seemed to want to hunt with the hounds and run with the hare. He told Howe that he approved of the commander-in-chief's change of mind, adding that the king "entirely approves of your proposed deviation from the plan you formerly suggested, being of the opinion that the reasons which have induced you to recommend this change in your operations are solid and decisive." He then added the poison—Howe could expect just twenty-nine hundred of the fifteen thousand reinforcements he had requested.

And where did all this leave Burgoyne? Was Germain
recommending incompatible plans to both British generals? Since 1777 Germain has been much criticized on this
score. He is frequently accused of having given Burgoyne
the go-ahead for the Albany campaign, while at the same
time agreeing to Howe's Philadelphia campaign in the
knowledge that there was no chance of Howe's offering
support to the northern army. Yet this accusation is unfair.
Burgoyne had been working with Germain on the Albany
plan and he must have known by now, in view of Howe's
letters, that the commander-in-chief was not in favor of it.
Possibly he presumed, because he had the backing of the
king and the colonial secretary, that Howe would simply
be ordered to support him. If this was so he was going to
be very disappointed. Either through sheer incompetence
or else something far more subtle and devious, Germain
never did order Howe to support Burgoyne, nor did he inform the commander-in-chief that the Philadelphia campaign was not going to be the prime British thrust for 1777.
In any event, from whatever cause, neither Burgoyne nor
Howe fully understood what the other was going to do. It
was a formula for catastrophe.

By the end of February Burgoyne had put the finishing
touches to the plans for his campaign and submitted them
to the king, under the heading "Thoughts for Conducting
the War from the Side of Canada." The planning seemed
sound, yet how convincing could it be when Burgoyne
added: "these ideas are formed upon the supposition that
it be the sole purpose of the Canadian army to effect a
junction with General Howe, or after co-operating so far as
to get possession of Albany and open communications to
New York, to remain upon the Hudson River, and thereby
enable the General to act with his whole force to the southward"? Here we face a problem of interpretation. Was Burgoyne suggesting that the Canadian army operate
independently of Howe? Or did he expect Howe to join him
at Albany? In either case, did Burgoyne's use of the word
junction necessarily mean that Howe had to advance to
Albany or was it sufficient for Burgoyne at Albany and Howe
at New York to be in close contact by courier? Again we
cannot be sure. But if the modern historian faces this problem of understanding, even with all the evidence to hand,
he can begin to appreciate how the two British generals

could fail to understand each other's intentions.

And was Germain—and the government of Lord North—playing entirely fair by its commanders? Why did Germain approve Howe's Philadelphia plan in his letter of March 9 and yet—at the same time—make it clear to Burgoyne that his plan was also approved? Certainly the government—and King George—would have welcomed two great victories in 1777—control of the Hudson Valley and the capture of the rebel capital. They could well end the rebellion at a stroke. Yet Germain had other reasons for acting as he did. By approving Howe's Philadelphia plan Germain was able to get away with sending the commander-in-chief just twenty-nine hundred reinforcements, whereas had he pressed him to go to Albany to support Burgoyne he might have had to provide far more men at a high cost. In addition, by giving Burgoyne the go-ahead on the Canadian plan he was inviting the ambitious general to risk everything on achieving success alone. If he succeeded then Germain and the government would earn the plaudits for approving the plan. But if he failed they would be able to point to the fact that Burgoyne had acted on his own and without Howe's help, making defeat a certainty. In that case all the opprobrium would fall upon Burgoyne.

Burgoyne, in any case, was confident that he could achieve the first stage of "The Grand Strategy" on his own. Once he reached Albany he could afford to wait until Howe found time—presumably after taking Philadelphia—to move up the Hudson from New York. In this way, Burgoyne was his own worst enemy, making the operation sound too easy. Yet he knew that if he were to show any doubts he would be replaced as commander or asked to wait until Howe could cooperate with him. In either case he would lose his chance of personal glory, and in pursuit of this he was prepared to take any risk. Like many an ambitious general he was faced with a make-or-break situation. In the event of success his reward would be ennoblement and a reputation to match his own vanity, but if he failed he would face the humiliation and perhaps poverty he had known from time to time in his early career. Burgoyne was a gambler and he knew the risks he was taking. But he was gambling this time with the lives of his soldiers and with the vital national interests of his king and country.

Part of Burgoyne's confidence was based on the knowledge that Howe would be keeping General George Washington's main rebel army busy in the defense of Philadelphia. This would remove the best American troops from blocking his advance and should make it relatively easy for his regulars to brush aside General Philip Schuyler's militiamen and continentals north of Albany. This overconfidence on Burgoyne's part probably encouraged Germain to let him go it alone. It is clear that the British government still believed—even as late as spring 1777—that Howe would eventually join Burgoyne at Albany, even if the commander-in-chief was delayed briefly by the capture of Philadelphia. Howe's arrogance—he compared the capture of the rebel capital to a mere jaunt—like Burgoyne's, served to misrepresent the true state of affairs entirely. Sir William Howe was not the sort to be unduly concerned by orders from a man like Lord George Germain, even if they did bear the stamp of the king. Nor was he likely to be concerned overmuch with the ambitions of John Burgoyne. He was already dissatisfied with the government's decision not to send him the reinforcements he had asked for, and he felt entitled to point out to Germain that without the extra men he would be unable to support Burgoyne.

With the king's support, Germain now drew up the plans for Burgoyne's campaign. In a letter dated March 26, Germain wrote to Sir Guy Carleton, governor-general of Canada, informing him that his original plan for a descent on Albany was now the property of John Burgoyne, who would command the expedition. Germain informed Carleton: "with a view of quelling the rebellion as soon as possible, it is become highly necessary that the most speedy junction of the two armies should be effected." Germain did not see fit to tell Carleton that Howe had other plans. Carleton was instructed instead to put all his resources at Burgoyne's disposal so that two separate expeditions could be launched simultaneously. As a diversion, Colonel Barry St. Leger would travel via the Saint Lawrence River to Fort Oswego and thence down the Mohawk Valley, while the main column under Burgoyne was to proceed to the Hudson River via Fort Ticonderoga. Germain—fatally—assured Carleton that he would inform Howe of these arrangements by the next packet. But he failed to do so. And from this moment the British grand strategy began to unravel.

It is doubtful that Germain's failure to write to Howe

stemmed from anything other than carelessness. But he had already been pilloried for his failures at Minden, and many writers have chosen to attribute Britain's disasters in the war against the American colonists to Germain's malign influence. It is far more likely that what happened was the result of incompetence rather than intention. Evidence from William Knox, undersecretary of state for the colonies, presented some five years afterwards, gives a far more convincing account of Germain's "lost letter" than the suggestions by some writers that Germain either deliberately withheld the letter or else "pigeonholed" and forgot about it. In Knox's account all the documents relating to Burgoyne's campaign were assembled for dispatch to Carleton:

> When all was prepared, and I had them to compare and make up, Lord Sackville came down to the office to sign the letters on his way to Stoneland, when I observed to him that there was no letter to Howe to acquaint him with the plan or what was expected of him in consequence of it. His Lordship started and D'Oyley [the deputy-secretary] stared, but he said he would in a moment write a few lines. "So," says Lord Sackville, "my poor horses must stand in the street all the time, and I shan't be to my time anywhere." D'Oyley then said he had better go, and he would write from himself to Howe and enclose copies of Burgoyne's Instructions, which would tell him all that he would want to know; and with this his Lordship was satisfied, as it enabled him to keep his time, for he could never bear delay or disappointment; and D'Oyley sat down and writ a letter to Howe but he neither show'd it to me or gave a copy of it for the office, and if Howe had not acknowledged the receipt of it... we could not have proved that he ever saw it. ...[1]

Without a copy of D'Oyley's letter we cannot be certain that Germain's intentions were clearly communicated to the British commander-in-chief. Even in an era of casual politics Germain's irresponsibility was shameful. From Knox's words we get a good impression of the man—not evil, perhaps, but careless and trivial, willing to set the future of his country at naught to avoid keeping his horses—or his whores—waiting. Such incompetence mocks the blood of brave men who were to die in the doomed campaign ahead.

On his return to Canada Lieutenant General John Burgoyne assembled his army at Montreal. He had at his command seven British regiments—the 9th, 20th, 21st, 24th, 47th, 53rd and 62nd—as well as eight German regiments, the latter raised as mercenaries from Hesse and Brunswick and commanded by Major General Baron von Riedesel. In total Burgoyne had 4,488 British and 4,699 German regulars, while he was later joined at Skenesboro by 148 Canadians, 500 Indians and some 682 Tory loyalists. It was a powerful professional force of more than 9,000 men, well disciplined and well led. In a European context it would have been a match for the best that France might have had to offer. Nor was Burgoyne the kind of European soldier who overlooked the different needs of campaigning in North American conditions, and it is unfair to criticize him in the way one might some British regular soldiers. Furthermore, the regular use he made of Indians and local loyalists saved him from some obvious errors.

A few days in advance of the main column, Colonel Barry St. Leger set out on his diversionary campaign. With 876 British regulars, St. Leger traveled down the Saint Lawrence River by boat, arriving at Fort Oswego on Lake Ontario, where he was met by the Mohawk chief, John Brant, with 1,000 Indians. St. Leger's first target was to capture Fort Stanwix before marching through the Mohawk River Valley to rendezvous with Burgoyne at Albany. But things did not go smoothly. In the first place, Burgoyne had completely miscalculated the effect that Brant's horde of redmen would have on the local settlers. Far from winning them over to the British side, Brant's braves only served to drive the settlers to enroll with the rebel militia in defense of their hearth and homes. When St. Leger reached Fort Stanwix, he found it defended by just 750 American continentals under the joint command of Marinus Willet and Peter Gansevoort. But help was at hand in the shape of the redoubtable Nicholas Herkimer, with 800 men from the New York militia. Herkimer advanced to the relief of the fort but was ambushed at Oriskany by Joseph Brant's Indians. Herkimer may have walked into a trap but he fought bravely and gave such a good account of himself that when Brant called off his braves the Americans were left in command of the field, though badly mauled. It was a serious setback for the rebels, but when the story reached General Schuyler at Stillwater he immediately dispatched another relief force of 950 continentals from Brigadier Poor's brigade, this time led by the formidable Benedict Arnold. News that Herkimer's relief force was advancing toward Fort Stanwix prompted the garrison to make a sortie, catching St. Leger by surprise and wrecking Brant's Indian camp. Marinus Willett left this account of the attack:

> About eleven o'clock three men got into the fort who brought a letter from General [Herkimer] of the Tyron County militia, advising us that he was eight miles off with part of his militia, and proposed to force his way to the fort for our relief. In order to render him what service we could in his march it was agreed that I should make a sally from the fort with 250 men, consisting of one-half Gansevoort's, one-half Massachusetts ditto, and one field-piece (an iron three-pounder).
>
> Nothing could be more fortunate than this enterprise. We totally routed two of the enemy's encampments, destroyed all the provisions that were in them, brought off upwards of 50 brass kettles and more than 100 blankets (two articles that were much needed), with a quantity of muskets, tomahawks, spears, ammunition, clothing, deerskins, a variety of Indian affairs and five colours. The Indians took chiefly to the woods, the rest of the troops then at their posts to the river. I was happy in preventing the men from scalping even the Indians, being desirous if possible to teach even the savages humanity; but the men were much better employed, and kept in excellent order.
>
> From these prisoners we received the first accounts of General [Herkimer's] militia being ambushed on their march, and of a severe battle they had with them about two hours before, which gave reason to think they had for the present given up their design of marching to the fort.[2]

While St. Leger was trying to recover his equilibrium Benedict Arnold was resorting to psychological warfare. Using a half-witted Dutchman—one Hon-Yost Schuyler—

to visit Brant's Indians, the half-wit spread rumors that a large American force was approaching, as numerous as the leaves on the trees, led by "Heap Fighting Chief" Arnold. So depressed were Brant's Indians that they broke off the siege and after raiding the liquor stores actually turned on their hitherto allies, the British. Faced with this Indian desertion, St. Leger had no alternative but to call off his expedition and withdraw to Canada via Oswego. The diversion, which had promised so much, had ended in fiasco.

Meanwhile, Burgoyne had set out from his base on June 20, traveling in a great fleet of gunboats and bateaux down the Richelieu River and Lake Champlain toward Fort Ticonderoga. Expecting a difficult siege, he took with him a heavy train of 138 pieces of artillery, but in fact Ticonderoga was lightly held by American general Arthur St. Clair with just twenty-five hundred men. On July 1 Burgoyne's main column—after a difficult and uncomfortable march from Crown Point—reached Ticonderoga only to find that St. Clair, overawed by the size of the British force, had withdrawn without a struggle. It was a promising start to the campaign, although the Americans had not so far contested the issue. St. Clair had put up a poor display, even leaving two of his regiments at Hubbardton—where they could do no good at all. These were quickly rounded up and captured by Major General Simon Fraser's light infantry, after a sharp encounter in which casualties were heavy on both sides. In Britain the news of the fall of Fort Ticonderoga was received with exaggerated displays of enthusiasm. It is reported that King George III entered his queen's apartments to tell her : "I have beat them. I have beat all the Americans." Lord George Germain even announced as much to the British Parliament, though the fact that such a minor event could have produced such transports of delight is an indication of just how far the British government was from understanding the real strategical situation in the American colonies.

Overconfident as Burgoyne undoubtedly was, he knew that the hardest part of the expedition lay ahead. He was still seventy miles from Albany and now faced an awkward choice, either to travel by water to Fort George and then march to join the Hudson River, or to march overland instead. After the skirmish at Hubbardton St. Clair had fallen back to form a junction with General Schuyler, commander of the Northern Department, who was holding Fort Edward. Burgoyne, meanwhile, had reached Skenesboro, where he was forced to delay for two weeks to allow supplies to catch up. After this, and under the not entirely disinterested direction of Philip Skene—a Tory loyalist leader—Burgoyne foolishly marched his men the twenty-three miles to Fort Edward over appalling terrain, being forced to build a road as he marched. He sent his heavy baggage and artillery by water to Fort George and might have been better advised to have taken his whole command in the same way.

By the time Burgoyne reached Fort Edward, on July 30, Schuyler had fallen even farther back to a defensive position at Stillwater and was awaiting reinforcements. So far Burgoyne had carried everything before him and the American regular troops had been unable to best the British regulars in battle. But Burgoyne had lost a lot of time through waiting for his supplies and it was time now that was against him. The longer he was on the campaign—and away from either Montreal or Albany—the more his men were forced to live off the country, which was notably difficult when the local people were so incensed against his Indians.

The march through the previously uncharted terrain south of Skenesboro was a nightmare for the German dragoons of Baron von Riedesel, who were dressed unsuitably for the conditions in thick woolen jackets, stiff leather breeches and heavy gauntlets, as well as thigh-length jackboots that weighed twelve pounds. As the dragoons marched through the forests their long feathered hats—which aroused the jealousy of the Indians—served only to make them more conspicuous for sharpshooters and frequently got knocked off by branches, while their swords, weighing ten pounds each, dragged along the ground, tripping them as they tried to march. Nothing was more obvious than the fact that these men needed horses—and the sooner the better. When word was received that a large supply of horses had been located at Bennington, in Vermont, Skene—acting as Burgoyne's political officer—advised the general that these horses could be easily won against opposition of little more than 400 militia. This advice—disastrous, as it turned out—persuaded Burgoyne to commit a ridiculously small contingent of 500 Germans under Colonel Frederick Baum. General von Riedesel, in his *Memoirs*, recounts the fact that he strongly disagreed with Burgoyne about this, telling him that Baum's force was much too small for the task. The Germans soon found that they were facing not 400 poorly motivated militiamen but 1,500 well-armed troops led by the fanatical New Englander John Stark. The march, supposedly conducted as a surprise attack, was a farce—with the dragoons like overloaded clotheshorses struggling to keep in step behind regimental bands proclaiming to every sharpshooter within earshot that the Germans were coming. Baum sent back requests for help to Burgoyne, who committed another 650 Germans under Colonel Heinrich von Breymann to go to his help. This was poor generalship, and on August 16 Stark first destroyed the courageous Baum and then Breymann, inflicting 527 casualties on the Germans against a loss of just 70 of his own men. Stark had incited his men with the words, "There, my boys, are your enemies. You must beat them, or Molly Stark sleeps a widow tonight." It worked. The skirmishes at Bennington were serious defeats for the British and were indications that Burgoyne was losing his grip on the campaign. Riedesel was furious when he found that Burgoyne was placing all the blame on the Germans. As he later wrote in his *Memoirs*:

> The English, as usual, endeavoured to lay the entire blame of the ill success of this expedition upon the Germans.... It is true that justice was done to the bravery of Colonel Baum, but they also said that he did not possess the least knowledge of the country, its people, or its language. But who selected him for this expedition?[3]

By the end of August, Burgoyne's position was far more serious than he imagined. Still convinced of his own capacity and that his troops could beat the Americans in open battle, the British general overlooked the fact that he had already suffered significant casualties—a seventh of his entire fighting force—and that the Americans would enjoy a substantial numerical advantage as the campaign progressed. But more than this, Burgoyne had now had definite news from Sir William Howe that he was going to Philadelphia and had no intention of advancing north to link with him at Albany. Howe's deputy—General Sir Henry

Clinton—promised to do what he could, which was not much. For Burgoyne to advance now with just 6,074 fit men—of whom only 4,646 were regulars—would be a very foolhardy action, unworthy of a professional British officer. To go on would almost certainly sever his communications and supply lines to Canada. Yet Burgoyne's visions of personal glory would not fade so easily. Even in spite of two further pieces of bad news he chose to move on. In the first place, news at last reached him that St. Leger had been completely outwitted by Benedict Arnold and had retreated to Oswego. The second problem concerned the beautiful fiancée of one of Burgoyne's Tory supporters—Jane McCrea—who had been murdered and scalped by Wyandoth Panther, one of the Indians accompanying the British army. Unwilling to punish the Indian, on the grounds that it would cause the rest to desert, Burgoyne won himself the hostility and contempt of the civilian population of the Mohawk Valley instead of, as he had hoped, winning the support of these people. Burgoyne found that many of them were rushing to supplement the militia and volunteers swelling Gates's army (Gates had only recently replaced Schuyler). Jane McCrea was becoming a rallying point for the resistance to the British, an "American Joan of Arc."

Burgoyne now had every reason to turn back, with no reason to expect help from New York, and with St. Leger retreating on the Saint Lawrence. Furthermore, the frontier settlers were in uproar as a result of his Indians, and his German contingents had been decimated at Bennington. The situation could hardly have been worse. Yet Burgoyne refused to give up, fearing to lose the king's favor, and claimed that his orders insisted that he should press on to Albany, whatever the cost. Consequently, Burgoyne wrote as follows to Germain:

Had I latitude in my orders, I should think it my duty to wait in this position, or perhaps as far back as Fort Edward, where my communication with Lake George would be perfectly secure, till some event happened to assist my movement forward, but my orders being positive to "force a junction with Sir William Howe," I apprehend I am not at liberty to remain inactive....

When I wrote more confidently, I little foresaw that I was to be left to pursue my way through such a tract

of country, and host of foes, without any co-operation
from New York....

Whatever may be my fate, my Lord, I submit my actions to the breast of the King, and to the candid judgement of my profession, when all the motives become
public, and I rest in the confidence, that whatever decision may be passed upon my conduct, my good intent
will not be questioned.[4]

On September 13, with more courage than good sense,
Burgoyne ordered his army to cross the Hudson River on
a bridge of boats not far from Saratoga. In three columns
he marched toward the American forces on the west bank
of the river. He knew that he would be facing Gates and
not Schuyler and he was convinced that he could best the
ex-British regular officer, whom he insisted on calling "the
old midwife." According to Madame von Riedesel: "General
Burgoyne was so certain of victory that the ladies [who
accompanied the army] were in high spirits."

General Horatio Gates, meanwhile, had moved his army
to a position known as Bemis Heights, which was strongly
protected by positions erected by the notable Polish engineer Colonel Tadeusz Kościuszko. Although Gates outnumbered Burgoyne by about two to one, some of his
troops were of questionable quality—apart from Colonel
Daniel Morgan's corps of outstanding frontier marksmen
from Virginia and western Pennsylvania. Buckskin clad,
and often fighting stripped to the waist in the Indian style,
Morgan's men were a law unto themselves. But if the mood
took them they could be formidable opponents, as they
were soon to prove. Morgan claimed to be able to control
his men without words of command and with his turkey
calls alone. Like many of the American frontiersmen—
indeed, like George Washington himself—Daniel Morgan
had fought on the British side against the French in the
Seven Years War. Again like Washington, he had survived
Braddock's massacre on the Monongahela in 1755 and had,
in addition, survived the attentions of the British provost
marshal by taking a full five hundred lashes across his
back. He had plenty of scores to settle with the British.

On September 19 Burgoyne ordered an assault on the
American position at Freeman's Farm. The British attacked
in three columns, led individually by Generals Fraser, Ham-

ilton and von Riedesel. The column led by the peerless Scottish commander Simon Fraser fell into an ambush, where it was devastated by Morgan's sharpshooters. But Morgan's men became overconfident and in pursuing the broken remnants of Fraser's force ran headlong into the massed volleys of Hamilton's brigade, which scattered them. This was not the kind of fighting that Morgan's men knew best, and the battle-scarred hero was left standing in tears as he tried to rally his men with his turkey calls. The battle was a seesaw affair with neither side able to establish a clear advantage, though American sharpshooters exacted a high toll of British officers, identified by the silver gorgets at their necks. Eventually Burgoyne was able to call in General von Riedesel on his left and it was artillery fire from the German guns that turned the fight, closely followed up by a bayonet charge by the Hessians. But the British had paid a high price for their victory, having lost six hundred men to the Americans' three hundred. Burgoyne knew only too well that he could not afford such losses against an enemy who was able to reinforce himself so easily.

Burgoyne's position was now very serious indeed. So serious, in fact, that a more prudent commander would have been looking to salvage what he could of his command. The Americans were fighting essentially on the defensive and it was unlikely that they would have been able to pursue him if he had organized a retreat. In the British camp supplies were so short that the specter of starvation reared its head and Burgoyne's generals—Phillips, Fraser, Hamilton and von Riedesel—advised retreat. But Burgoyne the gambler was prepared to risk everything on one final attack on the American positions. Meanwhile, he still clung to the faint hope that help would come from New York. General Clinton, Howe's deputy, had sent this message to Burgoyne on September 12:

You know my good will and are not ignorant of my poverty. If you think 2000 men can assist you effectually, I will make a push at Montgomery in about ten days. But ever jealous of my flanks if they make a move in force on either of them I must return to save this important post. I expect reinforcements every day. Let me know what you wish.[5]

In the desperate hope of Clinton's support Burgoyne postponed the renewal of the fight after the battle at Freeman's Farm, for which he has been much criticized. Some historians have pointed out that had he swiftly followed up the—admittedly Pyrrhic—victory at Freeman's Farm he would have found the Americans in disorder. There is truth in this, but how much better was the order in the British camp? The greater experience of the British veterans might have carried him through, but even if it had and he had pressed on toward Albany, he no longer had the strength to resist the growing tide of American resistance. Instead of a surrender at Saratoga there would probably have been a similar surrender only days later at Albany.

Meanwhile, on October 3 Clinton launched a most gallant "demonstration" on the Hudson River, in which he embarked three thousand troops in sixty vessels and sent them upstream to capture Fort Montgomery and Fort Clinton. Yet in spite of every effort, Clinton's New York garrison was eventually turned back forty-four miles south of Albany, effectively sealing Burgoyne's fate.

On October 7 Burgoyne proposed a reconnaissance in force by sixteen hundred picked men of the American positions at Bemis Heights. He might have been encouraged if he had known of the dissension in the American lines between two of the rebel generals, Gates and Benedict Arnold, which culminated in Arnold's being suspended from duty and confined to camp. But the irrepressible Arnold was not to be silenced so easily, and once the British reconnaissance began Arnold rode out to join his troops, closely pursued by one of Gates's aides with orders for Arnold to return.

Prominent among the British troops at Bemis Heights was General Simon Fraser, a commanding figure on a white horse. Arnold ordered one of the best shots in the American army—an Irishman named Tim Murphy—to cut down Fraser, which he did on his third attempt. It was a turning point in the battle. British resistance weakened with the wounding of Fraser, and with Arnold dominating the battlefield until he was wounded leading an assault on Breymann's redoubt, Burgoyne was forced to withdraw, having suffered over six hundred casualties.

It was the final straw for the British. In torrential rain and with his men suffering from starvation, Burgoyne was forced to begin his retreat. But it was far too late for that and American forces had already closed his escape route to the north. On October 17 he was forced to surrender his remaining five thousand men to General Gates at Saratoga. The American general, delighted and perhaps surprised at the completeness of his victory, offered generous terms to Burgoyne only for Congress to disgracefully repudiate his arrangements and send the British prisoners to camps in the south.

Burgoyne returned to London but he had to face both hostility and ridicule. He was subjected to the vicious banter of café society and to the satirical rhyme:

Burgoyne, alas, unknowing future fates,
Could force his way through woods but not through Gates.

The British defeat was decisive in at least two ways. In the first place, it breathed new life into the rebellion and persuaded Congress to accept the Articles of Confederation. Second, and perhaps more important, it encouraged France, along with other European powers, to recognize the new American confederation and join the war against Britain. French naval power added a decisive new aspect to the struggle, one that enabled the Americans to eventually gain their independence. But for Burgoyne and Germain in London it only remained to determine the guilt for the fiasco. Certainly Burgoyne's plan had had its virtues and it should have been possible to bring it to a successful conclusion. But mistakes were made so frequently that only the courage of the British—and German—soldiers enabled Burgoyne to get as far as he did.

In the first place, John Burgoyne was not the right commander for the operation. Vain and ambitious, he was prepared to cut corners on important military matters in order to press home his own personal advantage in the campaign. Without the guarantee of assistance from Sir William Howe at New York, Burgoyne was prepared to push on regardless, only looking for support from Clinton when matters had gone so far wrong that remedy was impossible. He took with him far more artillery than was needed to assault the feeble American defenses at Fort Ticonderoga and allowed himself to be sidetracked into marching through the wilderness from Skenesboro for the personal benefit of the local Tory squire. He took with him dismounted German dragoons whom he must have realized were unsuitably dressed and quite ill equipped for campaigning in American conditions. And when horses became available at Bennington he sent inadequate troops to collect them, allowing his German troops to be defeated in detail by the strong force of General Stark. Proper reconnaissance at this time would have shown him that Colonel Baum's German troops would be hopelessly outnumbered by the Americans.

Furthermore, hearing of St. Leger's failure at Fort Stanwix, he did not consider retreating while he still had a good chance of doing so. Bereft of St. Leger and Joseph Brant's Indians, he was always going to be heavily outnumbered by Horatio Gates's army. The sordid murder of Jane McCrea was similarly mishandled. Burgoyne should have realized the effect failing to discipline his Indians would have on the frontier settlers, who would reinforce Gates rather than side with the British. Short of men and supplies, Burgoyne still pressed on to confront superior American numbers at Freeman's Farm and Bemis Heights. In these two skirmishes Burgoyne showed more courage than tactical skill and his casualties were far too heavy to justify the Pyrrhic victory at Freeman's Farm. In the end, Burgoyne was forced to surrender because he had refused to take any of the numerous opportunities to end the expedition and cut his losses. Always a gambler, Burgoyne risked everything— even up to the last moment—in the hope that he could somehow wrest victory from the jaws of defeat. His personal courage was not enough to free him of a charge of gross irresponsibility. Nor was he entitled to blame Lord George Germain at home, for whatever the minister's failings, it was still the general who put his personal career before the welfare of his men and the interests of his country. And however awkward and uncooperative Sir William Howe proved to both Germain and Burgoyne, the latter could not rightly claim that he had much expectation that the commander-in-chief would come to his rescue at the eleventh hour. It was an age where generals still often chose to place self in the forefront of their campaigns. Benedict Arnold, one of the heroes at Saratoga, was one day to pay the extreme penalty for doing just this. Burgoyne,

on the other hand, paid up his fifty guineas to Fox and
slipped into obscurity—remembered as much for his plays,
one of which was attributed to Richard Brinsley Sheridan,
as for Saratoga, that "thunderclap which resounded 'round
the world."

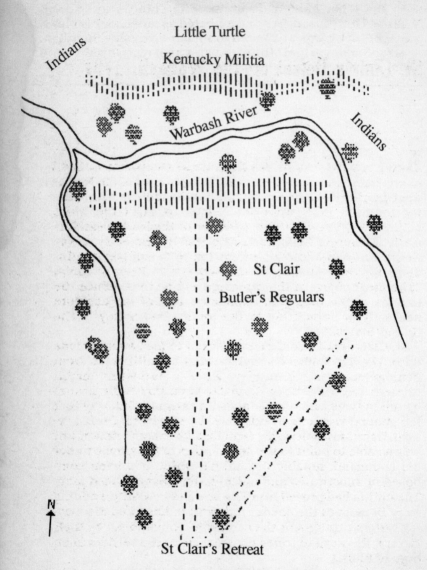

Little Turtle

Kentucky Militia

Indians

Warbash River

Indians

St Clair

Butler's Regulars

N

St Clair's Retreat

ST CLAIR'S DEFEAT 1791

St. Clair's Defeat on the Wabash, 1791

AFTER THE PASSAGE OF THE NORTHWEST ORDINANCE IN 1787 many Americans moved into the Ohio country of the Northwest Territory only to encounter hostile Indians who, fearing for their land, were determined to expel the white settlers. In June 1790 the governor of the Northwest Territory, Arthur St. Clair, was authorized by Secretary of War Henry Knox to equip an expedition to "chastise" the Indians for their attacks on the settlers. In Knox's words: "The great object of the campaign will be to convince the Indians of the futility of resistance, and of the absolute necessity of submitting to the justice and mercy of the United States."

St. Clair appointed General Harmar to lead a force made up of regular soldiers supplemented by militiamen from Pennsylvania and Kentucky. After a two-week march through the wilderness Harmar's force was badly beaten by the Indians and it was only with extreme difficulty that the general was able to extricate the survivors. On his return, Harmar was severely criticized for incompetence, but he was able to point to the deficiencies of the troops under his command, notably the militia, which had been composed of substitutes and officered by inexperienced men. The militia had proved troublesome and cowardly, running away in most of the encounters with Indians and disobeying orders throughout the campaign. Encouraged by their victory, the warlike tribes now turned on the settlers in an orgy of killing.

Smarting from this defeat Congress decided to try again the following year. St. Clair—now a major general—was to command the expedition himself, but again the quality of troops—mainly volunteers and militiamen—was so low that a repetition of Harmar's disaster was likely from the start. St. Clair was instructed to assemble an army of three thousand men, not including those soldiers who were to be used to garrison the forts that he would build as he cut his way through the dense forests north of Cincinnati. Knox was hoping to raise the troops fast enough to allow a departure in early July, but so slow was recruiting and requisitioning that the expedition did not set off until September 17—two months late and hardly any earlier in the year than the unfortunate Harmar in 1790.

Arthur St. Clair—a Scotsman by birth—had come to America as a regular British soldier in 1757 and had served under General Wolfe at the capture of Quebec. He resigned his commission in 1762 and settled in western Pennsylvania. During the War of Independence he sided with the rebellious colonists and served under George Washington at the battles of Trenton, Princeton, Brandywine Creek and Yorktown, rising to the rank of major general. But by 1791—in spite of his experience and seniority—he was not a healthy man, suffering severely from rheumatism and gout. In view of his poor health—and the fact that he had no experience of Indian fighting—he was an unwise choice to lead an expedition in the harsh conditions of a North American winter.

In his haste to have the Indians punished St. Clair ordered two punitive operations against the Kickapoo and Eel River Miamis, the first to be led by Brigadier General Charles Scott and the second by Colonel James Wilkinson. Both were successful in their way—villages were burned and prisoners taken. But they were of questionable military value, serving only to inflame the Indians—notably Little Turtle, chief of the Miamis—making it certain that they would be thirsting for revenge by the time St. Clair led the main expedition later in the year.

Meanwhile St. Clair's forces began to assemble at Fort Washington. With low pay and poor bounties it was difficult to attract enough of the right kind of recruits—many were poor Irish immigrants, others jailbirds or debtors. Even as late as August 1791 St. Clair had as few as six hundred regular soldiers and he and Knox were forced to consider supplementing the force with the much-hated militia.

These men had already demonstrated their incompetence on Harmar's unfortunate expedition, but both St. Clair and Knox realized that if they waited until they had recruited enough men freely it would be too late in the year and the whole expedition would have to be postponed until the following spring. In view of the pressure in Congress for the Indians to be subdued this was politically unthinkable. And so preparations were rushed and corners cut in equipping the force with food, munitions, clothing and transport. It was a recipe for catastrophe and Knox should have known that in his efforts to avoid political embarrassment he was courting military disaster. In fact, St. Clair's mission was as good as doomed from the start and Knox was as much to blame as his ailing general. Although the levies raised were untrained and as far from being useful soldiers as it was possible to get, St. Clair still preferred them to the militiamen who were eventually called on to swell the numbers. The militia seemed unwilling to accept either St. Clair's leadership or that of his second in command, General Richard Butler. During the expedition these men refused to accept army discipline, deserted when the fit took them, ran away in battle and, when reprimanded, threatened to plunder the supply column. One experienced soldier with St. Clair, Captain John Armstrong, thought the soldiers "the worst and most dissatisfied troops I ever served with."

Undisciplined as the men were, they had much to complain about. The difficulties faced by the quartermaster, Samuel Hodgson, meant that most of them were "badly clothed, badly paid and badly fed." Hodgson did not even arrive at Fort Washington until just four weeks before the expedition set off, and in that time he was faced by so many problems that he was quite unable to establish a system for his work. The men had short rations, defective powder and inadequate clothing for an autumn and winter campaign. The muskets and small arms were broken or defective, often lacking touchholes. The artillery carriages were rickety and sometimes lacked wheels. The horses were usually short of fodder and within weeks of leaving Fort Washington frost and snow was killing the edible grass along the forest paths.

The army that eventually left Fort Washington was a poorly trained rabble consisting of a mere six hundred regular infantry, eight hundred enlisted men—the "off-scourings of large towns and cities, enervated by idleness, debaucheries and every species of vice..."—and six hundred militiamen. St. Clair had been forced to move from his headquarters on August 7—even though he was not yet ready to begin the march—in order to remove his new recruits from the delights and temptations of the grog shops that abounded at and near the fort, and because his horses had exhausted the grazing. At Ludlow's Station—a mere six miles from Fort Washington—St. Clair wasted a further forty-one days of fine summer weather.

This time-wasting was driving President George Washington mad with anxiety. As a young officer Washington had accompanied British general Braddock's disastrous expedition to the Monongahela in 1755 and the horrors of that experience were seared in his brain. He had warned the stiff-necked British general of the dangers of campaigning in Indian country, only to have his opinion ignored—and it had fallen to Washington to bury Braddock after the British force had been cut to pieces. With this in mind he wrote to St. Clair, urging him to make haste before the weather turned against him. Washington and Knox had originally planned that the expedition should begin in early July and now it was past the middle of September! And even then some of the troops earmarked for the operation had not arrived at Fort Washington. It boded ill for St. Clair's success.

Once St. Clair left Ludlow's Station and began his march he proceeded at the rate of a mere five miles a day. The problem was that he was marching through heavily timbered virgin forest and a road had to be cut by woodsmen who preceded the soldiers. However, specialist woodcutters had been hard to find and the men consigned to the work were neither well equipped—the axes were of poor quality and broke easily—or well motivated. Nevertheless, after enormous labor the column reached the Great Miami River and work was started to build the first garrison post, to be known as Fort Hamilton. So far few Indians had been sighted and none of these had proved hostile. It was two weeks before the fort was completed, during which time most of the men simply sat around and watched. With a little foresight a labor force could have been sent out from Fort Washington in the summer to construct this fort—

which was not likely to be threatened by Indian attack. So
for the main party a further fortnight had been wasted and
the bad weather was beginning to close in. The cold nights
of October were already showing the men that their clothes
and their tents would be quite inadequate when the snows
came. Many began to desert. More Indians were now
sighted and they were increasingly hostile.

Before St. Clair set off from Fort Hamilton he was overtaken by a rabble of "debauched and idle-looking men"
who, it transpired, were newly enlisted reinforcements
commanded by Lieutenant Colonel William Oldham. He
can hardly have been pleased to see such an unsoldierly
addition to his command. In his diary Adjutant General
Sargent refers to these men as the merest "trash." Nor was
the military efficiency of the "army" improved by the camp
followers—always a feature of British armies, but usually
imbued with a severe self-discipline—a motley collection
of women, children and other hangers-on. Some of the
women were wives or mistresses of the soldiers and helped
the men as washerwomen, others were dissolute creatures
who succumbed to the harsh conditions and died unnoticed on the march.

From time to time St. Clair attempted to impose discipline on his men. Accustomed in his youth to the severe
discipline of the British army, he felt he could treat his
present command as he once would have the British redcoats—the "Bloodybacks"—but he was mistaken. Dealing
with such poor material—the human flotsam of a frontier
society—St. Clair found that his round of floggings only
served to make the men desert in droves. Officers were
court-martialed for minor offenses—one simply for bad lan-
guage to a superior—and on one occasion the whole army
was halted while a gallows was built and three men executed.

On October 13 St. Clair reached the site chosen for the
new Fort Jefferson, about forty-five miles to the north of
Fort Hamilton. This structure took a further ten days to
build thanks to the paucity of tools. In an army of three
thousand men there was just one saw, one grindstone and
sixty axes. When completed the fort was garrisoned by Captain Joseph Shaylor with ninety invalid soldiers!

While the work on the fort was taking place the weather
turned foul, with heavy rain and a bitter wind. The canvas

tents—each housing ten men—were soon leaking like
sieves. A few days of rain were then followed by heavy
frosts, chilling the men to their bones and turning the
soggy campsite into a skating rink. Many of the men lacked
coats, which had been promised but never supplied by the
quartermaster. But it was difficult and dangerous for them
to desert so far from Fort Washington and so chaos ensued
as many men tried to enlist in the regular regiments in
order to get proper clothing. All of this could have been
predicted before the expedition started. Secretary Knox
had earlier observed that the clothing allocated to the levies was "fit only for scarecrows." Yet nothing was done to
remedy this evil.

The late start and the twenty-four days spent in building
the forts had turned what had been intended as a summer
campaign into a winter one. And yet no allowances had
been made in terms of clothes and food allocation. Neither
Knox nor St. Clair had been prepared to compromise by
limiting their objectives to a few punitive raids in the fall
rather than a full-scale operation. Increasingly officers and
men lost faith in both their commander and his mission,
and St. Clair's health began to give way in the harsh conditions. Everything was in place now for the disaster that
was to follow.

When the march north from Fort Jefferson began St. Clair
was in no better physical state than the invalids he had
left behind to garrison the new fort. The route through the
dense, gloomy forest filled the men with foreboding. They
felt that there was an enemy behind every tree and that
they were constantly being watched. Overhead the rain fell,
occasionally turning to hail and snow. Stragglers began to
be picked off by the Indians. At night St. Clair took extra
precautions against Indian attack, ordering every man to
stand to his post just before dawn each morning—the most
popular time for Indian attacks. Even when twenty friendly
Chickasaw Indians joined the march, offering to act as
guides, St. Clair foolishly sent them on a scouting expedition so far from the main column that they were unable
to offer any real assistance.

When violent storms hit St. Clair's camp early in November it was the final straw for many of his militiamen, who
had been grumbling almost since they left Cincinnati.
When seventy of them decided to desert they threatened

that if St. Clair tried to stop them they would attack the supply convoy moving up from Fort Washington. In despair, St. Clair had to send some of his best regular soldiers back to defend the convoy against the militia. Fortunately the supplies arrived intact on October 31.

Snow had begun to fall as St. Clair pressed forward on November 2. After marching eight miles in terrible conditions he camped in the heart of hostile Indian country along the Wabash River. With the likelihood of attack very real, extra precautions were taken to protect the camp. The next day, after a few miles of trudging through the snow, they made camp again. But this time, through an almost total breakdown in reconnaissance, they were unaware that only two miles away there was a large encampment of Indian braves. Camped as they were in heavily wooded country, the Americans would be helpless against an attack from Indians advancing behind the cover of trees. Aware of what had happened to Braddock in 1755—something that Washington had taken extreme pains to point out to him—St. Clair considered surrounding his camp with trenches or breastworks. But his men were cold, exhausted and almost indifferent. At this, the most crucial moment of the march, the Americans were finally dropping their guard. Their defenses were purely routine, as if they were camping in friendly country instead of in a forest teeming with the most skillful woodsmen of their age. St. Clair might have expected more of his scouts but their performance mirrored the general lackadaisical attitude of their commander and his officers. Three senior officers—including General Butler—received reports that there were large groups of Indians in the forest, yet each decided against worrying St. Clair with the information. Had even one of them thought fit to send out patrols the alarm would have been raised in time to prevent the camp from being taken completely by surprise, as was shortly to happen.

Until November 4 the troops had stood to their posts ten minutes before daylight each day and then waited until sunrise before settling down for breakfast around the campfires. But on this one day—as fate would have it—the system was altered. Reveille was blown rather earlier than usual—presumably a sign of the uncertainty felt by the commanders—but in compensation the men were released earlier and retired to their campfires half an hour before sunrise. This was doubly worrying, for St. Clair now learned that the officer responsible for sending out morning patrols, Colonel Oldham, had failed to do so. With the men disarmed and seated around their cooking kettles, the Indians suddenly fell upon them. The first sign of their presence was the sound of bloodcurdling shrieks and war cries.

The Kentucky militia took the full force of the Indian charge, fired a few shots and then turned in panic and ran back across the Wabash River before crashing into the regular troops of Butler, Clark and Patterson. The flight of the militia spread confusion throughout the main camp. Sargent's comment on the militiamen was that they behaved like "a shameless lot of cowards." With a vengeful Little Turtle at their head the Indians now came up against the American regulars and were temporarily halted. But finding cover behind trees and fallen logs they soon began picking off the officers with remarkable accuracy until the regulars began to give way. The American artillery—three- and six-pounders—fired round shot and canister into the trees without doing any execution, while the Indians replied by killing everyone who served the guns. The newly recruited American soldiers now discovered why so much of army life was concerned with drill. Few of them knew how to use their muskets properly, misloading, misfiring, shooting friend and foe indiscriminately in their panic. According to one officer present the enlisted men did much slaughter on the "twigs and leaves of distant trees" but very little on the Indians who would soon take their lives.

When the troops on the left of the camp—Martz's and Purdy's detachments—caved in, the Americans were outflanked and in danger of being surrounded. There was little orderly resistance even though the Americans outnumbered the Indians by fourteen hundred to a thousand men. St. Clair was quite incapable—through ill health and fatigue—of commanding his troops. In the words of Colonel William Darke, "A general, enrapped ten-fold in flannel robes, unable to walk, placed on his car, bolstered on all sides with pillows and medicines, and thus moving to attack the most active enemy in the world was... tragicomical... indeed." Suffering so badly from gout that he could not walk, St. Clair was twice lifted onto a horse only for the poor beasts to be instantly shot. Suddenly the general discovered a new lease on life—his gout and rheu-

matism were forgotten—as a very natural desire to escape
from the Indians overtook him. As he said, "I could wait
no longer; my pains were forgotten, and for a considerable
time I could walk with a degree of ease and alertness that
surprised everybody."

While St. Clair was effecting this transformation, Colonel
Darke heroically charged the Indians and drove them back
across the Wabash, but there were too few men to support
him and once the Indians re-formed they attacked again
and closed in on the regular troops who had held their
ground to allow the retreat to continue. In the 2nd Regiment—a newly created force—only two officers escaped
and many men died like veterans who "had only been
months in uniform." St. Clair, meanwhile, bore a charmed
life. Unlike British general Braddock, who lost five horses
to Indian bullets only to die from a sixth bullet, which hit
him in the lungs, St. Clair had eight bullet holes through
his clothing and yet remained unhurt. His escape was undoubtedly due to the fact that he was wearing only a plain
coat and not the uniform of a commanding officer.

All around now the Indians were massacring their foes.
One American officer was scalped as he sat wounded
against a log and was later seen "sitting on his backside,
his head smoking like a chimney." General Butler was shot
twice but managed to reach a tent where two surgeons tried
to treat his wounds. As the camp was overrun Indians entered the tent and slew the surgeons before killing Butler
and eating his heart because of their respect for his great
courage. Butler paid a heavy price for his failures of reconnaissance the previous night. The camp followers, particularly the women, suffered a dreadful massacre, but not
before they had shown far more courage than the cowardly
militiamen they had followed. In fact, the women drove "the
skulking militia and fugitives of other Corps from under
wagons and hiding places" and back into the fight. Yet only
three women eventually escaped with their lives.

Desperate charges by a revitalized St. Clair, helped by
the heroic Colonel Darke, broke the Indian ring around the
camp to the south, allowing about two hundred or so soldiers to escape from the trap. But once they had gone the
Indians closed in for the kill and few others got away. What
followed was a dreadful scene of massacre, with the fren-
zied Indians torturing their victims with a refinement that

makes the flesh creep. Dancing and howling at the screams
of prisoners roasting at the stake, they eviscerated some
men while flaying others alive and hacking their limbs away
one by one. Babies and young children were whirled about
and smashed on tree trunks, while some of the women
were ravaged with pointed wooden stakes or "cut in two,
their bubbies cut off and burning."

The Indians were too intent on the slaughter of the camp
followers to attempt a pursuit and the survivors reached
Fort Washington unhindered. Only then was it possible to
compute the full extent of the disaster. Thirty-five officers
had died along with 622 soldiers and civilian employees.
Total casualties of 918 included soldiers wounded as well
as dead camp followers and women whose actual numbers
had not been officially recorded. The figures revealed that
the regular soldiers had borne the brunt of the fighting as
well as the casualties, while the militiamen had escaped
more lightly. St. Clair sent an aide, Major Ebenezer Denny,
to take news of the disaster to the president. On December
19 Washington was entertaining guests at dinner when
Denny reached Philadelphia—then the capital—and presented his message to Secretary Knox. Washington bore
the news bravely until his guests had gone, but then he
exploded with temper, showering curses on St. Clair and
reminding anyone who would listen that he had warned
the general to avoid being surprised. It was the Braddock
disaster all over again and with far less cause. St. Clair had
allowed his army "to be cut to pieces, hacked, butchered,
tomahawked, by a surprise, the very thing I guarded him
against! O God! O God! He is worse than a murderer! How
can he answer to his country?"

When he had recovered his temper Washington declared
that he would hear the general's report without prejudice,
and when St. Clair reached the capital in January 1792 the
president was as good as his word, though he did insist
that the ailing St. Clair resign his commission before the
hearing. A committee of the House of Representatives carried out a full investigation of the disaster and on May 8
reported that St. Clair should be completely exonerated of
any blame. The troops he had been given had been quite
unsuited to their task, the quartermaster and contractors
inefficient and the weather unexpectedly harsh. This was
little short of a whitewash. Even allowing for the failures

listed by the committee, both St. Clair and Knox—as professional soldiers—were culpable for allowing the expedition
to go ahead so late in the year. The low quality of the American troops—notably the levies and the militiamen—was
clear for everyone to see before they left Fort Washington.
To display surprise when these men broke in action was
simply dishonest. Knox knew the men were poorly armed
and dressed like scarecrows, and it was asking a lot for
such men to struggle through rain and snow in boots that
did not fit, sleep in leaky tents and face up to the fury of
an Indian attack in the dark forests in which the Indian
was the master. Nor was the weather unexpectedly harsh.
The expedition should have left in July or August. Once it
was decided to set out after mid-September, in the knowledge that roads needed to be cut through the forest and
two forts built and garrisoned, it was obvious to anyone
that the mission could not be completed before winter had
set in.

The exoneration of St. Clair was also less than just.
Though undeniably a brave man and, under some conditions, a capable commander, he was quite unfitted through
health and inexperience to lead green troops into Indian
country. His strict discipline—weakly imposed—only irritated the militiamen and drove them to mutiny and desert.
His procrastination caused delay after delay, making it certain that the expedition could not be completed before winter. Through personal faults he failed to weld his officers
into an efficient team and as a result allowed his army to
dissolve into a demoralized rabble. These criticisms may
seem severe when one considers St. Clair's age and physical condition. But one must be severe in assessing the
reasons for a disaster of this magnitude. Unfit for the command, he should have made it clear to Knox and Washington that this was so, and he should have supported the
appointment of a younger man. His poor health lost him
the respect of his men and contributed to the collapse of
discipline on the march. His campaign of floggings and executions failed to impress his men, who saw them merely
as cruel and unnatural.

If St. Clair's career ended in failure it was only partially
through his own fault. Certainly Knox had much to account
for. He knew as much about the condition of the army
before it left Fort Washington and thus should share much

of the blame, perhaps also for attempting to rush the dilatory St. Clair and forcing him to embark on the mission even after it was obvious that it was too late in the year. And even George Washington cannot avoid complicity in Knox's errors. Washington, after all, had seen the failure of a professional army under a British general when operating in the Indian's natural milieu, the forests. He had seen experienced regulars panic and flee, as much a prey to their own fears as to the Indians. Yet, having seen all this, he was content to allow a rabble led by an old and decrepit commander to march into the forests inhabited by numerous hostile Indians led by the able Little Turtle. It was all very well warning St. Clair not to be surprised on the march, but he must have known that if the Americans encountered the Indians many of the raw levies would run. Washington should have sent a commander experienced in Indian fighting and equipped him with regular troops or men whose heart or purse was involved in the campaign. An army of scarecrows led by a cripple met a predictable fate—and the buck stopped with the president and no one else.

The Expedition to Buenos Aires, 1806–1807

TODAY IT IS EASY TO FORGET JUST HOW ISOLATED MILITARY commanders were in the past, perhaps thousands of miles from their political masters and faced by problems of grand strategy they were often ill equipped to solve. Naturally only the man on the spot could be aware of a situation that changed hourly, or at least daily, so that orders dispatched from home in the pretelegraphic age might be weeks out of date before they arrived. This placed the local commander in a position of immense power—and frightening responsibility. His decisions could commit his country to a course of action involving the lives of millions of people, and the treasure of a whole empire. As a result, one might assume, a government would choose as commanders men with not only military ability but also some political sense. The fact that the British government failed to do this in 1806 is the subject of this chapter.

The sorry story of British intervention in South America began with a memorandum written in 1804 by Commodore Home Popham, an eccentric and restless naval officer who had spent long periods of service on the coasts of Africa and South America. There his eye for prize money and trading opportunities won him the respect of fellow officers and the affection of his crews. Popham's memorandum set out details for an expedition to South America to divert its great wealth from Napoleon's hands into Britain's, as well as to help the Spanish colonies in South America to drive out their unpopular Spanish rulers. The idea appealed to

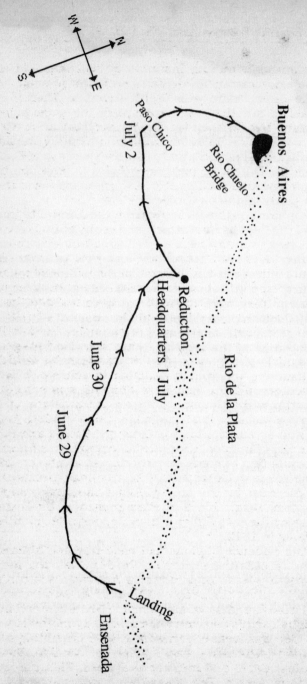

Whitelocke's March to Buenos Aires
28 June - 2 July 1807

the author's trading instincts by promising to create a whole new market for British merchants, previously barred from direct trade with South America. When his plans failed to stir the government with the same passion he himself felt for the idea, he decided to take matters into his own hands. In 1806, while commanding the fleet that had taken General Baird to capture the Cape of Good Hope from the Dutch, he persuaded Baird to lend him the 71st Regiment, under Colonel Beresford, to take over the Spanish possessions on Rio de la Plata.

Popham's prime directive from the Admiralty was to defend the Cape against attack, and yet he blithely abandoned this task even though a French squadron was known to be in the waters off Mauritius. So eager was he to begin his South American adventure that he left Baird's command at the Cape without a single man-of-war. In acting without Admiralty orders Popham must have realized that only a major success would save him from court-martial.

At this point it is as well to consider the task Popham and Beresford were setting themselves. Perhaps geography was not Popham's strong point. Certainly his ambition was outrunning the means available to achieve it. With just seventeen hundred soldiers Popham was setting out to overthrow the Spanish hold on the province of Buenos Aires, a vast area including almost all of modern Argentina, as well as the republics of Uruguay, Bolivia and Paraguay. The city of Buenos Aires, the largest in South America, had a population of some seventy thousand who could not be relied on to welcome the British troops as friends. Bounded to the west by the mighty Andes Mountains and to the north by Brazil, Rio de la Plata presented the British with a task little less difficult than Napoleon faced in invading Russia in 1812.

The evidence Popham had used to reach his optimistic forecast of British success in Rio de la Plata was unreliable, to say the least. Apparently an American sea captain had told him that the people of Buenos Aires were so hostile to Spain that they would welcome British intervention. An English ship's carpenter had reported that the city of Montevideo was weakly garrisoned, with crumbling defenses. British merchants had spoken of similar disaffection against Spain and military weakness. This was music to Popham's ears. But others were not convinced. Arthur

Wellesley, later to become Britain's greatest general, saw nothing but political problems for the British. The Catholic priests would inevitably be hostile, he said, and would stir up the people against the British. Without firm assurance on these matters, Popham and Beresford were embarking on an incredibly risky venture.

On June 24, 1806, Popham and Beresford arrived off Buenos Aires, and after minor skirmishes—and at a cost of just one man killed—forced the city to surrender. The Spanish viceroy, the Marques de Sobremonte, was taken completely by surprise. When he heard of the British landing he was with his family at the theater, celebrating the betrothal of his daughter. He immediately left the theater and fled into the interior with the bullion from the state treasury. It seemed that Popham's extraordinary coup had succeeded, particularly when Beresford sent back to Britain over a million dollars in prize money that Sobremonte had left behind. The people of Buenos Aires had also been taken by surprise: one Spanish lady only learned of the arrival of the British when she found one of their officers asleep on her sofa—with his dirty boots on one of her priceless quilts.

But the situation for the British was not as healthy as it appeared. Though poor in quality, the Spanish troops were numerous and were supported by thousands of Creole irregulars. Beresford had just seventeen hundred men, eight cannon and only sixteen cavalrymen to hold down the outlying areas. His control was therefore limited to the city of Buenos Aires and its immediate surroundings. The British were quite unable to contain the *gaucho* light cavalry, drawn from the families of small farmers or pampas cowboys. Although poorly armed, these riders and their tiny wild horses were entirely at home in their surroundings. Always staying just out of musket range, they chose their moments to rush in to attack when least expected. The few British cavalrymen found their European horses quite unsuited to the conditions and almost impossible to keep alive for lack of fodder.

When Popham's letters arrived in England, the government was faced with a *fait accompli.* They had not sanctioned Popham's action in seizing Buenos Aires and had no idea how the matter would turn out. Windham, the minister of war, cautiously sent instructions to Beresford not to interfere in any revolutionary movements in the colony and to await the dispatch of four thousand reinforcements under Sir Samuel Auchmuty. However, Beresford, unaware of this, was making his own arrangements. Realizing the danger that he was in, he urgently appealed for troops to General Baird at Cape Town. Baird reacted promptly by sending two thousand men from his own command.

Popham, meanwhile, seems to have been more concerned with advertising the financial potential of the newly won land than worrying about how he was going to keep it. He sent a circular to leading merchants in London telling them about the rich market that could be opened up to their products. In the euphoria that followed the fall of Buenos Aires, Popham appears to have completely lost his head.

Crisis point was reached when, at the beginning of August, the local commander, Captain Santiago Liniers, a Frenchman in the Spanish service who had expected the British to attack Montevideo first and had consequently moved downriver to protect that city, at last reached Buenos Aires with his force of regular and irregular troops. On August 12 the entire population of the city, some seventy thousand strong, took up arms against the British. Beresford decided to abandon the city and return to the ships but was held up by bad weather. Before he could move, the people—fighting from the flat roofs of their houses—began inflicting heavy casualties on his troops. After suffering the loss of 165 men Beresford was forced to surrender to Liniers on terms that would have allowed him to evacuate his troops to the ships. But Liniers was overruled by his Creole irregulars and instead Beresford and his men were taken inland as prisoners of the new revolutionary army. From his ship, anchored in the river, Popham could only fume as he saw his dreams of a new El Dorado fading before his eyes.

But time and distance were playing their tricks. A month later—a month he and his men had spent miserably as prisoners—Beresford's report of the capture of Buenos Aires reached London and took the nation by storm. Merchants and traders of all kinds took Popham's claims of a "New Arcadia" at face value and began to ship cargoes off to Buenos Aires in the hope of boundless riches. On September 20, the booty from Beresford's conquest was paraded through the streets of London in grand procession, bedecked with ribbons, flags and—prominent above all—the word *Treasure* spelled out in gold letters. The government, however, had its hands full with events in Europe and took a different view of this news of further territorial commitments. Prime Minister Grenville was of the opinion that Popham should be court-martialed. He did not blame Beresford, who was only acting under orders, but Popham and Baird should have known better.

Meanwhile, reinforcements were beginning to arrive at Rio de la Plata. Admiral Sterling came from England to replace Popham—recalled to face a court-martial for abandoning his station at the Cape of Good Hope. Ever resilient, and with the backing of the merchant community in England, Popham emerged with only a severe reprimand and continued to serve his country in the years ahead, notably during the disastrous Walcheren expedition in 1809. From the Cape fresh troops arrived at Rio de la Plata under Colonel Blackhouse, only to find to their astonishment that Beresford and all his men had been captured. After discussions with Sterling, Blackhouse landed his men and after a brief skirmish took possession of the small village of Maldonado, where he entrenched and awaited further orders.

In London the initial government reaction had mellowed somewhat as the financial implications became clearer. Popham's coup had proved to be tremendously popular in the country and by October the minister of war, William Windham, had "evolved one of the most astonishing plans that ever emanated from the brain of a British Minister of War." Robert Craufurd, commonly known as "Black Bob"— and later to be one of Wellington's most brilliant generals in the Peninsular War—was to be sent with four thousand men to effect a landing on the west coast of South America. His orders were to subdue the province of Chile, inform Beresford at Buenos Aires of his success, and secure by a chain of posts "an uninterrupted communication both military and commercial between Valparaiso in Chile and Buenos Aires." Windham can hardly have been aware that the distance between the two provinces was more than nine hundred miles and the terrain nothing less than the Andes mountain range! It was common for military commanders by their incompetence to place their political masters in difficult positions but surely never before had a minister, untroubled by the dangers and turmoil that a commander faced, set an officer such a completely harebrained task. One might have pardoned this as a temporary aberration had it not been immediately followed up by a plan from the prime minister for an attack on Mexico from both the east and the west coasts simultaneously. It seemed that Popham had been bitten and everyone else had gone mad!

Auchmuty, who kept a better sense of balance than most during the following events, arrived at Maldonado to relieve Blackhouse's besieged men. He had already learned about the capture of Beresford and felt that his forces were too weak to recapture Buenos Aires without reinforcement. He therefore decided to strike instead at the city of Montevideo. Contrary to Popham's reports, which claimed the city was weakly defended with crumbling walls, the defenses turned out to be in an excellent state of repair and the defenders had over a hundred pieces of artillery. What followed was a bloodbath. Though heavily outnumbered in both men and guns, the disciplined British troops forced a breach in the walls and took the city at the point of the bayonet. The enemy losses amounted to over 1,300 killed and wounded with 2,000 prisoners, while the British losses were heavy enough at 368.

While Auchmuty was consolidating his victory he was surprised by the appearance of Beresford and another officer, Colonel Pack, who had managed to escape their captors. Beresford's action reflected little credit on him, as he had clearly abandoned the troops under his command and acted entirely in his own interests. Significantly, a junior officer, Captain Patrick, when offered the chance to leave with Beresford and Pack, preferred to stay with his men during their captivity. In any case, Beresford was able to provide Auchmuty with valuable information before declining the offer of a command in the province and returning instead to England, having had more than enough of the Rio de la Plata.

In England the government had now decided to send a senior commander, Lieutenant General John Whitelocke, to take command of the forces at Rio de la Plata and to act as governor after the province had been subdued. Whitelocke was a most unwise choice. Although a capable officer, he had the unfortunate weakness of trying to cultivate a familiarity with the men under his command by swearing and cussing as heartily as any of them. This unusual trait earned him the contempt of the rank and file, who found his "coarse speech and manners" quite unsuited to an officer and a gentleman. It also created uncertainty in his relations with his brother officers, particularly with his second-in-command, Major General Leveson-Gower. Whitelocke, possibly with good reason, believed Leveson-Gower was no more than one of Windham's spies and treated him with mistrust and later hatred. As if this was not enough, Windham's instructions were nothing less than to recapture the province of Buenos Aires and yet not commit the British government to any form of protection over the colonists. This was ridiculous and presented Whitelocke with an impossible mission from which it is doubtful that even an able commander could have returned with his reputation intact.

By the time Whitelocke arrived at Montevideo to meet Auchmuty, on May 10, 1807, it was winter in South America, a fact that was certain to affect the conduct of the campaign. The Rio de la Plata was not an unknown river and there were many men available in London who could have briefed Whitelocke on the problems of climate and terrain. Incredibly, nothing of the sort seems to have been done. Lack of pasture posed a serious feeding problem for European horses, yet no special efforts were made to obtain local horses. This oversight hampered transport and communication, as well as rendering the British cavalry ineffectual against the well-mounted irregular horsemen of the enemy.

When Craufurd's transports arrived at Montevideo, on June 14—having been redirected from their original destination in Chile—some of his troops had been on board ship for nine months and were quite unfit for strenuous military service. Yet General Whitelocke worked Craufurd's half-fit men harder than the troops who had been ashore for months and were thoroughly acclimatized.

Faced with the problem of approaching Buenos Aires by river, Whitelocke decided that the troopships would not be able to carry the troops farther than a point twenty-nine miles below the city, as the water was too shallow. Beresford, it should be noted, had landed at Point de Quilmes, only eight miles from Buenos Aires, but that landing point was now covered by enemy artillery. No thought was apparently given to the possibility that the fleet could break the enemy hold on Point de Quilmes. In any event, Whitelocke's decision to land at Ensenada instead was a serious mistake.

Lack of reconnaissance meant that Whitelocke was preparing to move through hostile country, against irregular forces who knew the land well and over terrain that presented considerable and unexpected difficulties, without any attempt to ascertain enemy strength and disposition. Furthermore, he was committing his troops to a mud bath. From his point of disembarkation at Ensenada to as far as Buenos Aires the riverbank—to a distance of four miles—was low-lying and marshy, no more than two feet above water level. Added to this inconvenience, the damp and cold of the winter months ate into the bones of the British soldiers and lowered morale. The lack of trees made it impossible for them to find fuel for fires or for shelters so that they were rarely able to eat hot food or sleep in dry blankets. Whitelocke, himself, was obsessed with the effects of rainfall, prompting him to impose—apparently in the men's interests—a savage regime of marching to find cover, which exhausted the newly arrived men of Craufurd's force.

In view of the hostile conditions, the timing of the attack was crucial. The rainy season was beginning and river transport would become even more difficult in the gales and storms. Everything pointed to the need for a delay but Whitelocke insisted that the defenders of Buenos Aires would benefit from such a delay more than the British. Pack, who had been with Beresford when he escaped and knew the conditions better than anyone, disagreed. He pointed out that an attack on a strongly garrisoned city in wintry conditions gave all the advantages to the defenders. Whitelocke discounted his advice; his decision to attack straightaway was based on a fear that he would be unable to feed his force during the winter.

Up to this point little had happened to suggest the disasters that were to follow and for which Whitelocke was to be blamed. He had encountered difficulties from weather and terrain that were common to anyone campaigning in the Rio de la Plata region. His troops were not the best the army had to offer but they were infinitely better than any possessed by the enemy. He had with him able and professional commanders, particularly men like Craufurd and Auchmuty, on whom he could rely for advice, if he was prepared to ask for it. He had the support of a powerful fleet and a secure base at Montevideo. Yet, from this moment, his behavior becomes irrational and his incompetence contributes substantially to the failures of the campaign.

Under Whitelocke's direction, the army was now formed into four divisions—commanded by Craufurd, Lumley, Auchmuty and Colonel Mahon—while a garrison of thirteen hundred men was left in Montevideo. In his allocation of troops Whitelocke allowed personal factors to affect his judgment. Lord Muskerry, who knew the country between Ensenada and Buenos Aires better than anyone in the British force, was deliberately chosen to command the garrison at Montevideo after he had expressed the view that anyone attempting a landing at Ensenada in midwinter must be mad. Whitelocke also left behind two companies of the 38th—Muskerry's regiment—and the 47th, some of the best soldiers in his command.

On June 28, the disembarkation at Ensenada began and soon turned into a fiasco. In trying to occupy the heights that ran alongside the river at a distance of four miles, the British troops found that the intervening ground was merely swamp, at least two feet deep in water. As more and more men tramped through the swamp it churned up into a filthy treacle that sucked men, horses and baggage down at every step. The guns stuck fast and could not be dragged clear even by double teams of horses, while most of the provisions were ruined by a combination of muddy slime and seawater. Relations between Whitelocke and Commissary Bullock—already strained before the troops disembarked—broke down completely when the problem of transporting rations arose. Many of the local horses, still unbroken, would not bear a saddle and ran away, kicking madly and tipping their packs into the ooze. Of eight tons of biscuit disembarked just one ton reached the army intact, while mule carts were equally unable to transport the supply of spirits. Only the sustained labor of hundreds of men served to rescue the guns.

By the morning of June 30 the horrors of the swamp were past and Whitelocke was able to advance toward the village of Reduction. But the problems caused by the dis-

embarkation had a habit of repeating themselves. Faulty
staff work meant that many troops did not receive orders
to bring three days' rations with them, while others had
lost theirs in the march through the swamp. The result
was that the troops found themselves without food while
at least two days' march from Reduction, the first place at
which they could reopen contact with the fleet and get more
supplies. Whitelocke was furious, but as Auchmuty
pointed out to him, "If a General does not himself attend
to the supply of his troops, Sir, they will often want provisions." One can imagine—but scarcely print—Whitelocke's reply. A chance discovery of a flock of sheep provided
some men with meat but most went hungry or were not
given the time to cook what meat they could find.

In the march to Reduction Whitelocke showed little common sense. Craufurd's exhausted troops were pressed into
the advanced guard and hurried forward to where the commander knew provisions could be found. However, these
underfed and poorly conditioned troops wilted under the
pressure and—to ease their burdens—Whitelocke ordered
them to abandon their blankets and march on with just
their greatcoats. In view of the weather and the season of
the year the effect of this decision was disastrous. At last,
on July 1, the village of Reduction was reached but here
mud was still the enemy. Between the troops at Reduction
and the landing point at Port Quilmes there were two miles
of swamp over which all the provisions had to be carried.
Whitelocke now ordered a halt to allow the unloading to
take place and allow the artillery, which was lagging behind, to catch up. The men, tired after a long march and
without food, were now ordered to struggle through to Port
Quilmes to carry back the supplies through the swamp.

Whitelocke ordered his second-in-command, General
Leveson-Gower, with the advanced divisions of Craufurd
and Lumley, to cross the Chuelo River at the first ford and
take up a position near the northern suburbs of Buenos
Aires. Once in position they were to call on the Spanish
commander to surrender. The order was taken to Gower
by Quartermaster General Bourke, who felt Whitelocke was
acting unwisely. In his opinion the men needed rest and
the country ahead needed proper reconnaissance. Furiously Whitelocke ordered him to mind his own business,
and though Leveson-Gower tended to agree with Bourke,

he obeyed the orders. Whitelocke was eager to get his men under cover before the winter rains broke in earnest and this became an obsession with him. On one occasion, when sensing rain, he ordered his entire force to march on—without rations—leaving on the ground recently cut meat from captured oxen. With large numbers of enemy irregulars in the countryside ahead, for all he knew he might be advancing into a trap with starving and exhausted men.

Meanwhile, Leveson-Gower's advanced guard was rapidly dwindling as more and more stragglers fell by the wayside. Of his sixty mounted men no more than a handful remained to maintain communications with the rest of the column, which was now constantly harried by enemy horsemen. Nevertheless, by an extraordinary piece of luck, Whitelocke was about to be presented with the chance of winning the campaign almost bloodlessly. Rarely can a commander have been given such a chance, yet even then he could not see that Dame Fortune was smiling in his direction for the last time. Faced by the difficult passage across the swirling waters of the Chuelo River, Craufurd's scouts spied a retreating enemy cavalry squadron at the Paso Chico ford. Scarcely believing his luck, Craufurd ordered his men to follow. This removed the last obstacle to the British troops before the city of Buenos Aires itself and gave Craufurd a chance to take the city unassisted.

Having crossed the river, Craufurd proceeded to clear the heights of enemy troops and seeing them begin to break he ordered a pursuit which Leveson-Gower tried unsuccessfully to stop. On reaching a large open space known as the corral—generally used as the city slaughter yard—Craufurd was fired upon by a Spanish cannon, whereupon his brigade charged the nearby hedges and cleared them of enemy infantry, pursuing them hotly into the outskirts of the town. Again Leveson-Gower sent orders for Craufurd to withdraw but by this time the Scotsman was convinced he had taken the enemy by surprise and the city was his. In fact, Craufurd was right. The Spaniards had massed nine thousand men and fifty guns by the bridge over the Chuelo and his lucky crossing by the ford had outflanked them. On hearing that the British had crossed the river Liniers rushed a column of troops back to the corral and it had been these men that Craufurd had routed. Ironically, Liniers had been defending the northern face of the city, having clearly got details of Whitelocke's plan from a captured British officer. The extraordinary chance by which Craufurd had found the ford had enabled him to approach the city from an unexpected direction. But Leveson-Gower's caution, understandable as it was, prevented Craufurd from taking the city and realizing the purpose of the entire expedition.

Meanwhile, in spite of Craufurd's successes, Leveson-Gower's position was extremely difficult. His troops were now concentrated in the corral, the city's slaughter yard, sleeping amidst the putrid remains of the dead animals. Moreover, he had no idea where Whitelocke was with the main column. In fact, Whitelocke had halted for the night in order to rest and feed the men. Although he heard firing ahead it seemed not to occur to him that his advanced column might be in trouble and so he sent no messenger to Leveson-Gower to learn his situation. Leveson-Gower, as ordered, had demanded the surrender of Buenos Aires but had met with a defiant refusal.

On July 3, Whitelocke at last made contact with Leveson-Gower. He asked him if he had had any thoughts of a plan to attack the city. Leveson-Gower unfortunately had. Whitelocke, after consulting him, abandoned his own plan and called a meeting of officers for the next morning. Leveson-Gower's plan, in fact, ranks as one of the most ridiculous in the whole of military history. He proposed nothing less than that the British troops should enter Buenos Aires from thirteen directions, in thirteen different columns, down thirteen separate streets. No arrangement was made to allow communications between the separate columns; each was to be entirely on its own. Once inside the city they were bound to be swallowed up by the superior numbers of the enemy. One column was instructed to seize the commanding buildings in the Plaza de Toros, while the others pushed on to the river's edge, capturing the buildings there and forming up on the roofs. What was to happen next was anyone's guess. Whitelocke—outside the city and with no communications with any of the columns—had accepted the role of a passive spectator.

Satisfied with Leveson-Gower's plan, Whitelocke instructed his brigadiers that the attack would begin at noon. Auchmuty, arriving late at the conference, was amazed. His officers had had no time to acquaint themselves with the plan, nor reconnoiter the ground, and surely midday was an extraordinary time to assault a heavily populated city like Buenos Aires. Reluctantly, Leveson-Gower agreed to delay the attack until first light the next morning but there were to be no other changes, even though Pack, Beresford's companion in his escape from captivity and the only British officer with a thorough knowledge of the city, thought the plan insane.

Why Whitelocke accepted such a plan is difficult to understand in view of the fact that on his arrival at Rio de la Plata he had pointed out to Craufurd that the construction of the local houses—with flat roofs surrounded by parapets—made them ideally designed for defense against just such an attack as Leveson-Gower envisaged. He had even added that he would never expose his own troops to the unequal contest of street fighting against irregulars on rooftops. His own plan, as far as one can tell, would have involved a heavy and prolonged bombardment, possibly in conjunction with the naval forces on the river, before his assault troops were committed. Why then did he adopt Leveson-Gower's harebrained scheme?

Whitelocke, it seems, was becoming uneasy about the condition of his men; they were tired, short of provisions and exposed to the rigors of the rainy season. He had found it very difficult to maintain links with the fleet and to transport supplies to the troops on the march. Rather than find a solution to the supply problem he preferred to risk everything on winning a quick victory. Once the city was captured his problems would disappear, as his troops would be able to shelter and feed in some comfort. The fact that he did not expect to meet much opposition is made clear by his comments at his court-martial. He had underestimated his enemy with little justification in view of the fact that they had defeated and captured Beresford as well as strongly resisted Auchmuty at Montevideo.

During the afternoon of July 4 an extraordinary interview took place between Whitelocke and Leveson-Gower. Whitelocke was clearly at the end of his tether and demanded that Leveson-Gower should testify to the soundness of his orders and dispositions throughout the campaign. Leveson-Gower was not prepared to do this, claiming that as an inferior officer he was not qualified to comment on his superior. Whitelocke furiously denounced him as an enemy and said that he would replace him as soon as he could. On this unhappy note they parted, to prepare for the assault.

Everywhere, officers were desperately trying to make some sense of the plan. Bourke was instructing them on which roads were to be followed but this was no easy task, as flanking attacks from adjoining streets and at junctions were bound to occur as the enemy retreated. The fact was that the enemy would know the layout of the city infinitely better than British troops entering it for the first time, and ambushes were certain. Leveson-Gower just would not accept this and brushed aside the objections, insisting that the plan must go ahead unaltered.

Clearly he had made no allowance for the columns to be held up by enemy action in the narrow streets of the city. He should have realized that besides the fire from regular soldiers the British might expect to face, they would also encounter missiles of every kind, from grenades to chamber pots, from tables and chairs to porcelain vases, thrown by almost every able-bodied civilian man, woman and child. Without some form of artillery bombardment the British troops were throwing away their technological advantage and fighting an enemy who had the advantage of the high ground. Even more incredible was the decision taken by Leveson-Gower to order the troops to remove the flints from their muskets before entering the city. Although the flints were later returned to them, the original aim was to take the city at the point of the bayonet. Two reserve companies, in the heat of the moment, were sent into action without their flints and were quite unable to use their muskets against the enemy.

According to Leveson-Gower's plan, on the northern side of Buenos Aires, Auchmuty was to send the 38th Foot to seize Plaza de Toros with the surrounding ground and to hold it at all costs. Next to the 38th, in succession, came the 87th, 5th, 36th and 88th Foot, each of which was divided into two wings and was ordered to advance down eight parallel streets to the south of the 38th. Auchmuty accompanied the right wing of the 87th; Lumley the right wing of the 36th.

Next to these came the 88th Foot in two wings, on the extreme right of the left side of the attack. The four central streets were left vacant, except that the street that ran di-

rectly from Whitelocke's headquarters to the fort was to
be occupied but not traversed by the Carabiners, with two
guns, who were to make a false attack.

The first street to the south of the four central streets
was allocated to a part of the Light Brigade under Pack,
the second to the remainder of that brigade under Craufurd, each column taking with it one three-pounder field
gun. The two wings of the 45th were to move parallel with
the Light Brigade down the two next streets, then join together to march to the last square of houses on the river
and to form up on the roofs of the buildings. If any failed
to penetrate so far, they were to lodge themselves at the
farthest point to which they were able to advance.

A general instruction said that in all cases of doubt the
detachments were to incline outwards; that is to say, Auchmuty's and Lumley's brigades, which formed the left wing,
were to bear to their left, the remainder, which formed the
right wing, to their right. But this order was so confusing
and obscure that Craufurd's staff officer simply left it out.

At Whitelocke's court-martial details of the following
misleading order emerged:

> Each officer commanding a division of the left wing,
> which is from the 88th to the 87th inclusively, to take
> care that he does not incline to his right of the right
> wing, that is Light Brigade and 45th to the left.[1]

This is very unclear. And if the British were uncertain
what they were supposed to do they had given even less
thought to what their enemy might do. The plan needed
the closest possible contact between the various columns,
so that each could adapt quickly to changed circumstances. It also needed the commander to be able to follow the
progress of the advance from close quarters, because the
whole situation might change many times in as many minutes. Reports from the fighting men would be hopelessly
out of date by the time they could be received by Whitelocke
and acted upon. In this way his own brigade commanders
were as much cut off from him as he was from his own
political masters in London. In simple terms, Whitelocke
had decided to fight the battle blindfolded!

The Spanish defenders of Buenos Aires were prepared
to defend every street in the city and had organized them-

selves accordingly. Cannons were placed at the ends of the
streets and trenches were dug across the main streets leading to the Great Square. Houses were barricaded and missiles of every kind were assembled on the flat roofs to hurl
on the advancing British infantry. Moreover, the morale of
the defenders was far higher than that of the dispirited
British. Priests had aroused the people to a religious fury
and everyone was willing to play their parts in defending
their city. There may have been as many as fifteen thousand
Spanish and irregular troops in the city, commanded by
Liniers, but there were thousands more ordinary citizens
who would join in when the time came. The British had
lost the moral advantage of being seen as liberating the
people from the Spaniards. They were now simply regarded
as foreign invaders—and enemies of the Catholic faith, at
that.

The British had about five thousand men to carry out the
assault, with something over one thousand kept in reserve.
Each column was to be led by two corporals equipped with
crowbars, presumably to dismantle barricades. At six-
thirty in the morning they advanced into the city, which
for all its population of seventy thousand was deathly silent, with scarcely even a scavenging dog to be seen. The
sound of marching soldiers and cannons being dragged
over the cobbles echoed in the stillness. On the left, Auchmuty advanced a mile without meeting any resistance until
suddenly two cannons opened up on his columns, followed
by heavy fire from hidden musketeers. Simultaneously, firing burst out from many parts of the city as if by prear-
ranged signal and there were shouts and screams of anger
from the rooftops as Negro slaves, women and even children joined the attack. Within minutes Auchmuty's force
was decimated and he led the remnants of the 87th into a
large house down by the river, where he was able to deduce
that the heavy fire he had encountered had come from the
Plaza de Toros, which according to Leveson-Gower's map
should have been three streets to his left and not straight
ahead! Meanwhile, to the south of Auchmuty, the 5th had
reached the river by 7:15 A.M. without encountering any
opposition at all. They raised a flag from a house top and
entrenched in a nearby church. Their right-wing column,
led by Major King, also occupied a house near the river

and raised its flag but this only served to bring down heavy fire from troops in the Plaza de Toros.

On the extreme left the 38th, under Colonel Nugent, found itself in a narrow lane leading to the Plaza de Toros and faced by a large house filled with enemy snipers. Staggering through the thick mud of the street, many soldiers lost their shoes, but the regiment battled on and was able to open heavy fire on Spanish troops in the bullring. With the timely assistance of Auchmuty and some of the 87th, the defenders of that building were forced to surrender.

So far, for all the absurdity of Leveson-Gower's plan, things were going well. This probably resulted from the fact that neither the 38th nor the 87th had gone where he had ordered them; in any case, the Plaza de Toros had been captured and Auchmuty had taken over one thousand prisoners and thirty-two guns. However, British casualties had been very heavy.

To the south of Auchmuty, Lumley's brigade, the 36th and 88th, had encountered strong opposition. The 36th had fought its way through to the riverbank and had hoisted its colors over a tall building there. However, this action brought down on it a hail of fire from cannons in the fort and marksmen in all the surrounding houses so that Lumley could do no more than hold his position.

The 88th was in even more trouble. Its left column, under Major Vandeleur, advanced under a hail of bullets, grenades, stones and every kind of missile, while it was raked by cannon in the Great Square. With great courage Vandeleur led his men over a sandbag defense in the road only to discover that they were trapped, with no outlet to the river. After fighting their way into a nearby house, it soon became apparent that they had no hope of escape and so were forced to surrender. Colonel Duff led the right column of the 88th, which was so depleted in men that its numbers were supplemented by two reserve companies. On their arrival, Duff discovered that their muskets were unserviceable because Leveson-Gower had ordered their flints to be removed. For a while Duff's troops were not molested, until they reached the gates of their original target—the Church of La Merced—whereupon they were hit by volleys of musket fire from the adjacent houses. Failing to break the well-barricaded doors of the church, Duff had no alternative but to surrender, having lost nearly two hundred out of his original five hundred men.

On the extreme right of the British line, the 45th advanced on the Residencia in two columns, under Colonel Guard and Major Nichols, and occupied this building within an hour and with light casualties. This was an important achievement as it gave Whitelocke a strong point on the southeastern flank of the city, within easy reach of the fleet. To the north, the Light Brigade had advanced in two columns, one of six hundred men under Colonel Pack, the other under the personal direction of Craufurd. Both of these columns advanced unmolested as far as the beach. Upon reaching it there was immediate confusion. Craufurd wanted to advance on the fort and ordered Guard to support him with the 45th, ignorant of the fact that Guard had been ordered by Leveson-Gower to occupy the Residencia. Certainly there was no mention of this in the general orders. Pack, meanwhile, assuming that the Great Square and the fort were his targets for attack, turned northwards until, near the Franciscan church, an outburst of firing wounded him and wiped out half his force. Pack tried to convince Craufurd that the situation was hopeless and a withdrawal to the Residencia was advisable, but the general decided instead to advance to the Convent of St. Domingo. Here Craufurd occupied the building and fortified it, but his men were under constant fire from surrounding houses. At noon a Spanish officer, showing a flag of truce, brought a message from Liniers, which Craufurd assumed was a Spanish capitulation. Instead it was a demand for a British surrender. Although Craufurd rejected it, by 3:30 P.M. it was apparent that his position was hopeless and he surrendered. This action marked the final episode in the chaotic assault on Buenos Aires.

Throughout the fighting Whitelocke had simply paced up and down at his headquarters awaiting news. In fact, no reports reached him because none of the commanders in Buenos Aires knew where he was. So confused was the fighting in the city that messengers could not have reached him anyway, and if they had their messages would have borne witness only to the narrow horizons of the officers who sent them, trapped in a maze of roads, shot at from all sides and above or holed up in churches or houses for protection. Once they entered the city Whitelocke's troops were beyond his control.

At nine o'clock Whitelocke sent his aide-de-camp, Captain Whittingham, toward one of the central streets but he was driven back by heavy fire. Whittingham later climbed to the top of a nearby house and was able to report British colors flying in various places, which seemed encouraging but was in fact merely a sign of heroic defiance. Five more hours passed before Whitelocke called for a volunteer to try to gain news of Auchmuty. Whittingham, with an escort, was able to fight his way to Auchmuty and back with news of mixed fortunes: the 87th had been successful but the 88th had been captured. What had happened to Craufurd nobody seemed to know.

Whitelocke, from his distant command post, had been unable to influence affairs one way or the other. Via Whittingham, Auchmuty advised him to move into the Plaza de Toros at once but he refused, hoping that better news might yet reach him. Instead there arrived a letter from Captain Liniers that dashed all his hopes. Liniers stated that he had captured Craufurd and well over one thousand men but was prepared to free not only them but also the survivors of Beresford's command if Whitelocke would remove all his troops from the province. Whitelocke refused this offer at first, suggesting instead a twenty-four-hour truce in order to collect and succor the wounded.

By the time Whitelocke and Leveson-Gower met Auchmuty at Plaza de Toros to assess their situation, it was apparent that British casualties amounted to nearly three thousand, with over four hundred killed. On the other hand, the Spaniards had lost heavily themselves and the British were in possession of strategic points on both sides of the city. It was only a matter of time before the city fell, but Whitelocke was not to be granted that time. His troops no longer had any confidence in him. According to the story told by Rifleman Harris, Craufurd was so furious with his commander that he had ordered his own men to shoot Whitelocke if they got the chance! Everywhere, troops began scrawling graffiti on walls suggesting that Whitelocke was "either a coward, or a traitor, or both." However, frustrating as the general's decision appeared to his troops, it was by now apparent that even if they completed the capture of the city they could not hope to control the whole province without committing the British government to a wholly disproportionate military effort. Whitelocke therefore signed an agreement with Liniers to restore all prisoners and to evacuate the province within ten days, though Montevideo was to be held for a further two months. A proposal for liberty of commerce for British traders was utterly rejected by the Spaniards, and so ended Popham's dreams of commercial empire.

Curiously, Whitelocke was attacked as much for this settlement as for his incompetent handling of the military situation. Really he had no alternative, although his own troops vilified him as a traitor. When the news reached London the reaction was predictably hostile and was heightened by financial loss. Whitelocke's greatest critics were those who had foolishly believed Popham's promises of unlimited wealth and had staked their life savings in this South American venture. Nothing less than a court-martial would satisfy such a wave of public indignation and it duly took place on Whitelocke's return, under the presidency of General Meadows.

Whitelocke faced four charges:

1. That he had driven the people of Buenos Aires to resistance by making excessive demands upon them.

2. That he had mishandled the military operations and had ordered his troops to attack Buenos Aires with unloaded arms.

3. That he had made no effectual effort to control or support the columns once inside the city.

4. That while still in a position to capture the city he had deliberately preferred to evacuate the country.

The sense of national humiliation felt by the British public undoubtedly influenced the findings of the court, which found Whitelocke guilty on all counts except the second. In fact, little consideration was given to the difficulties he had faced, otherwise he could scarcely have been found guilty on point one. It was most unlikely that the Spanish colonies, having freed themselves from the corrupt rule of Spain, would have immediately accepted rule by Britain. Only a form of independence under British protection might have been acceptable and it was precisely this sort

of commitment that the British government was not prepared to make—and indeed had told Whitelocke so.

In the other charges there is far more substance. In spite
of his difficulties with climate and terrain, it is obvious
that Whitelocke did not make the most of what advantages
he did have. The knowledge of Pack and Muskerry, as we
have noted, which could have been vital throughout, was
contemptuously ignored. Instead, much to his cost,
Whitelocke relied on Leveson-Gower. Leveson-Gower was
"as conceited as he was unpractical" and "as overbearing
as he was incompetent." Despite the fact that Leveson-
Gower owed his appointment to Windham, the minister of
war, Whitelocke should have asserted himself and not
come to depend on somebody so obviously inept in military
planning.

Leveson-Gower's plan for the attack on Buenos Aires and
Whitelocke's acceptance of it are evidence of military incompetence. A Spanish commentator thought that half as
many troops could have taken the city and said that "ten
thousand English sheep came to present their throats to
the knife." Why Whitelocke's army needed to be divided
into thirteen different columns is known only to Leveson-
Gower, for the commander himself had earlier in the campaign rejected just such an idea of street fighting, where
the advantage would always rest with the irregulars firing
from the flat roofs of the houses. Why he therefore ordered
an attack that by his own reasoning had to fail is inexplicable.

Whitelocke was understandably criticized for not accompanying his forces into the city and at least keeping in
touch with one or two of the columns. Once the force was
divided into thirteen parts he was certain to lose contact
with all of them. Why was no system of signaling or maintaining communication arranged? Moreover, what added
to the confusion was the additional verbal orders given by
Leveson-Gower to some individual commanders and not
to others. This resulted in the confusion between Craufurd
and Guard at the Residencia. Having confused just about
everybody with his plan, his verbal instructions and his
inaccurate maps, Leveson-Gower now joined Whitelocke
in trying to blame Craufurd and Pack for causing the disaster by disobeying orders. This is easily said, but to the
soldier caught up in the complexities of street fighting or-

ders need to be both simple and clear, which is something
Leveson-Gower's were not. Craufurd defended himself vig-
orously against his accusers, yet in doing so he was placing
too much stress on his orders, which did not constitute a
plan of operations at all. The judge advocate commented
on Craufurd's and Pack's courage and devotion to duty
rather than to the letter of their orders:

> General Whitelocke... imputes the surrender of those
> columns, to a disobedience of the orders he had given:
> he states, that, when the two divisions of the light bri-
> gade had arrived at the river, they turned to the left,
> instead of following the directions he had given, of in-
> clining to the right. I must entreat the Court to consider
> a little what the circumstances were, under which
> those columns found themselves, and most particu-
> larly that division of the light brigade, which was under
> Brigadier General Craufurd... (when) he arrived at the
> Plata... the enemy was all to the left. The Court will
> see, by the plan, that the high buildings, which he was
> directed to occupy, were all to the left; that Colonel
> Pack's division, which he states to you was then en-
> gaged with the enemy... were all to the left. What was
> any officer to do in that situation?[2]

Craufurd could hardly have achieved much by turning
his back on the enemy and following orders based on inaccurate mapwork. Moreover, Pack's decision to turn to
the left was based on the fact that the high buildings he
was supposed to occupy were on the left and there were
no high buildings to the right. Leveson-Gower and Whitelocke had no real idea how victory was going to be achieved.
They simply assumed that the effect of thirteen columns
of British troops advancing through the city would have
been enough to silence obviously second-rate opponents.
Whitelocke was paying the price of undervaluing the enemy, which is a fault that has contributed to military incompetence throughout the ages.

However, the debacle at Buenos Aires was not simply the
result of incompetence on the part of Whitelocke or of
Leveson-Gower, it was also the result of a failure in grand
strategy. The ministers in England had acted in complete
ignorance of the true state of affairs in Spanish South

America. They had considered plans not only for the conquest of Rio de la Plata but Chile as well, without thinking for one moment of the vast distances involved, the terrible climate the British troops would encounter, terrain ranging from almost tropical jungle in places to frozen wastes in Chile, and the great barrier of the Andes Mountains. How could Britain, engulfed in a "life or death" struggle with Napoleonic France in Europe, provide sufficient troops to hold down such a vast area of land?

Whitelocke's instructions were in themselves products of confused thinking. He was ordered to conquer the province of Buenos Aires by force and exile those who had imprisoned Beresford. However, in doing so he was not to cause too much distress to the enemy or occupy too much of his territory. He was to convince the population of the merits of British rule, without committing Britain to any kind of protectorate over them in the event of a Spanish attempt to reestablish their authority. This required a capacity for sleight of hand that eluded General Whitelocke. Perhaps Auchmuty, had he not been superseded, would have managed the military side of the equation, but he would have found politics a far more dangerous arena than the Plaza de Toros in Buenos Aires.

The Loss of Detroit, 1812

At the outbreak of war between the United States and Britain in 1812 there was a general feeling among American nationalists, inspired by the hawkish Senator Henry Clay of Kentucky, that the conquest of Canada would prove to be little more than a military exercise for the new republic. In 1810 Clay had declared: "The conquest of Canada is in your power. I trust I shall not be deemed presumptuous when I state that I verily believe that the militia of Kentucky are alone competent to place Montreal and Upper Canada at your feet."

The American war plan for 1812 was based on a three-pronged attack on Canada from separate points on the border: Detroit, Niagara and Lake Champlain. Unfortunately, to lead the three attacks the Americans had chosen a trio of incompetent commanders: at Detroit, General William Hull, the governor of Michigan Territory; at Niagara, General Stephen Van Rensselaer; and on Lake Champlain, the nominal commander-in-chief of American forces, General Henry Dearborn. In fairness to the men who suffered under their commands it is as well to point out that rarely has any nation suffered, even at the outbreak of a war, from three such nincompoops. If Van Rensselaer and Dearborn had a single virtue it is perhaps that they were more able than William Hull, whose failure is the subject of this chapter. William Hull had been a capable soldier in his youth and had fought with distinction in the War of Independence, but now, at age fifty-eight, he felt quite unequal to the task that lay ahead. Only pressure from President Madison had convinced him to accept the governorship of Mich-

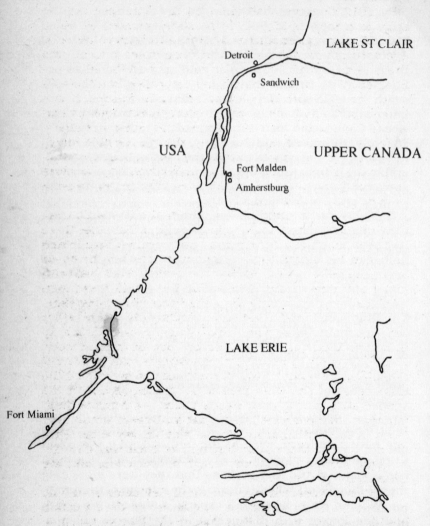

LAKE ST CLAIR

Detroit

Sandwich

USA

UPPER CANADA

Fort Malden

Amherstburg

LAKE ERIE

Fort Miami

GENERAL HULL'S INVASION OF CANADA 1812

igan and command of the American left flank in the attack on Canada.

By 1812 Congress had enlarged the American regular army to a total of 35,000, to be supplemented by up to 100,000 militia and a further 50,000 short-term volunteers. Against such numbers—impressive on paper at least—the British had just 12,000 regular soldiers and Canadian militiamen. With Britain thoroughly embroiled in a life-and-death struggle with Napoleonic France in Europe, it was impossible to find any more British regular troops for service in Canada and recourse was made to Indian irregulars, generally of limited military value, though the able Shawnee chief Tecumseh was to earn the rank of Brigadier General in the British army. But America's advantage was more apparent than real, and as in previous wars, her militiamen were to prove a doubtful asset.

Hull was due to begin his two hundred-mile march from Cincinnati to Detroit on June 15, though at that stage there had been no official declaration of war against Britain and he began his march in total ignorance of when he could begin offensive action against the enemy. Hull had with him 1,500 men of the Ohio militia but found these men troublesome, particularly when they were not paid on time. The Ohio men found his ideas on military discipline rather odd—as, for instance, when he tried unsuccessfully to stop them from "tarring and feathering" one of their officers. Eventually, only by using regular soldiers could he prevent the militia from mutinying. A court-martial sentenced the ringleaders of the Ohio men to be drummed out of the service after having their heads shaved—a humane punishment when compared with what mutineers would have faced in the British army of that time. In any event, Hull did not impose these punishments; he knew that if he did it would drive a permanent wedge between him and the Ohio men.

Hull's northwestern army eventually left camp at Urbana on June 15, 1812, to begin a long march to the Canadian border and their target—Fort Malden (Amherstburg). Muster rolls indicate that Hull commanded 2,075 men in all, though it is doubtful if he ever had so many with him at any one time. The march proved extremely hard—they were obliged to build a road as they went, and as a result averaged just three miles a day. The rainfall was torrential, bringing out hordes of blackflies and mosquitoes to plague the men as they struggled on through the wilderness. As they marched they were aware that Indians were watching them from behind trees, but no attempt at hostility was shown by either side.

On June 27 the army reached the area known as Fallen Timbers where "Mad Anthony" Wayne had defeated Blue Jacket's Indians in 1794. Even this close to Lake Erie, Hull had still not been informed the war had broken out. This perhaps explains his next decision. Spying a schooner at anchor in the river—it was the *Cayacauga*, owned by Captain Chapin of Buffalo—he decided to requisition the boat for a sum of sixty dollars to transport the officers' baggage, the medical supplies, the tools and a trunk containing the army muster rolls—these contained the full details of the column and Hull's official orders and campaign details— to Detroit. Hull was taking an enormous risk, one so serious that he is greatly to blame for what happened next. On the evening of July 1 Captain Chapin in the *Cayacauga* entered the Detroit River and passed under the guns of the British at Fort Malden, little expecting danger. Suddenly a longboat rowed swiftly out into the schooner's path and redcoats poured aboard. The American ship was captured without bloodshed and the whole valuable cargo fell into British hands—muster rolls and all. In addition, thirty sick regular soldiers were taken, along with a motley group of passengers, the chaplain and three officers' wives. Hull had blundered—but was it really his fault?

On July 2 a galloping messenger entered Hull's camp with the news that war with Britain had indeed broken out—some two weeks before. Hull was handed the following message from Secretary of War William Eustis: "War is declared against Great Britain. You will be on your guard—proceed to your post with all possible expedition, make such arrangements for the defence of the Country as in your judgement may be necessary, and wait for further orders."

Why had Hull not been told sooner about the outbreak of hostilities? The fact is that the secretary of state for war had sent the vital information in the ordinary mail to Cleveland, with the request "please forward" to Detroit by the normal post. Fortunately, at least one American had a sense of urgency, and the postmaster at Cleveland sent a special messenger to find Hull. Incredibly, the War Department had not seen fit to inform American frontier garrisons at Fort Wayne, Fort Dearborn and Fort Michilimackinac either, and Hull chose not to interfere with their control of affairs by taking the initiative and sending messengers himself. Aware now that he must place his command on a war footing, Hull marched on to the river Raisin, learning from friendly Indians the dismal fate of the *Cayacauga*.

While the Americans dawdled toward their date with destiny the British and the Canadians—heavily outnumbered—made the best of their resources. The British administrator for Upper Canada—Major General Sir Isaac Brock—had known of the state of war since June 25 and had quickly alerted his garrisons. At Fort Malden, the British commander, Lieutenant Colonel Thomas St. George, had heard the news four days before Hull and had been waiting for the *Cayacauga* with open arms. The loss of the schooner was a bad blow for the Americans, costing them all the official correspondence relating to the expedition, as well as the muster rolls for Hull's force. In this way Brock soon knew more about his enemies than they knew about themselves.

On July 6, Hull sent two of his officers to Fort Malden to ask if the British intended to hold the baggage captured aboard the *Cayacauga*. The Americans were disappointed to be told that the British had already sold most of it and distributed the profit as prize money to the crew that had captured the schooner. Meanwhile Hull faced more serious problems. As he approached Detroit he was leaving the British base at Fort Malden to his rear, allowing the British to threaten his supply line back to the Ohio River. Moreover, he was giving the British too long to organize their own defenses at the fort. To make matters worse, he was already encountering difficulties with the Ohio militia, whose officers informed him that their men would be unwilling to attempt to face British regulars with the bayonet. Any assault on Fort Malden at this stage would therefore have been certain to fail. Hull abandoned plans to attack the British fort and instead marched straight to Detroit, arriving on July 7. So far he had done well with limited resources, but two errors had been committed—not entirely to be laid at his door—that were to have serious consequences: the loss of the schooner *Cayacauga* with his official correspondence and, even more worrying, the fact that the British were in a position to dominate his supply lines to the south.

The town of Detroit, with its fort, had a population of perhaps 800 souls and lived mainly through trade. Originally built by the French in 1701, the town's fortifications were in good repair and were protected by some forty pieces of artillery. So far so good. But Hull soon discovered that he was entirely bereft of naval support and that the British completely controlled the waters of Lake Erie. Nevertheless, he could field over 2,000 soldiers—450 regulars, 1,450 Ohio militia and some 200 militia from Kentucky—and with this force he should have been immune from attack by the British forces at Sandwich and Fort Malden, which were far inferior in numbers, probably no more than 300 regulars when Hull first arrived at the lake. On the other hand, British naval strength was quite formidable, consisting of the brig *Queen Charlotte*, mounting sixteen guns, the schooner *General Hunter*, with six guns, and numerous smaller craft and armed merchantmen. If the British were weaker by land and stronger by sea than their American opponents, their most substantial advantage was in the quality of their commander. Sir Isaac Brock was an outstanding officer who was to outmaneuver William Hull at every turn.

On his arrival at Detroit, Hull faced an immediate problem—namely, how to supply his army. The town was accustomed in peacetime to importing its foodstuffs and now faced an unprecedented increase in population. With the lake a "no-go area" to the Americans, the vital supply route to Ohio assumed even greater importance. Meanwhile, Hull had his orders from Eustis to "take possession of Malden and extend your conquests as circumstances may justify." This might have seemed simple while poring over a map in distant Washington, but Hull was aware of just how difficult his task would be. He had a number of options. Given an indefinite amount of time he might have consolidated his hold on Detroit and—by constant drilling—turned his militiamen into soldiers before attempting to seize Fort Malden. This had its advantages but missed the vital point that the British could similarly consolidate their defenses and, moreover, could tighten their grip on the American

supply lines and possibly starve Detroit into surrender. A
second option—one both hazardous and daring—would
have involved an amphibious landing on the far shore and
an immediate assault on the British positions. This was a
desperate option but would have exploited American advantages in numbers, provided that it could be carried out
when the British ships were off their guard. A third option,
which Hull may well have preferred, would have seen him
fall back along his supply line and reprovision his army at
Miami Rapids. Unfortunately, orders from Eustis had absolutely forbidden Hull to abandon Detroit. Eventually Hull
decided that the most viable plan was to cross the water
to the British fort at Sandwich, drive the British out and
establish enough artillery there to remove any threat to
Detroit and to dominate both sides of the river. Furthermore, Hull believed that many Canadians would welcome
his army as liberators and would turn against the hated
British. Hull therefore issued a proclamation offering to all
Canadians who did not oppose him freedom and protection
in their property and persons. Unwisely, Hull included a
"no quarter" clause that was to rebound on him later, saying that no mercy would be shown to any white man who
fought alongside the Indians.

At dawn on July 12 the American troops prepared for
their crossing of the river opposite Sandwich. But Hull now
encountered an unexpected problem. A hundred of his militiamen refused to cross into Canada on the grounds that
it was illegal to ask them to serve outside the borders of
the United States; others admitted to being deserters from
the British service who would be shot if recaptured. Incredibly, one soldier named Blackhall Stephens petitioned
Judge Woodward of Detroit for protection against General
Hull and had his request upheld. Secretary Eustis even had
to warn Hull in the middle of his campaign not to violate
the man's civil rights. A militia officer was court-martialed
for not carrying out Hull's orders but was promptly re-
elected by his men and Hull was helpless to do anything
about it.

When Hull at last succeeded in getting his men across
the river he found that the British had abandoned the fortress at Sandwich and withdrawn their troops within Fort
Malden. Hull now devoted his attention to the next stage
in his campaign: the assault on Fort Malden itself. However,

far to the north at the head of Lake Huron a decisive event
was taking place that was to change the balance of power
in the campaign. The small British post at St. Joseph Island
was commanded by Captain Charles Roberts with just
forty-six regular soldiers. When Roberts received news
from General Brock that war had broken out he decided to
undertake a daring attack on the American post at Fort
Michilimackinac, where American Lieutenant Porter
Hanks with a small garrison of sixty-one men was blissfully
unaware of the outbreak of conflict with Britain. Taken completely by surprise, the Americans were forced to surrender. The significance of this bloodless victory went beyond
the capture of a fort, for the neighboring Indians, eager to
be on what they thought the winning side, flocked to the aid
of the British at Amherstburg (Fort Malden). Hull would
soon find himself outnumbered. On August 2 the Wyan-
dots—previously friendly to the Americans—changed
sides, and with them came many of the tribes that lived
along the American supply route south from Detroit. Several times Hull's mail was captured by the Indians and
presented to the British, and he could no longer expect to
receive food supplies unless he sent substantial escorts
south to ensure their safety. Hull's situation had taken a
decisive turn for the worse and he now decided to move
the bulk of his force out of Sandwich and back across the
river to Detroit.

While Hull was achieving nothing at Sandwich and Detroit, nemesis was approaching in the persons of two great
soldiers: Sir Isaac Brock and the Shawnee chief Tecumseh.
The latter, on meeting the British general for the first time,
declared "There is a man" and committed his warriors to
serve the British against the Americans at Detroit. Unable
to capture Fort Malden by going forward, or to ensure his
supply line by going backward, poor William Hull now
found that it was not even safe to stand still. His own men—
notably the Ohio militia—had lost all confidence in him
and now looked for a way to be rid of him. The colonels
who led the Ohio militia circulated a "round-robin" letter
of no confidence in Hull "requesting the arrest or displace-
ment of the General, and developing the command on the
eldest of the colonels, McArthur." Even the inhabitants of
Detroit joined in by agreeing amongst themselves "to seize
General Hull and depose him from command."

While Hull faced this threat to his authority, Brock arrived at Fort Malden and made his plans for an assault on Detroit. With the confidence that Hull could no longer feel, Brock bestrode the stage like a Titan, offering amnesty to deserters who had joined the Americans and now wanted to return, promoting officers on merit and inspiring the Canadian militia to acts that would have been unthinkable for the men from Ohio. By August 14, Brock even had one thousand Indians at his disposal and had persuaded their leader, Tecumseh, to join him in the capture of Detroit. Leaving just a token force at Fort Malden, Brock ordered his troops to advance on Sandwich. With their gunboats controlling the river, the British easily retook the fort that they had abandoned just four weeks before. Brock now assembled his artillery to fire across the river at Detroit and prepared his men for an assault on the American town the next day.

Hull's position was growing more desperate as every hour passed. At Raisin River to the south a provision train commanded by Captain Henry Brush was attempting to force its way through Indian ambushes to Detroit. On August 14 Hull sent a strong force of four hundred militia under Colonels McArthur and Cass—significantly, the two officers most deeply involved in the plot to remove him—to relieve Brush and escort him to Detroit. But neither of the militia colonels was eager to leave the town, for obvious reasons. Even though Hull probably was aware of the two colonels' disloyalty, he found himself in an impossible position. If he had attempted to arrest them their men would have mutinied and the entire American position would have collapsed. On the other hand, the colonels were probably his most able subordinates and to order them south—while relieving him of the choice of arresting them or submitting to them—would rob him of their services at the very moment they were most needed. Eventually Hull decided to insist that the men march to the relief of Captain Brush and chose to face the British threat alone.

Across the river General Brock was using psychological warfare to the full, dressing local villagers in red tunics to resemble British regulars and allowing a letter to fall into Hull's hands that said that there were now five thousand Indians at Malden and that more would be superfluous. Hull's nerves seemed to crack and he began to see visions of thousands of British regulars facing him as well as hordes of blood-crazed Indians. The presence of his daughter and grandchildren in Detroit must have further sapped his confidence, two hundred miles from his base and heavily outnumbered. The truth—which he was no longer able to see—was that British strength was approximately equal to his own.

On August 15 Brock must have felt that he had "softened up" his opponent enough, for he sent the following message to the American general:

> The force at my disposal authorises me to require the immediate surrender of fort Detroit. It is far from my intention to join in a war of extermination, but you must be aware, that the numerous body of Indians who have attached themselves to my troops, will be beyond control the moment the contest commences. You will find me disposed to enter into such conditions as will satisfy the most scrupulous sense of honour. Lieutcolonel McDonnell and Major Glegg are fully authorised to conclude any arrangement that you may lead to prevent the unnecessary effusion of blood.[1]

It is doubtful if Brock thought that Hull would respond to this rather cheeky surrender demand, but he knew that the thoughts of an Indian massacre must have played on the old general's mind. While Hull thought matters over, Brock was actively completing British gun emplacements for the bombardment of Detroit, should it prove necessary. Eventually the American commander returned his reply to Brock, bravely declaring: "I am prepared to meet any force which may be at your disposal." Almost immediately a barrage broke out from the British gunboats. It was answered by the American artillery. For two hours the fire continued, providing as noisy and harmless a display of pyrotechnics as the very best fireworks parties, and injuring just a single man on each side. With the drama halted for a while, Brock continued his psychological assault on General Hull's nerves.

Meanwhile, McArthur and Cass were wending their way south to rendezvous with Captain Brush and the supply column. Unknown to them, the captain had abandoned his attempt to leave Raisin River, and when scouts returned with the news that the column was nowhere to be seen, they turned back. Just before dark, they received a message from Hull ordering them to march back to Detroit as fast as possible. They marched into the night and camped just three miles from Detroit, though—either through incompetence or treachery—they failed to inform the general that they were so close to the fort.

The British had already decided to begin their attack on Detroit at three A.M. the next day and arrangements had been made for them to cross the river under cover of the naval guns. As dawn broke Hull saw that three brigades of British regulars had crossed the river and were approaching Detroit, accompanied by Indians on all sides. Brock's plan was for the British to assault the fort while the Indians took the town. Hull's position was now desperate. He could try to meet the British in the open, though his troops were unlikely to stand a bayonet assault by British regulars. On the other hand, he could surrender the fort to Brock and save the lives of the inhabitants of Detroit. The first case might be suicidal but the second was certainly treasonable. It was a difficult choice for a gentle old man whose nerve had been broken by both the efforts of his supposed friends and those of his enemies. Eventually, Hull decided to play for time in the hope that McArthur and Cass might return. He ordered all of his men to withdraw into the fortress and attempt to withstand the British assault. But this was as suicidal as the bayonet charge. Within minutes the British would simply pulverize the fort and all the defenders with their artillery, while the Indians had a free hand to massacre the townspeople. When the news reached him that the Michigan militia had abandoned their posts Hull exclaimed to one of his officers, "My God! what shall I do with all these women and children?" The question was rhetorical; there was no way out now. Suddenly a British shell exploded inside the fort, causing several casualties, and without firing a shot in return Hull ordered a white flag to be raised. Brock could hardly believe his luck. Without thinking, Hull had given his own men the impression that a total surrender was planned, instead of which he still hoped to win concessions from Brock. Perhaps, even now, McArthur and Cass—just three miles away but more involved with their breakfast arrangements—would come in the brink of time. In defense of the two colonels, it must be said that when they sent out scouts they were told by a Frenchman that Detroit had already fallen. Yet it must also be said that it was the belief that the two colonels with their four hundred men were at Raisin River rather than forty minutes' march from Detroit that convinced Hull that he had no alternative but to surrender. The American regular soldiers became prisoners of war, though much to their relief—and the frustration of the Indians—private persons had their property respected. In an attempt to prevent Tecumseh's Indians from moving south and destroying McArthur's and Cass's column, Hull included them all in the surrender document.

While the British raised the union flag over Fort Detroit and their bands celebrated the event with a rendering of "God Save the King" General Hull and his officers were taken aboard the *Queen Charlotte* en route for Montreal. The fate of the Ohio militia—whose part in this sorry tale was far from praiseworthy—was the kindest of all. While far worthier men went into captivity, they were shipped by the British beyond the fear of Indian attack and allowed to return to their homes. Colonels McArthur and Cass, on returning to Detroit, were amply repaid for their disloyalty to Hull by finding that they also were prisoners of the British.

The surrender of General William Hull at Detroit in August 1812 was just one—if perhaps the most ignominious—of a number of disasters that overtook the American armies on the Canadian border at the start of the war. On his return from captivity, Hull was court-martialed for cowardice and sentenced to be shot, but President Madison showed clemency to him on the grounds of his fine record in the War of Independence. Yet like Lear it can be said of Hull that "he was more sinn'd against than sinning." Eventually, faced by a more able commander and possibly more numerous troops, short of provisions and with the responsibility of saving hundreds of civilians from an Indian massacre, Hull had chosen to display moral rather than physical courage. He had made many mistakes on the expedition, but his failures had been compounded by difficulty in dealing with militiamen noted for their intransigence. He had lacked authority and had failed to impose himself on his officers, but their duty had surely been to obey him rather than to behave like unruly schoolchildren and see how far they could go in disobeying their leader. The general who fails receives little pity from his fellow professionals. As American General James Wilkinson wrote of Hull: "Hull's misfortunes grew out of too much precipitancy, too much confidence and too little foresight—I knew him a good officer, but he has forgot his trade..."

Wilkinson's words could just as aptly be applied to the American army as a whole. The Americans had entered the War of 1812 without due consideration of what the war might involve. They lacked able commanders and relied too heavily on militiamen whose performance in previous encounters—notably with the Indians—had often been deplorable. Lacking discipline, the militia was quite incapable of fighting regular soldiers. Hull was a convenient scapegoat for the failures on the Canadian border in 1812 but he was no coward. Hull was the governor of Michigan Territory as well as a general, and this dual responsibility made it difficult for him to risk a desperate defense of Detroit that in all probability would have ended with the massacre of the very people he was supposed to protect. The disloyalty of his officers and the weakness of the American military machine as a whole were not factors for which he alone can be held responsible. Hull's failure at Detroit was symptomatic of a malaise that afflicted the entire American army in 1812. Perhaps it would have been instructive for Henry Clay to have watched the militiamen of Michigan and Ohio as they abandoned their posts and betrayed their leader.

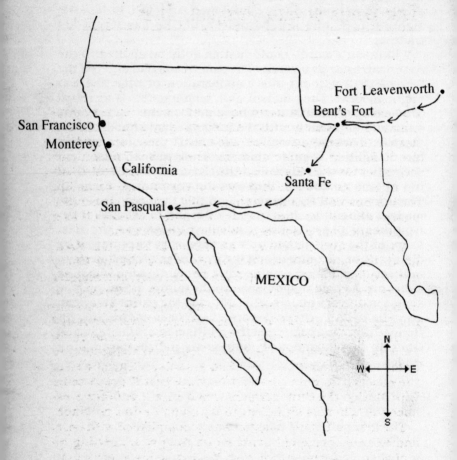

Fort Leavenworth •

Bent's Fort

San Francisco •

Monterey •

California

Santa Fe •

San Pasqual •

MEXICO

N

W ← → E

S

KEARNEY'S MARCH TO SAN PASQUAL 1846

The Battle of San Pasqual, 1846

As a substitute for rational thinking some military commanders fall back on racial stereotypes by which they can assure themselves that "man for man" their own soldiers are in some way superior to the enemy. Such a man was Brigadier General Stephen Watts Kearney, who, at the battle of San Pasqual, in 1846, was guilty of such contempt for his Spanish-Californian opponents that he suffered a sharp reverse—and still had the effrontery to claim it as a victory and gain promotion for his "achievement."

With the outbreak of war with Mexico in 1846, U.S. President James K. Polk and Secretary of War William Marcy decided to send Colonel Stephen W. Kearney, commander of the 1st Dragoons at Fort Leavenworth in Kansas, to march into New Mexico and to occupy Santa Fe. After seizing and garrisoning New Mexico, Kearney—now promoted to Brigadier General—was ordered to press on from Santa Fe with his "Army of the West" deep into California, in order to seize Monterey and San Francisco. Speed was of the essence as Polk wanted to ensure that if peace came with Mexico the United States would have a military presence in California sufficient to lay claim to that province.

The first part of his mission was accomplished with ease, and Kearney occupied Santa Fe on August 18, setting up a civilian government for New Mexico before pressing on into California just four weeks later. With him now rode a mixed group of civilians and soldiers: three hundred dragoons, a party of engineers led by Lieutenant Emory with two small howitzers, and hunters and guides under the experienced Antoine Robidoux and Jean Charbonneau. Unfortunately the party was very poorly mounted for the thousand-mile journey to the coast, many riding "devilish poor" mules, some of which broke down less than a day out of Santa Fe. With difficulty the party moved deeper into California through desert country until, on October 6, they encountered a group of riders who approached them yelling and whooping like Indians. It turned out to be the legendary frontiersman Kit Carson, with a nineteen-man escort, who was taking a message overland to Washington from Commodore Stockton at San Diego. It seemed that the struggle for California was over and that Stockton had raised the American flag in the harbor at San Diego. With John Charles Frémont already penciled in for governor, Kearney's "Army of the West" was no longer needed.

Kearney sent back the bulk of his force to Santa Fe and, keeping with him just 121 men and Kit Carson as guide, he pressed on toward San Diego, sending ahead by the hand of an Englishman named Stokes news that he had annexed New Mexico and established a civilian government there. In his letter to Stockton, Kearney asked for some well-mounted volunteers as an escort. Stockton reacted promptly, sending Lieutenant Archibald Gillespie with a party of thirty-seven volunteer riflemen and a field gun. Gillespie told Kearney about the state of the country ahead and warned him that a band of insurgents led by Andrés Pico was no more than six miles away at San Pasqual. In spite of torrential rain, which had lowered morale in Kearney's party, the general could not resist the opportunity of engaging the Californians. He called a council of war and planned a reconnaissance of the enemy camp, prior to an attack the following morning. A captain named Moore was loud in his opposition to this plan, trying to convince Kearney that he was underestimating the enemy, who were superb horsemen and far too strong for the American troops on their feeble mounts. It would be better to take the camp by surprise and strike the Californians while they were dismounted. Once on their horses the Californians would prove the masters. But Moore was overruled and Kearney insisted on reconnoitering the Californian camp.

Gillespie offered the services of his "mountain men" who could get in and out of the camp without arousing suspicion, but Kearney insisted that the task should be carried out by regulars—his ADC, Lieutenant Thomas Hammond, with six dragoons and the Californian deserter named Rafael Machado—a most unfortunate choice, as it turned out. Machado led Hammond and his party into the valley of San Pasqual, to within half a mile of an Indian camp. The deserter learned from the Indians that Pico and his men—one hundred strong—were resting nearby, completely unaware of the American presence. But Machado was taking too long and Hammond's impatience got the better of him. He rode into the Indian camp with his men, swords clanking, setting the dogs barking. The commotion alerted the Californians, who leaped up shouting, "*Viva California, abajo los Americanos.*" By sheer stupidity Hammond had blown Kearney's cover. As he and his dragoons turned and rode for their lives, pursued by Californian lancers, one of Pico's men found a blanket marked "U.S." and a dragoon jacket dropped in the flight. Pico was now convinced that Hammond's party was merely scouting for a much larger American force. The Californians rounded up their horses and prepared to abandon their camp.

Hammond returned to Kearney's camp to warn him that Pico had broken cover and the general now decided on an immediate attack, even though it was past midnight and the weather was so cold that the bugler could not even sound reveille. Some of the American troopers could hardly hold the reins of their horses, which, with the mules, were in no better state themselves—cold, sore and weak from lack of adequate fodder. Even worse, nobody had seen fit to check the American firearms, which had received a thorough drenching not long before. Unknown to Kearney, he was leading a virtually unarmed force against an unexpectedly dangerous enemy.

Once the Californians had been alerted and surprise was lost, the Americans had little to gain by pursuing them. Yet Kearney was able to convince himself that Pico was barring the road to San Diego and therefore had to be driven off. In fact, nothing could have been further from Pico's mind, which was concerned simply with escape. It was merely the poor impression the American soldiers made on him that tempted him to stand and fight. Kearney—aware of the deplorable state of his mules—was also keen to remount his troopers by capturing some of the horses the Californians had with them. But most telling of all was the impression given to Kearney that the Californians were cowards and no match for his men. How much this impression was gained from listening to men like Kit Carson we cannot be sure, but what is certain is that Kearney underestimated his enemy and failed to take precautions before encountering him. Kit Carson had certainly told the general that "all Americans had to do was to yell, make a rush and the Californians would run away." Nor was Gillespie free of blame, having expressed the view that "Californians of Spanish blood have a holy horror of the American rifle." In fact, Kearney may well have succumbed to the enthusiasm of some of his men, bored after a long march and eager for action. In any case, it was his decision to initiate the action and he was to blame for what happened next. In the words of one observer, "Kearney, having made one of the longest marches in the history of the United States, was spoiling for a fight and intended to have it."

Kearney's men reached a ridge between Santa Maria and San Pasqual still in good order, and it was here that the general had his last opportunity to instill some discipline into his force. Informing them how much their country expected of them and encouraging them to charge with the point of the saber, he gave orders to surround the Californian camp and take as many men alive as possible. The column then began to descend the rocky path into the valley, and soon became blanketed in low clouds and fog. Confusion reigned. An order from the general to begin to trot was misinterpreted by Captain Johnston's men at the front and the captain suddenly drew his sword and shouted "Charge!", even though he was over a thousand yards from Pico's camp. Kearney was heard to exclaim, "O heavens! I did not mean that!" One of the camp followers later wrote in his private journal what happened next:

> Those which were passably mounted naturally got ahead and they of course were mostly officers with the best of the dragoons, corporals and sergeants, men who had taken most care of their animals and very soon this advance guard to the number of about forty got far ahead—one and a half miles at least—of the main body while the howitzer was drawn by wild mules. In the gray of the morning the enemy was discovered keeping ahead and with no intention of attacking but their superior horses and horsemanship made it mere play to

keep themselves where they pleased. They also began to discover the miserable condition of their foes, some on mules and some on lean and lame horses, men and mules worn out by a long march with dead mules for subsistence.[1]

Instead of proceeding as a compact force of riders, Kearney's men lost all cohesion and charged hell-for-leather after the Californians. An advance guard of twelve dragoons under Captain Johnston soon broke away from the men mounted on mules, and with everyone riding madly forward on as unimpressive an array of quadrupeds as ever graced the field of honor, it must have resembled a gold rush rather than a cavalry charge. Behind Johnston—a long way behind, as it transpired—rode Kearney, Lieutenant Emory, and the engineer, William Warner, while behind them, laboring along on mules exhausted by their thousand-mile journey, were a further fifty dragoons. At the back, dragging the guns, came Gillespie with his volunteers.

Captain Johnston rode straight into a party of Pico's men who opened fire, killing him instantly. Seeing more Americans approaching, the Californians rode off again as if in retreat and Captain Moore ordered his men to continue their charge. The chase lasted for another mile, until the American force was stretched out down the valley. Suddenly the Californians wheeled their horses around and charged the leading Americans, lances at the ready. The shock of seeing their fleeing foe turn and confront them made some of the Americans try to fire their rifles, only to discover that their powder was so damp it would not ignite. Thus disarmed, the dragoons were forced to resort to sabers and rifle butts, which were no match for Pico's lances. Captain Moore encountered Pico himself but his pistol misfired and before he could strike with his saber he was speared sixteen times by lances and fell dead from his saddle. The Americans were quite unaccustomed to this kind of melée in which the advantage always rested with the Californians' longer weapon. Almost every dragoon in the forward party suffered from the points of the willow lances. Even more surprising for the Americans was the use made of the lasso, or reata, which Pico's men cast with unerring accuracy, pulling the dragoons from their horses and making them easy targets for the lancers. Seeing Moore mortally wounded, his brother-in-law, Lieutenant Hammond, rode to his side and died with him, pierced through and through by the lancers.

By the time Kearney reached the scene of the action chaos reigned and he was unable to give any coherent commands. It was every man for himself. Matters grew graver as Kearney himself succumbed to a lance thrust in the back. Gillespie and his mountain men were singled out by the Californians, who bitterly hated them, and Gillespie himself suffered numerous wounds, including a lance thrust over the heart. Crippled but undaunted, Gillespie fought his way back to the artillery pieces, which had by now arrived, and brought one into action with the help of a naval midshipman, James Duncan. The Californians, dragging off one of the guns, now broke off the engagement and rode away down the valley. It had been a brief encounter—possibly lasting less than fifteen minutes—but American casualties had been very severe. No more than fifty of the Americans had come into action, but of these twenty-one died and seventeen were seriously wounded. Losses among the officers and NCOs were particularly severe: Captains Johnston and Moore, Lieutenant Hammond, two sergeants and a corporal were all killed by lance thrusts. General Kearney and Captains Warner, Gillespie and Gibson were all seriously wounded, along with Antoine Robidoux.

It had been a thoroughly bad battle from the American point of view. It has been claimed in Kearney's defense that because Pico abandoned the field the Americans were thereby victorious, but it is a ridiculous assertion. Pico had never intended to fight; his only concern was to escape from his pursuers. In his own words he "could not resist the temptation" to attack the Americans because their pursuit was so disorderly and their appearance—on mules—aroused the contempt of his followers, men born to the saddle. Kearney had seriously underestimated his opponents—always a serious mistake in a commander—and knew little of their technique of fighting. His advantage rested in the training of his professional troops and in his own appreciation of the military art. It did not consist in chasing thoroughbred horses on blown mules, or matching damp powder and sabers against lassos and lances. Gillespie should have been able to tell him something about

the way the Californians fought, but it is clear that Kearney
was not in a hurry to listen. Dr. John S. Griffin, who was
present at the battle, mournfully commented, "This was
an action where decidedly more courage than conduct was
shown." One of Moore's dragoons put it more pointedly:
"such another fight was unknown—it was a disgrace";
while a number of his men felt that it would have been no
more than he deserved had the general died from his
wounds. Had he waited for daylight, they suggested, there
would have been far fewer casualties. Kearney blithely reported the battle as a victory, "but [we] paid most dearly
for it."

Kearney's performance at San Pasqual earned him promotion, but might instead have won him a court-martial
for incompetence. In almost every way his leadership was
at fault. The bloody skirmish at San Pasqual was an unnecessary battle, fought to satisfy a general's ego and to
indulge the jaded appetites of a group of adventurers mas-
querading as soldiers. As a professional soldier himself
Kearney made almost every mistake in the book. When
Pico's camp was discovered he ignored Gillespie's offer of
help and allowed the blundering Hammond to alert the
Californians to his presence. He took up the challenge of
pursuing an enemy of unknown numbers and firepower by
night and with a force inadequately mounted and with rifles
soaked by torrential rain. Even though an alternative route
to San Diego was available he claimed that Pico was barring
his route to the coast and had to be challenged. Having
conceded advantages in mobility and firepower to the enemy, Kearney also prepared to fight them on unknown terrain and in such poor visibility—from darkness and mist—
that his own men had great difficulty in telling friend from
foe. But above all—and this is unforgivable in any commander—he allowed the prejudices of others (notably Kit
Carson) to persuade him that his enemy was unworthy of
respect. Underestimating the qualities of the Californians—notably in their horsemanship and in the superiority
of the lance and lasso in close-quarter fighting—he allowed
his force to rush blindly to destruction. Once in action
Kearney failed to impose himself on his men and allowed
Johnston's erroneous order to disrupt the actions of the
entire force. A swift countermand might have brought up
even the advance guard in its tracks. Better by far to allow

the Californians to escape than to allow his own force to be cut up piecemeal.

With General Kearney incapacitated, Captain Turner—the ranking officer—sent an urgent message to Stockton at San Diego asking for help, but before the news of the disaster reached Stockton the "Army of the West" had clashed again with Pico's force near Rancho San Bernardo. Kearney's force was now surrounded by the Californians, who obviously hoped to starve them into surrender. Fortunately, within two days, Stockton's relief force of one hundred sailors and eighty marines led by Lieutenant Gray of the U.S.S. *Congress* raised the siege and escorted the exhausted survivors of Kearney's "army" into San Diego. Kearney's march from Fort Leavenworth had been a triumph of exploration and endeavor, and the general had shown astuteness in dealing with his civil duties in establishing a government in New Mexico. Unfortunately, it was as a military commander that he failed both himself and his men in the wholly unnecessary battle at San Pasqual.

The Battle of Gettysburg, 1863

Bʏ Jᴜɴᴇ 1863 ᴛʜᴇ Wᴀʀ Bᴇᴛᴡᴇᴇɴ ᴛʜᴇ Sᴛᴀᴛᴇs ᴡᴀs ɪɴ ᴛʜᴇ ʙᴀʟ-
ance. In Virginia the Confederates under Robert E. Lee were
at the high point of their success, fresh from whipping the
Federal Army of the Potomac under "Fighting Joe" Hooker
at Chancellorsville. But in the Mississippi Valley they were
facing potential disaster as Union commander Ulysses S.
Grant tightened his grip on the Confederate fortress of
Vicksburg. Unless the siege of Vicksburg could be lifted
the whole of the Mississippi would be in Union hands, cutting the Confederacy in two. Confederate president Jefferson Davis faced a dilemma. Should he call on Lee for troops
to help the defenders at Vicksburg and by so doing blunt
his only sharp weapon in the South's struggle for survival?
Or should he leave Vicksburg to fend for itself and invest
everything in his premier commander? When Davis explained his predicament to his cabinet he was delighted to
hear that Lee already had a plan to take the war into Pennsylvania by pursuing the Union Army of the Potomac and
defeating it once and for all in a decisive battle. Lee's home
state of Virginia had already suffered such devastation in
the previous two years that it was incapable of sustaining
his army there any longer. It would be better by far, Lee
considered, to live off the rich lands of Maryland and Pennsylvania. In any case, if he did not harass the beaten Army
of the Potomac it would regain its morale, perhaps under
a new commander, and resume its drive on Richmond. By
striking north Lee could at least relieve the pressure for a
while. As he wrote to James Seddon, the confederate secretary of war:

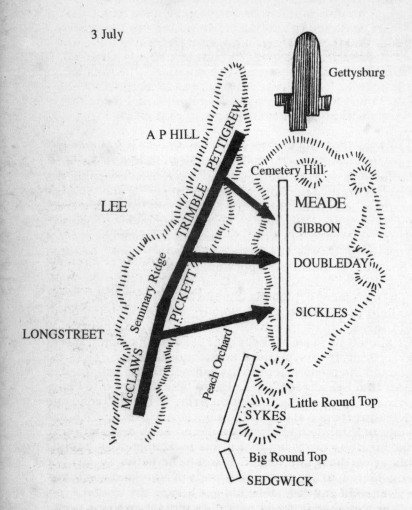

3 July

Gettysburg

A P HILL

PETTIGREW

TRIMBLE

Cemetery Hill

MEADE

LEE

GIBBON

Seminary Ridge

PICKETT

DOUBLEDAY

LONGSTREET

SICKLES

McCLAWS

Peach Orchard

Little Round Top

SYKES

Big Round Top

SEDGWICK

THE BATTLE OF GETTYSBURG 1863

As far as I can judge, there is nothing to be gained by
this army remaining quietly on the defensive, which it
must do unless it can be re-enforced. I am aware that
there is difficulty and hazard in taking the aggressive
with so large an army in its front, intrenched behind
a river, where it cannot be advantageously attacked.
Unless it can be drawn out in a position to be assailed,
it will take its own time to prepare and strengthen itself
to renew its advance upon Richmond, and force this
army within the intrenchments of that city.[1]

Davis was immediately attracted by Lee's proposal to
take the war into the North, threatening the security of
Washington and possibly even forcing President Lincoln's
administration to negotiate a peace settlement. A display
of Confederate strength in the heartland of the North might
even be enough to persuade foreign powers like France and
Britain to recognize the South and offer financial, even
military, assistance.

But both Davis and Lee were chasing shadows. Even an
overwhelming disaster in Pennsylvania would have done
no more than make the North dig deeper into its bottomless
reserves. This—the first of all modern wars—could not be
decided by a single victory or defeat. And to turn away from
the plight of Vicksburg was supreme folly. Nothing Lee
could achieve in Pennsylvania would cause Lincoln to
withdraw troops from around Vicksburg or in any way relax
Grant's relentless grip on the fortress. Time was on the
side of the Union. With her warships controlling the Mississippi and blockading the coasts of the South, she could
afford to wait and take her victories where she found them.
The pressure was on Lee to manufacture victories, to force
the issue and to take the initiative. Could the master of the
riposte, of the masterly maneuver and of the counterstroke
do just as well when he was faced with the urgent need to
win a battle and destroy his opponents?

Abraham Lincoln was one of the few Northerners to really
appreciate the dilemma facing the South's greatest general
as he moved into Pennsylvania in June 1863. So great was
Lee's reputation that for many Northern politicians news
of his coming was as welcome as rumors that the Four
Horsemen of the Apocalypse had been sighted on Pennsylvania Avenue. Instead Lincoln saw Lee's invasion as an

act of desperation. By coming north Lee was exposing his army to defeat and destruction as never before. Deficient in numbers and now robbed of his right-hand man, Thomas "Stonewall" Jackson—killed at Chancellorsville by a Confederate bullet—Lee had come scavenging into his enemy's backyard. Was Lee overconfident and was he losing his poise? Lieutenant General James Longstreet, Lee's stalwart I Corps commander, certainly thought so. Longstreet felt the invasion plan too risky and made his views very clear, but he was overruled and Confederate president Jefferson Davis gave Lee the go-ahead.

The army Lee led north was comprised of 76,224 men and 272 guns, organized into three infantry corps: I Corps under Longstreet, II Corps—for so long "Stonewall" Jackson's—now under Lieutenant General Richard Ewell, and III Corps led by the pugnacious Lieutenant General A. P. Hill. The cavalry division of 12,000 was commanded by the brilliant and dashing "Jeb" Stuart, generally described as the best cavalry leader ever foaled in North America. The Confederate Army of North Virginia was a veteran force, accustomed to victory but perhaps grown overconfident as a result of Lee's string of victories over second-rate Union commanders. Facing Lee, Union commander "Fighting Joe" Hooker—soon to be replaced by George Meade—fielded 90,000 Union troops in seven infantry corps—each smaller than their Confederate equivalents: I Corps was led by John F. Reynolds, II Corps by Winfield S. Hancock, III Corps by Dan Sickles, V Corps by George Sykes, VI Corps by John Sedgwick, XI Corps by Oliver Otis Howard, and XII Corps by Henry W. Slocum, with Major General Alfred Pleasanton in command of the cavalry.

Lee began his invasion of the North on June 3, leaving A. P. Hill's III Corps in position at Fredericksburg to delay the Union army's response. Longstreet's I Corps moved along the eastern edge of the Blue Ridge while Ewell's II Corps moved down the Shenandoah Valley. However, at this moment Lee made the first of the mistakes that were to litter this campaign. Stuart was given permission to take his cavalry division around the right flank of the Union army and carry out a raid in the area of Harrisburg. But this was not enough for Stuart and—forgetting his vital role as the "eyes" of Lee's army—he set off to make war on his own terms. Soon he was raiding the outskirts of Washington and had captured a supply train of 125 wagons no more than ten miles from the unfinished Capitol Building. Carefree Jeb Stuart, a showy dresser who often rode into battle accompanied by a man playing the banjo, sometimes had more courage than sense. And this was one of those occasions. Content to cut telegraph lines, rip up railway tracks and generally enjoy himself, Stuart was not keeping Lee apprised of enemy movements.

Meanwhile Lee and his three corps crossed the Potomac but—short of Stuart's cavalry—were not certain where the Union army was. In fact, Meade had established his headquarters at Taneytown—fourteen miles south of Gettysburg—and his seven corps were widely spread over the countryside between his headquarters and Gettysburg. Lee decided to concentrate his forces around the towns of Cashtown and Gettysburg in Pennsylvania and the battle that ensued on July 1 was entirely fortuitous, for neither commander had a clear idea of the whereabouts of his opponent.

Meade guessed that the only way in which he could effectively defend Washington, as well as Philadelphia and Baltimore, was to find Lee's army and force it to give battle, preferably at a place of his choosing. Sending Buford's cavalry division across Lee's anticipated line of march, Meade hoped to draw the Confederates into battle and then feed more and more men into the struggle as he pinned his opponent down. Supporting Buford would be Major General John Reynolds, at one time considered for Meade's job himself, with the I, III and XI Corps under his command. Buford's advanced guard reached Gettysburg only to find that a few miles to the west of the town were large bodies of Confederate troops—in fact, units of Hill's III Corps. Buford dismounted his men and lined the hedgerows along the Chambersburg road with marksmen. Knowing that he might soon be outnumbered, he sent a messenger to Reynolds asking him to move up in support. Reynolds acted promptly, riding at the head of Brigadier General Wadsworth's division, which contained the famous "Iron Brigade," made up of Midwestern troops kitted out in black hats, and reputedly the toughest fighters in the Union army. The battle of Gettysburg was about to begin as an "encounter battle."

On June 30, one of Hill's divisional commanders, Henry

Heth, had received news that there was a large consign-
ment of shoes in Gettysburg and sent a brigade into town
to secure them. It was these men, marching along the
Chambersburg road, who were fired on by Buford's dismounted troopers. The next day, Hill sent more of Heth's
division to test out the Union defenses and these were soon
engaged in a slugging match with Buford's men, who were
strung out along McPherson Ridge. For two hours Buford's
men held the Confederates at bay until Major General Reynolds arrived with reinforcements from I Corps. No sooner
had Reynolds begun to deploy his men than he was shot
through the head by a Confederate sharpshooter.

While this sharp encounter was taking place both sides
were receiving reinforcements, the Confederates from
Hill's corps to the west and the Federals from the south.
The next Union corps to arrive was Howard's "Dutch" XI
Corps, which deployed north of Gettysburg only to be shattered by Ewell's II Confederate Corps marching south from
Carlisle. Howard, finding himself on Reynold's death the
senior Union commander present, ordered I and XI Corps
to fall back from their positions north of Gettysburg to take
up defensive positions on Cemetery Hill and Cemetery
Ridge.

By the late afternoon Lee had reached the battlefield in
time to see the defeated Union troops streaming through
the deserted streets of Gettysburg. With a number of hours
of daylight left he must have had visions of a sweeping
victory before sunset. All that was needed was for Ewell's
corps north of Gettysburg to maintain their momentum
and the Unionists would never be able to establish defensive positions. The battle would be lost before the rest of
Meade's army even reached the field. But speed was of the
essence, and Lee sent a message to Ewell telling him to
press home his advantage "if possible" but to avoid "a
general engagement" until reinforcements arrived. At this
moment—the first crisis of the battle—Lee failed to impress on his lieutenant just how much was at stake. Accustomed to leaving much to the initiative of men like Jeb
Stuart and Stonewall Jackson, Lee made the mistake of
leaving too much to Ewell's discretion. Ewell was new to
his post and needed the security of an order rather than a
suggestion. Lee's message left Ewell in a quandary. His
own troops had suffered heavy casualties but had beaten

the Yankees, and their morale was high. On the other hand, Lee had suggested waiting for reinforcements. Perhaps caution was called for. In the confusion of the battle Ewell had a far less clear view of the situation than one of his divisional commanders, Jubal Early, who was close to the abandoned Culp's Hill. The hill was covered in woods and so Early could not be certain that the Unionists had fled, but he should at least have found out. This vital position was lost to the Confederates by sheer lack of initiative on the part of Lee's junior commanders.

The first day of fighting drew to a close and by the time Meade arrived on the battlefield—at about one A.M.—it was to find that, partly by chance and partly by the choice of corps commanders like Howard and Hancock, the Union army had occupied a powerful defensive position. South of Gettysburg—on the right of the line—Howard's XI Corps occupied a semicircle around Cemetery Hill reaching back to Culp's Hill, where Slocum's XII Corps was to take up position a few hours later. To Howard's left—along Cemetery Ridge—stood the remnants of I Corps, Hancock's II Corps, and at the extreme southern flank the III Corps of Dan Sickles. Behind Sickles, Sykes's V Corps was in reserve until the later arrival of Sedgwick's VI Corps the following afternoon. It was a surprisingly strong position considering the speed with which it had to be established and should have been sufficient to keep even the redoubtable legions of Robert E. Lee at bay but for two glaring errors. In the first place, through an oversight, two strategically vital hills—Round Top and Little Round Top—had not been occupied by Union troops. Possession of these points would have allowed Confederate gunners to enfilade the troops on Cemetery Ridge and undermine the entire Union position. The second error was the responsibility of Major General Dan Sickles. Ordered to occupy the southern edge of Cemetery Ridge, Sickles was convinced that a far better position existed a thousand yards farther forward—on Seminary Ridge—where the land overlooked his allocated position. He requested Meade's permission to advance but when Meade's answer was inconclusive he took the matter into his own hands and moved his entire corps into a virtual no-man's-land along the Emmitsburg road and with both his flanks in the air. When Meade saw what Sickles had done his temper got the better of him—not for the first time—but by then it was too late to fall back.

As dawn broke on July 2 Lee was confident that he could turn the previous day's advantage into a smashing victory. In a series of battles against these same Union troops he had always gained the advantage and he could see no reason for changing his opinion that—man for man—his men were better than the Yankees and his commanders far more able than their Union counterparts. But his judgment was clouding. He was being drawn into an attritional battle in which his numerically weaker Army of North Virginia was bound to suffer casualties it could ill afford. Robbed of his cavalry "eyes" and his capacity for maneuver, he was opting for battle against a Union army fighting in strong defensive positions and on its own soil. Meade was inviting him into a clinch where the attacking qualities of his men would be ground down. Nor could he afford to wait before attacking Meade. Living off the country imposed its own time limits, and without an immediate victory Lee would be forced to retreat into Virginia, the whole campaign a failure, with all that that would mean for a Confederacy bracing itself for news that Vicksburg had at last fallen. The situation was such that Lee can hardly be blamed for wishing away his darker thoughts and committing everything to an outright victory on July 2.

The absence of Jeb Stuart—and the death of Stonewall Jackson at Chancellorsville—had removed one of Lee's usual options: the decisive maneuver and the lightning strike by Stonewall's hard-marching II Corps. Thus, as General Longstreet rode up to join Lee on July 2 he found his chief unusually inflexible. To Longstreet the situation seemed clear. The Federalists were in a strong defensive position that precluded frontal assaults. The obvious move was to march round the Union left flank and hit them from the rear. Lee listened patiently to his deputy, pointing out that his ignorance of the precise whereabouts of all of Meade's corps left him open to the possibility of being struck in the flank as he marched south. Without Stuart to reconnoiter for him the option of turning a flank—though attractive—was too risky. Instead he would attack both flanks of Meade's army and hope to break them with frontal assaults. He was confident that his men could do it; after all, when had they failed him in the past? Longstreet was not so confident. Gazing through his telescope at the Union position on Cemetery Ridge he thought it far too strong to attack. There was a danger that the battle could become a Fredericksburg in reverse, with his own men dying on Cemetery Ridge just as Ambrose Burnside's bluecoats had died on Marye's Heights the previous year. Surely it would be better to turn the Union's southern flank? But Lee was adamant and he gestured at Cemetery Hill, saying, "The enemy is there, and I am going to attack him there." Longstreet replied in anguish, "If he is there, it is because he is anxious that we should attack him; a good reason, in my judgement, for not doing so." Longstreet was disappointed to find that Lee was exchanging the rapier for the hammer. Whether he was sulking when he left the meeting with Lee we will never know for sure. But certainly his heart was not in the plan that Lee had adopted, and he has been roundly criticized for the way in which he implemented it.

Lee's plan was for Longstreet to march south down Seminary Ridge before turning to attack the Union III and V Corps at the extreme left of the Union position. Simultaneously Ewell would attack Culp's Hill on the Union right flank, while Hill's corps would launch attacks supporting either flank attack. But the fighting could not begin until Longstreet got his men into position and Longstreet was in no hurry to oblige. Although Lee never criticized his corps commander for the delay that ensued, military historians have been quick to point out that in the time wasted Sykes's V Corps reached the field and came to the help of Sickles's stricken III Corps, and—at two P.M.—Sedgwick's VI Corps arrived to form a vital reserve. Had Lee's instruction for a morning assault been carried out it is difficult to see how the Union army could have avoided disaster. As it was, it was not until four P.M.—at least five hours after Longstreet received his order—that the bulk of the Confederate I Corps struck Dan Sickles.

Before Longstreet launched his attack Confederate gallopers brought him the startling news that both hills to the south—Little Round Top and Round Top—were unoccupied. His divisional commanders—McClaws and Hood—urged him to disobey Lee's orders and turn the Union's left flank. But Longstreet refused. He had already tried to change Lee's mind once on that score and would not try again.

At four P.M. Longstreet ordered his corps—twelve thou-

sand strong—to attack Sickles head-on. While his artillery
pounded the Union position, Hood's division struck from
the south and McClaws from the west. In some of the bloodiest fighting of the whole war the Federals were pushed
back from the peach orchard and wheatfield, falling back
into a rocky area later ominously known as the Devil's Den.
Sickles was carried from the field with a shattered leg, but
as III Corps began to crack under the relentless pressure
Meade fed in a division from Hancock's II Corps and the
whole of Sykes's V Corps. And then occurred one of the
chance events that frequently play such a part in deciding
the outcome of battles and for which no planner can make
allowance. Dan Sickles's advance from Cemetery Ridge had
uncovered the two Round Top hills, and with Hood's men
swarming around the Devil's Den it was only a matter of
time before they occupied these strategic high points. The
situation was saved by Meade's chief engineer—General
Gouveneur Warren—who discovered that the vital hills
were unprotected at the very moment that a brigade of Al-
abamians was advancing to seize them. Showing initiative
sadly lacking in Ewell and Early the previous day, he redirected the 20th Maine Brigade to defend the hills,
where—for the next two hours—they fought a ferocious
and successful battle against the Alabama troops. Inspired
by their commander, Colonel Joseph Chamberlain—a pro-
fessor in civilian life—they drove the Confederates back at
bayonet point and finally captured many of them. But if the
crisis on the left of the Union line had been averted, cracks
were appearing farther north where Hill's III Corps was
threatening to break the Union center. Desperate to plug
the gaps here, Meade took the dangerous step of with-
drawing XII Corps from the right of his line, facing Confederate II Corps. This was exactly what Lee was hoping
would happen and now the opportunity to exploit the situation fell once again to Ewell.

Ewell's orders from Lee had been to demonstrate against
Cemetery Hill and to await the outcome of Longstreet's
attack on the left of the Union line. If, through pressure
elsewhere, Meade was forced to transfer troops from his
front, Ewell was ordered to exploit any gaps. Ewell had had
ample time to brief his divisional commanders and reconnoiter the ground ahead, but through slackness this was
not done. Even though Longstreet's attack had gone in at

four P.M. it was not until ninety minutes later that Ewell
ordered his men forward. Even then one of his divisions—
Johnson's—was a mile away from its starting point, ensuring another hour's delay. When the attack finally took
place Early's division was unable to make any progress
against Cemetery Hill but Johnson's gained a foothold on
Culp's Hill. Yet by now it was too late to exploit even this
minor success. And what Ewell did not know was that of
the sixty-four hundred Union troops who occupied Cemetery Hill at four P.M. there were just twenty-nine hundred—
without reserves—holding it by the time he launched his
tardy attack, and the situation was much the same on
neighboring Culp's Hill. If Ewell had launched his attack
simultaneously with Longstreet, Meade would have faced
the impossible task of shoring up the Union lines everywhere and a Confederate breakthrough somewhere would
have been certain. In fact, had Ewell started earlier it is
difficult to see how he could have failed to take both Cemetery Hill and Culp's Hill. His handling of his corps had
been disappointing, to say the least, and the confusion
between his divisional commanders combined with a general lack of initiative probably cost Lee victory on July 2.

As the second day ended there was little elation in either
camp. The Confederates had had their chances to win but
had so far not taken them. The Unionists were relieved not
to have lost, and Meade for one wondered whether they had
done enough already and should withdraw rather than see
the battle through to its conclusion. At a conference with
his generals in a farmhouse on Cemetery Ridge, Meade
suggested the possibility of withdrawal to a better position
at Pipe Creek but was persuaded to stay. General Doubleday—present at the meeting—recorded Meade's final words
as he left the meeting: "Have it your own way, gentlemen,
but Gettysburg is no place to fight a battle." If true, this is
an extraordinary description of the wonderful defensive
position chosen for him the day before by Howard and Hancock.

By July 3 Lee had lost his way. Tired and ill with diarrhea,
he was allowing Meade to dictate how the battle would be
fought. The master of the rapid deployment had become
little more than a head-down slugger. Cemetery Ridge was
an obsession with him that loomed larger and larger all
the time. Instead of planning to outflank Meade he was con-

tent to batter away at the Union defenses in search of the
decisive victory that he felt would end the war. Now reinforced by Stuart's cavalry—at last—and Pickett's division, he planned for the third day of the battle a huge
artillery bombardment of the ridge to be followed by a frontal attack on what he took to be the weak center of the
Union line. Longstreet was speechless with fury when he
heard, and he argued vehemently for an attack on Meade's
left flank but Lee would not listen. He was convinced that
the center must be weak now that Meade had directed so
much of his strength to his flanks. He ordered Longstreet
to attack the Union center on the ridge with the fifteen
thousand men of Pickett's division, supported by brigades
from Pettigrew's and Trimble's divisions. Speaking as if for
posterity, Longstreet told his commander, "General Lee,
there never was a body of fifteen thousand men who could
make that attack successfully." Lee simply replied that his
men could do it. Longstreet reported later, "That day at
Gettysburg was one of the saddest of my life."

From the start everything went wrong. Coordination,
which had been bad the previous day, was again lacking.
Ewell's attack on Culp's Hill, which should have been timed
to coincide with Pickett's assault at one P.M., began just
after dawn. This time the fault was Lee's, not Ewell's. He
should have known that once there was enough light the
fighting around Culp's Hill would begin again. The two
sides were too close for any extended truce. By four A.M.
men of the Union's XII Corps were fighting with Johnson's
division in an effort to clear them from their partial occupation of Culp's Hill. All morning long the fighting raged
on this front, but by midday Ewell had been well and truly
driven back. Lee could expect no more success on the
Union right flank.

Around lunchtime a hush fell on the battlefield. Whether
he was aware or not of the gamble he was taking—for Lee's
mind seems to have been far from clear on this third day
at Gettysburg—the Confederate commander was about to
risk everything on a single head-down charge against a
strongly defended Union position. The great captains of
history must have covered their eyes. Lee was about to
make the kind of mistake that had seen Burnside cursed
as a butcher for Marye's Heights—or, more kindly, a buffoon. But this was Bobby Lee—proving himself as

wretchedly human as the next man, obsessed by a target from which he should have turned his head in contempt. Even his most loyal subordinate—"Old Pete" Longstreet— could do nothing to turn him from catastrophe. He was staking the future of the Confederacy on a throw of the dice. And should Pickett fail and Meade prove less cautious than expected, the whole Army of North Virginia could be swept away and the war lost. It was a risk unworthy of so great a commander and so gentle a man. He was expecting his men to walk on water, to march through fire, to defy death itself, because he willed it. It was hubris and it was heartbreaking.

At one A.M. the Confederate artillery—General Alexander's 138 guns—opened the biggest bombardment ever heard on the American continent. A torrent of shells fell on the Union positions on Cemetery Ridge, particularly on the divisions of Hancock's II Corps. But impressive as it was—and to observers it seemed that nothing could have survived such a bombardment—the Confederate gunners were overshooting and the frontline troops suffered relatively light casualties. In the face of Lee's guns Meade's 80 artillery pieces were almost silenced. But the Union gunners were waiting for a much more valuable target: the infantry they knew would begin their assault when Alexander's guns stopped firing.

Once the guns were silent and the smoke had begun to drift away from the valley between the two armies, the Union troops saw a massive force of fifteen thousand Confederate infantry—a mile in width—assembling along Seminary Ridge. It was the all-Virginia division of General Pickett, supported by brigades from Pettigrew's and Trimble's divisions. Even at this late stage Longstreet wanted to spare his men this martyrdom, but orders were orders. When Pickett asked him, "General, shall I advance?" Longstreet was so choked with emotion that he could not reply. Pickett repeated his question but all he could get from "Old Pete" was a desperate look and a quick nod of the head. Mounting his horse, Pickett rode out at the head of his men. Pickett's charge at Gettysburg is an American epic—as magnificent and as futile as the charge of the Light Brigade at Balaclava. In this single action Lee was squandering the cream of his army and accepting casualties the South could not afford. At this moment the men of the Old

South—veterans of all Lee's victories—were being cast to the winds in a lost cause. The scene had a certain tragic grandeur, yet had the men marched on the orders of an Ambrose Burnside, a John Pope or a Benjamin Butler, the charge would have been denounced as the merest butchery. The fact that it was Robert E. Lee who sent them to needless death makes Pickett's charge the stuff of tragedy.

As Pickett's men crossed the valley toward the clump of trees on Cemetery Ridge that was their target they soon realized that their artillery had failed them. The Union guns were intact and soon opened a devastating fire of grape and canister that cut swathes through their lines. Worse, with both flanks in the air, men from Union XI Corps on Cemetery Hill opened a steady fire that shattered Pettigrew's men on the left of the line, while on the right the men in gray were harried by the artillery and infantry fire of Union III Corps. In places—notably where Colonel Armistead heroically led a brigade with his hat held aloft on his sword—the Confederates reached the Union guns, but in most places they were sent tumbling down the slopes of Cemetery Ridge. Reluctantly—with more than two thirds of his force gone— Pickett ordered the retreat, and his sullen troopers stumbled back toward their lines.

A British military observer, Colonel Freemantle, was standing with General Longstreet and witnessed the charge and its repulse. He remarked to Longstreet, "I wouldn't have missed this for anything." Longstreet replied, "The devil you wouldn't! I would like to have missed it very much; we've attacked and been repulsed; look there!" Freemantle then saw Lee arrive at the front:

He was engaged in rallying and in encouraging the broken troops and was riding about a little in front of the wood, quite alone, the whole of his staff being engaged in a similar manner further to the rear. His face, which is always placid and cheerful, did not show signs of the slightest disappointment, care, or annoyance; and he was addressing to every soldier he met a few words of encouragement, such as: "All this will come right in the end; we'll talk it over afterwards; but in the meantime all good men must rally. We want all good and true men just now." He spoke to all the wounded men that passed him, and the slightly wounded he exhorted to "bind up their hurts and take up a musket" in this emergency. Very few failed to answer his appeal, and I saw many badly wounded men take off their hats and cheer him.

He said to me, "This has been a sad day for us, Colonel—a sad day; but we can't expect always to gain victories." I saw General Willcox come up to him and explain, almost crying, the state of his brigade. General Lee immediately shook hands with him and said cheerfully: "Never mind, General, all this has been *my* fault— it is I that have lost this fight, and you must help me out of it in the best way you can."[2]

Such behavior at times like this was sublime—but sadly it concealed military mistakes for which the description "ridiculous" might not be too hard. Longstreet had warned Lee what would happen and yet he persevered because his belief in himself and in his men went beyond rational thought. As he later said, "I thought my men could do anything."

With Ewell pegged back on the Union right and Longstreet's corps in disorder after the shattering defeat of Pickett's charge, Lee was beaten and he knew it. At any moment he expected the blue lines on Cemetery Ridge to roll down in a relentless and unstoppable charge that would have broken his army once and for all. But Lee was saved by his own reputation. Meade could not believe what had happened. So often had the Army of the Potomac suffered at the hands of Bobby Lee and these same invincible gray warriors that he could not accept the thought that they had been well and truly whipped. And as the situation became clearer to him he clung ever more firmly to the fact that he had won the battle and beaten Bobby Lee. Certainly it was only a defensive victory, but he was unhappy at the thought of risking any victory in pursuit of so dangerous an opponent. Meade was by nature a cautious commander and his army had suffered tremendous casualties—perhaps as many as twenty-three thousand men. Nor could he know that Lee had suffered even more, perhaps 33 percent of his total force. It was all very well for President Lincoln in Washington to curse and rail at his caution, but Meade had achieved what no other Union commander had achieved so far in the war—a clear and decisive victory over the Army of North Virginia with Lee at its head.

The fourth day of July, 1863, was the blackest day of the war for the Confederacy. If Lee's invasion of the North had been aimed at diverting Union strength from the siege of Vicksburg, it had failed, for on this day—with Lee's army broken but defiantly holding its ground at Gettysburg—Vicksburg and its garrison of thirty thousand Confederate soldiers fell to Grant and the worst fears of Jefferson Davis were confirmed. Now there would be no foreign recognition, no sudden British intervention to turn the tide of war. The South would have to fight alone and Lee would have to withdraw his army from Pennsylvania and return to Virginia to protect the capital.

Already the wagons—crowded with the wounded of Gettysburg—were heading back toward the river crossings of the Potomac. Still Meade did not attack, and Lee began to dare to hope that he would be allowed to withdraw from the stricken field unchallenged. Lee could not fathom Meade's mind. Meade was happy enough to see the Confederates retreating and leaving Northern soil. But Abraham Lincoln despaired of his generals: "Will our generals never get that idea out of their heads? The whole country is our soil." In the words of historian Bruce Catton, "The Union was endangered, as Lincoln saw it, not because Lee's army was north of the Potomac but because Lee's army existed at all."

Lee's campaign in Pennsylvania was a flawed conception. It merely directed *attention* away from the vital siege of Vicksburg; it directed no actual soldiers or war materials away from the South's vital fortress on the Mississippi. Even had Lee succeeded at Gettysburg there were other Union armies and better commanders than Meade. The North was more than a general, an army, a battle or even a capital city—it was an idea. And while Abraham Lincoln clung to his view of the Union no amount of Confederate victories could secure them what they sought—independence.

Gettysburg was a personal defeat for Robert E. Lee. His subordinates—so reliable in numerous encounters—drew little inspiration from their great commander. The absence of Stonewall Jackson and Stuart's dereliction of duty robbed Lee of much of his luster. Ewell—uncertain on both the first and second day's fighting around Cemetery Hill and Culp's Hill—was no substitute for the man whose absence, Lee believed, cost him the battle. And Stuart had left Lee blind at vital moments throughout the fight, notably by the lack of reconnaissance that would have enabled Longstreet to turn the Union left flank at the Round Tops on July 2. Longstreet often acted from pique throughout the encounter, and if he was proved right on two separate occasions, it added nothing to the efficiency of Lee's army that its generals could not see eye to eye. But if his subordinates failed Lee, he failed them also, seeming to lack inspiration and falling back on the most basic form of command, the frontal charge and the attempt to break the enemy by main force. Against a more numerous enemy, entrenched in strong positions, Lee was asking his army to fight the wrong kind of fight. In the business of butchery Meade was his equal, and in an attritional battle the Union would win every time. Lee lost more than a battle at Gettysburg, he lost an army and a war. He would have more successes in the months to come but they were limited, temporary ones. After Gettysburg it was only a matter of time before the enormous advantages of the Union—in numbers, materiel and wealth—would grind Lee down in the dreadful attritional struggle around Richmond in 1864 and 1865.

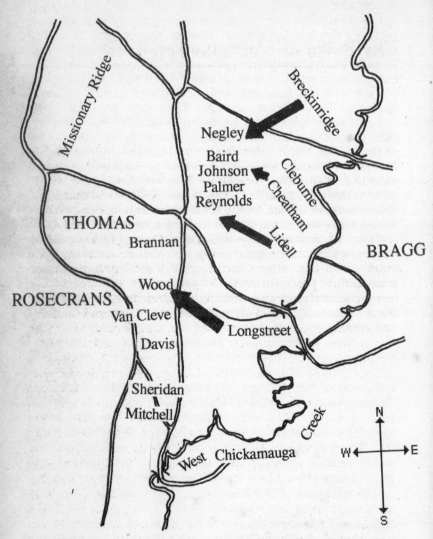

The Second Day of the Battle of Chickamauga, 1863

The Battle of Chickamauga, 1863

THE BATTLE OF CHICKAMAUGA WAS NOTABLE MORE FOR THE courage of the fighting men than for the skills of their generals. Both Union commander William Starke Rosecrans and his Confederate opponent, Braxton Bragg, made mistakes that, if exploited, would have led to their defeat. Rosecrans, made overconfident by his bloodless victory at Tullahoma, seemed to think that war could be reduced to the movement of armies like flags on a map. Convinced that intellectual defeat must have reduced the Confederates to a desperate rout, he divided his army in the face of the enemy and pushed separate corps and divisions through gaps in the Cumberland Mountains like "rats popping out of a hole." The fact that he got away with it says much for the confused thinking of the Confederates and the fact that Braxton Bragg neither trusted nor was trusted by his subordinate commanders. Whether Bragg was to blame for his failure to crush the Army of the Cumberland in detail before Chickamauga, or whether—as Bragg insisted—it was the fault of men like General/Bishop Leonidas Polk, who failed to carry out his orders, is an academic point. The fact was that Rosecrans was able to reform his army and fight the battle of Chickamauga. His subsequent martyrdom—and that of the right wing of the Union army—happened because a simple misunderstanding (not unlike Lord Raglan's confusing order that caused the charge of the Light Brigade at Balaclava) was visited with punishment so severe that it seemed as if the hand of God had smitten the Union army with a biblical destruction not unlike that of Pharaoh's army in the Red Sea. But if Bragg did not deserve to win the battle, Rosecrans deserved to lose it. In any event, it was James Longstreet—sojourner from Lee's Army of North Virginia—who really gained the victory, and George Thomas—the Virginian Unionist—who saved the army, became a legend and was eventually selected by Lincoln to replace the broken Rosecrans.

July 1863 was a tragic month for the Confederacy. As a leading Confederate, Josiah Gorgas, wrote on the twenty-eighth day of that month:

> Events have succeeded one another with disastrous rapidity. One brief month ago we were apparently at the point of success. Lee was in Pennsylvania, threatening Harrisburg, and even Philadelphia. Vicksburg seemed to laugh all Grant's efforts to scorn... Port Hudson had beaten off Banks' force... Now the picture is just as sombre as it was bright then.... It seems incredible that human power could effect such a change in so brief a space. Yesterday we rode on the pinnacle of success—today absolute ruin seems to be our portion. The Confederacy totters to its destruction.[1]

On July 4, coinciding with the fall of Vicksburg, news reached President Abraham Lincoln of another Union victory—a bloodless one—by which General William Rosecrans—"Old Rosey"—had completely outmaneuvered Confederate general Braxton Bragg in eastern Tennessee, forcing him to abandon his defenses around Tullahoma. With Union general Ambrose Burnside and the Army of the Ohio threatening to move through the Cumberland Gap to occupy Knoxville—a center of pro-Union sentiment— Rosecrans now planned to move on to the vital railway junction of Chattanooga, where Bragg was making a stand. It had been a masterly campaign and Rosecrans was incensed at how little personal credit he gained for it as compared to Meade at Gettysburg and Grant at Vicksburg. As he told Union Secretary of War Stanton, "You do not appear to observe the fact that this noble army has driven the rebels from Middle Tennessee.... I beg in behalf of this army that the War Department may not overlook so great an event because it is not written in letters of blood."

But Rosecrans, pleased as he was with himself and his

men, was in no hurry to pursue Bragg. Six weeks were
allowed to pass before he reopened the campaign. Then
McCook's XX Corps and Thomas's XIV Corps made a right
flanking march, crossing the Tennessee River below Chattanooga, while Crittenden's XXI Corps moved toward the
city. Again, Bragg found himself outmaneuvered, and with
his communications with Atlanta threatened, he was
forced to evacuate Chattanooga, allowing Crittenden's
corps to occupy the city on September 9.

With matters growing serious in Tennessee, Jefferson
Davis took the opportunity provided by the deadlock along
the Potomac after Gettysburg to reinforce Bragg from Lee's
Army of North Virginia. Davis detached two divisions from
Lieutenant General James Longstreet's I Corps and rushed
them by railroad to join Bragg. Forced to bypass eastern
Tennessee, which had been occupied by Burnside, Longstreet's men had to endure a rail journey of nine hundred
miles through North Carolina, South Carolina and Georgia,
using as many as ten different lines to reach Bragg. Only
half of Old Pete's men arrived in time to fight at Chickamauga, but even so their presence was to prove decisive.

Rosecrans was unaware of these troop movements, by
which Bragg's army would soon number seventy thousand
men, more than the fifty-nine thousand of his own Army
of the Cumberland. But more serious than that, he was
suffering from the delusion that his masterly maneuvers
had sent Bragg reeling back in disorderly defeat. It was on
this erroneous assumption that he allowed himself to be
drawn into the mountains south of Chattanooga with his
three corps spread out across a fifty-mile front, just asking
to be defeated in detail. Rosecrans was more confident than
some of his officers, and when word of their uncertainty
reached Washington, Assistant Secretary of War Dana was
sent from the capital to investigate. At last the truth was
revealed: Bragg was no longer retreating but had instead
withdrawn to Lafayette, and on hearing that he was to be
reinforced by Longstreet began to plan an offensive.

Bragg was by nature a gloomy and despondent man who
enjoyed poor relations with his corps and divisional commanders. His many retreats had made people doubt his
abilities and had alienated his men, who lacked confidence
in his appetite for the war. He considered himself particularly ill served in this campaign, for several times between

September 10 and 13 he had been shamefully let down by his corps commanders, who failed to crush isolated parts of the Union army. On September 10 Major General James S. Negley escaped from certain destruction at McLemore's Cove, as did Major General Thomas L. Crittenden at Gordon's Mills three days later. Claiming that their orders were discretionary, Bragg's corps commanders had apparently decided that discretion was the better part of valor and declined to join battle with the Union troops.

Union XIV Corps commander George Thomas, for one, breathed a sigh of relief, commenting that "nothing but stupendous blunders on the part of Bragg can save our army from total defeat." According to Confederate general D. H. Hill, these blunders can be laid at Bragg's door:

So far as the commanding general was concerned, the trouble with him was: first, lack of knowledge of the situation; second, lack of personal supervision of the execution of his orders. No general ever won a permanent fame who was wanting in these grand elements of success, knowledge of his own and his enemy's condition, and personal superintendence of operations in the field.[2]

Bragg seemed to be getting out of his depth:

General Bragg had said petulantly a few days before the crossing into Will's Valley: "It is said to be easy to defend a mountainous country but mountains hide your foe from you, while they're full of gaps through which he can pounce upon you at any time. A mountain is like the wall of a house, full of rat-holes. The rat lies hidden at his hole ready to pop out when no one is watching. Who can tell what lies hidden behind that wall?" said he, pointing to the Cumberland range across the river.[3]

Hill was also highly critical of Bragg's failure to comprehend the opportunities he was facing:

The truth is, General Bragg was bewildered by "the popping out of the rats from so many holes." The wide dispersion of the Federal forces, and their confrontal of him at so many points, perplexed him, instead of being a source of congratulation that such grand opportunities were offered for crushing them one by one. He seems to have had no well-organized system of independent scouts, such as Lee had. . . . For information in regard to the enemy, apparently, he trusted alone to his very efficient cavalry. But the Federal cavalry moved with infantry supports, which could not be brushed aside by our cavalry. So General Bragg only learned that he was encircled by foes, without knowing who they were, what was their strength, and what were their plans.[4]

According to Hill, Major General Hindman's failure to destroy Negley's Second Union Division at McLemore's Cove was the result of errors by Bragg himself. Bragg had instructed Hindman "to retire if he deemed it not prudent to attack"—hardly the orders of a general committed to a decisive victory. On September 13, Hill writes, Polk had been ordered to attack Crittenden at Lee and Gordon's Mills. Bragg had sent the following order to Polk:

GENERAL: I inclose you a despatch from General Pegram. This presents you a fine opportunity of striking Crittenden in detail, and I hope you will avail yourself of it at daylight tomorrow. This division crushed, and the others are yours. We can then turn again on the force in the cove. Wheeler's cavalry will move on Wilder so as to cover your right. I shall be delighted to hear of your success.[5]

Polk was slow to react and this order was repeated twice:

The enemy is approaching from the south—and it is highly important that your attack in the morning should be quick and decided. Let no time be lost.[6]

But Polk was frustratingly unaware of the great opportunity he was missing, as Bragg later complained:

At 11 P.M. a despatch was received from the general [Polk] stating that he had taken up a strong position for defence and requesting that he should be heavily reinforced. He was promptly ordered not to defer his attack—his force being already numerically superior to the enemy—and he was reminded that his success depended upon the promptness and rapidity of his movements. He was further informed that Buckner's corps would be moved within supporting distance the next morning. Early on the 13th I proceeded to the front ahead of Buckner's command, to find that no advance had been made upon the enemy and that his forces (the enemy's) had formed a junction and recrossed the Chickamauga. Again disappointed, immediate measures were taken to place our trains and limited supplies in safe positions, when all our forces were concentrated along the Chickamauga threatening the enemy in front.[7]

Aware of just how lucky he had been to avoid being destroyed piecemeal, Rosecrans drew his army together again just west of Chickamauga Creek, on a six-mile front from Lee and Gordon's Mills to Pond Springs. Bragg, having missed his chance, now concentrated on the east bank of the Chickamauga, planning to turn the left flank of the Union army, cutting it off from Chattanooga. But in the dry late-summer weather the Confederate troops threw up vast columns of dust, allowing Rosecrans to clearly identify Bragg's movements. On September 18, with the arrival of the first of Longstreet's divisions—under John Bell Hood—Bragg had moved most of his army across the creek and desultory fighting had broken out on the Union left where Forest's dismounted cavalry had been in action against Thomas's reconnaissance forces.

The following day, September 19, Rosecrans brought his full strength into action, except for Granger's small corps of six thousand men, which was held in reserve on the Ringgold road, two miles from the main battlefield. Because of the confused nature of the fighting, Rosecrans had allocated the command of the left of his army to George Thomas, while Alexander McCook took the right. On the Confederate side, Bragg had reached a similar command decision, allocating the right to Leonidas Polk and the left to Longstreet. Throughout the day, Polk continued his attempts to turn the Union left flank and there was savage fighting but without result.

The next morning Bragg ordered Polk and Longstreet to attack successively on each wing, beginning at daybreak. But Polk—claiming to have received no order from Bragg—was slow in getting his men into action, and it was nine-thirty A.M. before he did, only to find that the Union soldiers had built breastworks overnight. Bragg rode over to see Polk at eight A.M. to inquire why the attack had not started. As he later wrote: "I found Polk after sunrise sitting reading a newspaper... two miles from the line of battle, where he ought to have been fighting." Nevertheless, when the fighting did begin it was so intense that eventually—at eleven-thirty A.M.—Thomas sent a galloper to Rosecrans asking for reinforcements. Rosecrans seems to have responded by losing his head. He had already become convinced that the Confederates were massing all their strength against his left. Without informing McCook, he had been feeding troops from his right flank to support Thomas all morning. Now there occurred one of the most extraordinary mix-ups in all military history. Rarely has any battle been so completely turned by a single error of a commander.

In the center of McCook's line was the division of Brigadier General Thomas J. Wood, a veteran officer from Kentucky with a hitherto blameless war record. But providence had reserved a particularly unkind fate for Thomas Wood. As one of George Thomas's staff officers—Captain Kellogg—rode into Rosecrans's headquarters, he brought startling information. As he had ridden behind the lines he had noticed a gap—perhaps four hundred yards wide—in the Union lines, between the division of Wood and that of Brigadier General Thomas J. Reynolds. Rosecrans was thunderstruck and, without even sending to see if the staff officer was correct, he ordered an aide—Major Bond—to direct Wood to close up on Reynolds and support him. Had he checked he would have seen for himself that the so-called gap was illusory, and was actually filled by Brigadier General John M. Brannan's division, slightly to the rear of Wood's men.

When Wood received the order to close up on Reynolds he was mystified, knowing of course that Brannan was there. But the middle of a battle was hardly the time to be questioning decisions made at headquarters. Clearly Rosecrans must know something that was not apparent to Wood. Obeying his orders to the letter, Wood pulled his men back from the fighting, marched them to the rear and around the back of Brannan's division, and set off on the eight hundred-yard march to support Reynolds. Had fate been kinder to Wood the mistake might have gone unnoticed. Instead it was about to be exploited in the most remarkable way.

Only a few hundred yards from the Union line where Wood's division had been, and completely hidden by the trees, James Longstreet and Major General Simon B. Buckner were preparing the left wing of the Confederate army—eight brigades in a column of attack eight hundred yards wide—to strike Rosecrans's right wing. Just as they were about to begin the great assault, gallopers reached them with the startling news that facing them was a gap—at least four hundred yards wide—in the Union line. This was luck indeed, and Longstreet did not need a second summons. He launched his men at the gap in the Union lines and cut Rosecrans's army in half at a single stroke, certainly the most shattering single blow of the entire war. Led by Brigadier General Bushrod Johnson, the Confederates swept out of the woodland and in Johnson's own words: "The rush of our heavy columns sweeping out from the shadow and gloom of the forest into the open fields flooded with sunlight, the glitter of arms...the shouts of hosts of our army, the dust, smoke, the noise of fire-arms...made up a battle scene of unsurpassed grandeur...."

The shock was tremendous, and the entire Union right was swept away as if by a tidal wave. According to Union Brigadier General Thruston:

The woods in our front seemed alive. On they came like an angry flood. They struck McCook's three remaining brigades, the remnants of the Federal right. Under the daring personal exertions of McCook and Davis, they made a gallant but vain resistance. The massed lines of the enemy swarmed around their flanks. Pouring through the opening made by Wood's withdrawal, they struck his last brigade as it was leaving the line. It was slammed back like a door, and shattered. Brannan, on Wood's left, was struck in front and flank.[8]

Rosecrans, with his corps commanders McCook and Crittenden, was caught up in the general debacle—along with four divisional commanders and a third of the army—and all were driven off the field toward Chattanooga. For what Rosecrans was thinking as he was swept back we must rely on Thruston again:

All became confusion. No order could be heard above the tempest of battle. With a wild yell the Confederates swept on far to their left. They seemed everywhere victorious. Rosecrans was borne back in the retreat. Fugitives, wounded, caissons, escort, ambulances, thronged the narrow pathways. He [Rosecrans] concluded that our whole line had given way, that the day was lost, that the next stand must be made at Chattanooga. McCook and Crittenden, caught in the same tide of retreat, seeing only rout everywhere, shared the opinion of Rosecrans.[9]

Longstreet was content to let them go, for he still had a battle to win—if Bragg would let him. Just five Union divisions remained under Thomas's command and the Federals were in danger of suffering a classic double encirclement—an American "Cannae." Thomas, ignoring Rosecrans's panic-stricken order to retire, had formed what remained of the Union army into a semicircle around Horseshoe Ridge and later Snodgrass Hill, and prepared to make a last stand. He was helped by the arrival of Gordon Granger's small corps from the Ringgold road. Acting without direct orders, Granger had "marched to the sound of the guns" and had arrived in time to stem Longstreet's assaults on Snodgrass Hill. By the time night fell, Thomas—who earned immortality as "the Rock of Chickamauga"—and Granger had saved the army, and they were able to disengage in the darkness and fall back toward Chattanooga.

Longstreet and Confederate cavalry commander Nathan Forrest pressed Bragg to pursue the beaten Union army to prevent it from reorganizing itself at Chattanooga, but Bragg was unconvinced and could only see disaster all around him. His losses had been heavy and he thought in terms of defeat rather than the crushing victory that presented itself. Forrest remarked, "What does he fight battles for?" Certainly Bragg was missing a great opportunity to restore the South's fortunes after the disasters of July.

Recriminations were widespread and Bragg's headquarters became a new battleground. Bragg suspended Leonidas Polk—the two had a history of bitter disagreement—for disobeying orders and for being too slow to carry out the dawn assault on September 20. There was truth in this, but much of it stemmed from the fact that nobody trusted Bragg's capacity to give orders anymore. The fiery Nathan Forrest fell out with the commander for failing to follow up the victory at Chickamauga and refused to serve under Bragg in the future. As he told him, "I have stood your meanness as long as I intend to. You have played the part of a damned scoundrel.... If you ever again try to interfere with me or cross my path it will be at the peril of your life." Longstreet—soon to return to Virginia—petitioned the Confederate secretary of war to ask for Bragg's removal. As he put it, "nothing but the hand of God can save us or help us as long as we have our present commander." Surely it was the hand of God that had prompted Rosecrans to move Wood's division at the very moment that Longstreet was ready to strike. Yet the Confederates had failed to exploit their success. In the end, so great was the hostility to Bragg that Jefferson Davis was forced to travel from Richmond to interview Bragg's four corps commanders at the commander's headquarters. Possibly Davis hoped to persuade Longstreet to take over, but Old Pete was already yearning to return to Virginia, and declined. In any event, Bragg remained, much to the disgust of his men.

The disaster at Chickamauga—"disaster" because it was both more than and less than a defeat for the North—was too much for Rosecrans. At the end of the first day's fighting he had informed Washington that he had been attacked but was holding his ground and hoped to win on the second day. But on September 20 his dispatch spoke only of disaster and that he doubted that he could even hold Chattanooga. In Lincoln's choice phrase, he had become "confused and stunned like a duck hit on the head." Rosecrans was ashamed to have left the field and fled eight miles to Chattanooga while other men—notably George Thomas and Gordon Granger—had stayed to fight. Thomas had limited the damage to the Union side as well as prevented the victorious Bragg from exploiting his success. In a sense, he had picked up the mantle of command that Rosecrans had left abandoned on the battlefield and made it his own.

The Cherokee Indians had named the little creek that flowed across the battlefield Chickamauga—meaning "river of death"—as if some ancient prescience had foreseen the bloody sights of September 19–20, 1863. Both sides had suffered heavy casualties, and the victory had been dearly won by the Confederates, who lost 18,454 men to the 16,179 from the Army of the Cumberland. Many of the Confederate casualties had been suffered during Polk's relentless struggle with Thomas on September 19 and on the morning of September 20. Yet when victory came to the Confederates, it came gift wrapped and with very little to pay. The South's tragedy was that it was a victory without consequences, and for that Braxton Bragg could blame only himself.

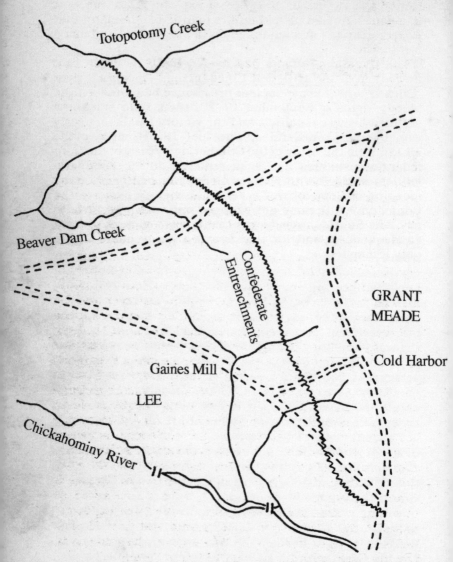

The Battle of Cold Harbor, 3 June 1864

The Battle of Cold Harbor, 1864

T HE UNION VICTORY AT GETTYSBURG ON JULY 3, 1863, AND
Grant's capture of Vicksburg a day later had given many
people in the North the impression that the war was as
good as over and the South beaten. But nothing could have
been further from the truth. In fact, the South had been
forced to temper its search for a decisive victory—which
would bring the Yankees to their knees—with a new strategy based on willpower. Jefferson Davis—and Robert E.
Lee—had been forced to sheathe their rapiers and adopt
instead the tools of the blacksmith—the hammer and the
anvil. They no longer counted on military victory, nor the
intervention of foreign powers. Instead they hoped to keep
the war going long enough for the war-weariness that was
apparent throughout the North to bring about a negotiated
settlement. Not victory, perhaps, yet if Abraham Lincoln
failed to win reelection in 1864 and was replaced by a Democratic politician then peace with honor might prove an
acceptable alternative. And so the South fought not to win
but to deny victory to her opponent, in the hope that victory
of a sort would attend her cause: essentially a Clausewit-
zian solution. When it is claimed, therefore, that the attritional fighting of 1864 was at the instigation of Ulysses S.
Grant, the argument is one-sided. Robert E. Lee was no
unwilling victim, drawn struggling to the "wearing-away"
fights at the Wilderness, Spotsylvania and Cold Harbor.
Refusing to fight in the open against overwhelming odds,
Lee left Grant with no alternative but to "grapple."

On March 9, 1864, Ulysses S. Grant was appointed a lieutenant general—a rank previously held only by George

Washington—and placed in total command of the Union armies. But Grant had no intention of becoming a desk-bound general and kept Henry Halleck to handle the paperwork in Washington as his chief of staff. Grant's place of work would be in the field, with the Army of the Potomac, though he did not assume command from Meade, who had done a fine job at Gettysburg and afterward in molding the army into a fighting force equal to the best that Lee could offer. What the army needed, in Grant's opinion, was steel in the soul, and that he intended to provide. Like John Pope in 1862, Grant came to the Army of the Potomac with a reputation based on brilliant victories in the West. His new corps commanders—mainly veterans of thirty months of fighting against Lee's Army of North Virginia—were hoping that he would soon appreciate what they had been up against. Instead, Grant spoke of Lee with no greater respect than he had of an earlier opponent—Braxton Bragg—boasting that he would soon crush Lee's army and bring the war to a close. By May 1864 Grant was so confident that he told Halleck:

Lee's army is really whipped. The prisoners we now take show it, and the action of his army shows it unmistakably. A battle with them outside of intrenchments cannot be had. Our men feel that they have gained the morale over the enemy and attack with confidence. I may be mistaken, but I feel that our success over Lee's army is already insured.[1]

Men like Meade had heard it all before—and had seen a succession of Union generals dance to Bobby Lee's tune before losing their seats when the music stopped. Yet Grant was different. He was a fighter, not a dancer, and the Southern capital of Richmond held no special charms for him, as it had for McClellan and Hooker. As he told Meade, "Lee's army will be your objective point. Wherever Lee goes, there will you go also." Grant had come east to fight and to beat Bobby Lee, and whatever the price he would willingly pay. If Lee wanted attrition Grant was happy to oblige. Nevertheless, after his shattering repulse at Cold Harbor, Meade wryly observed, "I think Grant has had his eyes opened, and is willing to admit now that Virginia and Lee's army is not Tennessee and Bragg's army."

Grant joined the Army of the Potomac in its camp at Culpeper Court House on the northern bank of the Rapidan River. Facing it, across the water, was Lee's Army of North Virginia. Both armies had received recent reinforcements: Burnside's IX Corps had joined Meade, bringing his strength up to a total of about 120,000 men, while Lee had been joined by Longstreet's corps, fresh from its triumphs at Chickamauga in Georgia, and stretching Lee's numbers to about 60,000.

Grant had made no secret of his intention to cross into Virginia and bring Lee to battle, and to keep on fighting him until he was destroyed. In the meantime, in Lincoln's marvelous phrase, "Those not skinning can hold a leg." While Grant was in the process of "skinning" Lee, he had proposed that other Union forces keep the Confederates busy, Ben Butler on the James River south of Richmond, and Franz Sigel on the Blue Ridge. Unfortunately, Butler and Sigel found the task of "holding legs" beyond them, and both suffered unnecessary defeats at the hands of inferior forces. So it was left to Grant—and Meade—to skin Bobby Lee alone.

On May 4, the Army of the Potomac crossed the Rapidan and began to march south toward Richmond. It was Grant's intention to bring Lee to battle in the open, but the Confederates forced the Union army back into the junglelike stretch of land known as the Wilderness. Here the advantage lay with the Confederates, who were more accustomed to this kind of fighting—"bushwhacking" as one soldier described it—and although outnumbered two to one, Lee won a two-day battle and inflicted seventeen thousand casualties on the Yankees. Grant was particularly frustrated at the effect that Lee's presence had on his own men. To one of his own brigadiers he said:

> I am heartily tired of hearing what Lee is going to do. Some of you always seem to think he is suddenly going to turn a double somersault and land on our rear and on both our flanks at the same time. Go back to your command, and try to think what we are going to do ourselves, instead of what Lee is going to do.[2]

By May 7 everyone in the Army of the Potomac was ready for retreat: the men had seen it all before under McClellan and Hooker. But things had changed. Grant had had his nose bloodied but no more than that—the advance would go on. He had promised Lincoln, "Whatever happens, there will be no turning back." This time Grant was heading for Spotsylvania Court House, to the southwest of Fredericksburg. If he could get there first he would be between Lee and Richmond, and then the Confederates would be forced to fight on Grant's terms.

In fact, Grant's defeat at the Wilderness had been a strategic victory. In terms of maneuvering for position Lee still held the inside track, but Grant was advancing and he was setting the pace. Where he went Lee had to follow: at last the Confederate leader was dancing to a Union general's tune. As Grant told Lincoln, "I propose to fight it out on this line if it takes all summer." He continued his attempts to turn Lee's right flank but Lee was still reading Grant's intentions and, by determined night marching, his men reached Spotsylvania just before the Federals and won a sharp skirmish that prevented their flank from being turned. What followed was the fiercest fighting of the whole war— a twelve-day bloodbath at Spotsylvania—with neither side gaining the upper hand. While the infantry slugged it out like two heavyweight boxers blinded by their own blood, Grant's new cavalry commander—Phil Sheridan— won a decisive victory over Jeb Stuart's Confederate horse at Yellow Tavern. Even more telling from the South's point of view was the death of Stuart himself, to add to Lee's cup of sorrow, which seemed to overflow with the news that "Old Pete" Longstreet had been seriously wounded by friendly fire.

Stymied at Spotsylvania, on May 20 Grant ordered his army to move south from the Spotsylvania battlefield in the direction of Hanover Junction, but again Lee beat him to it, and by the time the Federal troops arrived they found the Confederates waiting for them behind powerful defenses. Grant probed these positions before deciding to continue on his march, crossing the Pamunkey River at Hanover Town and then heading toward Cold Harbor. It was still his aim to turn Lee's right wing, but using interior lines Lee was always able to react to Grant's moves before the Union commander was able to complete them.

Nevertheless, Grant's confidence was still high and it was infectious. Union officers began to talk of final victory and said that prisoners were being taken in droves. And these Confederate prisoners spoke only of defeat, as Assistant Secretary of War Dana said: "They were more discouraged than any set of prisoners I ever saw before. Lee had deceived them, they said, and they declared that his army would not fight again except behind breast works...."

There was some truth in what the Federals were saying. The war had changed. Robert E. Lee, for so long the man who made things happen—who held the initiative against every previous Union commander—had been forced to accept a defensive role and was now simply reacting to whatever the Northern commanders threw at him.

But Grant's patience was growing thin. Frustrated by his inability to get between Lee's army and Richmond, he decided to try to break through the Confederate lines at Cold Harbor before driving to the Chickahominy. Grant's decision was partly based on the fact that he had just received reinforcements from Butler's Army of the James—W. P. F. "Baldy" Smith's XVIII Corps, some eighteen thousand strong. Grant decided to use Smith, along with the corps of Hancock and Warren, to strike the Confederate lines at four-thirty A.M. on June 2. But Grant faced frustration as his corps commanders let him down. Having just arrived, Smith claimed his men were not ready, lacking ammunition and transport, prompting an infuriated Meade to exclaim, "Then why in Hell did he come at all?" To add to the confusion, Hancock's II Corps was facing a nine-mile night march to get into position and was making a poor job of it. Meade sent an urgent order to Hancock:

> You must make every exertion to move promptly and reach Cold Harbor as soon as possible.... Every confidence is felt that your gallant corps of veterans will move with vigor and endure the necessary fatigue.[3]

Unfortunately there was more "veteran" than "vigor" on the march, and when the engineer officer sent to guide them tried a shortcut through the unmapped woods he got totally lost. A huge logjam of men, horses, wagons and guns now piled up in the darkness, with men and animals panicking and officers riding madly to and fro trying to give orders, and eventually being knocked from their mounts by the branches of trees. There was no alternative but to turn around and retrace the original march, thereby turning the nine-mile march into a fifteen-mile nightmare. Even so, by forced marching the corps reached its position by seven A.M., exhausted and in disarray—and just two and a half hours late! Meade was beside himself with anger, commenting—unfairly—that the men were exhausted before they had even started the march and: "Our men no longer have the bodily strength they had a month before; indeed why they are alive I don't see." There was no point now in ordering an attack when the men were so clearly unfit to carry it out, and the assault was put off until four P.M.

As the day wore on Union VI Corps took up its position, but to its right "Baldy" Smith was pleading to be left out of this attack. He claimed that of his eighteen-thousand-man corps battle losses and straggling had reduced him to just nine thousand and these were so shaken that he could not guarantee that they would be able to hold off a determined Rebel attack. Meade must have thought he was hearing things. When he reminded Smith that it was his force that was supposed to be attacking he was told, "An attack by me would be simply preposterous." Grant wrote to Meade postponing the attack for the second time that day.

This was a truly tragic decision, as Grant was soon to realize. Meanwhile, even the heavens seemed to have turned against the Federals. Torrential rain now soaked the men as they lay in their positions awaiting the dawn.

All of this was doubly frustrating because the Confederates had been at their weakest on June 2—just 40,000 men holding a line six miles long against Grant's 100,000, with 50,000 concentrated on a three-mile front to hit the Confederate lines to the west of Cold Harbor. Had the Union attack gone in it is difficult to see how Lee's men—however firm their entrenchments—could have resisted such overwhelming strength. But with twenty-four hours of grace, Lee was reinforced by three divisions—14,000 fresh men buoyed up by their recent successes over Butler and Sigel.

Grant would have done better to cancel the attack completely. The whole situation had changed and it is difficult to avoid the conclusion that the Union commander was acting from pique. As it was, instead of the relatively weak Confederate lines they would have encountered the pre-

vious day, the assault troops now faced tremendous obstacles. Lee's men had worked day and night to strengthen
their positions and both Meade and Grant are culpable for
having failed to study the terrain over which the assault
troops would have to advance at first light. The Confederates had taken great pains to position their entrenchments
to take advantage of the swampy ground, the watercourses,
the ravines and the clumps of trees that were to be found
between the Chickahominy Swamp on the right of their
line and the Totopotomoy Creek on the left. In just twenty-
four hours the Confederates had created a perfect killing
ground over which the Union troops would advance to their
deaths.

Grant and Meade had left reconnaissance to their corps
commanders, but their assumption that this would be carried out as a routine measure was mistaken. Incredibly,
over fifty thousand Union troops were going to march toward the Confederate lines completely unaware of what
they might have to face. Yet many of them had a good idea.
One of Grant's staff officers found them writing their names
on pieces of paper and stitching them to their coats so that
their bodies could be identified after they had been killed.
It was Fredericksburg all over again—as if nobody had
learned the lesson of Marye's Heights.

Just before dawn a single cannon was fired in the Union
positions as a signal for the assault to begin, but ominously
it acted instead as a warning to the Confederate defenders
who now manned their positions, and on a two-mile front
thousands of musket and rifle barrels could be seen, tipped
with bayonets, glinting in the early rays of the sun. As soon
as the lines of blue began to advance they were hit by the
most intense fire of the entire war, likened by some to an
exploding volcano or a clap of thunder. Its effect was devastating. In the words of one of the survivors:

> To give a description of this terrible charge is simply
> impossible, and few who were in the ranks of the 12th
> [New Hampshire] will ever feel like attempting it. To
> those exposed to the full force and fury of that dreadful
> storm of lead and iron that met the charging column,
> it seemed more like a volcanic blast than a battle, and
> it was just about as destructive.[4]

The Federal attack was soon broken up into a series of charges by individual groups, some achieving local success—a brigade from Hancock's corps even entered the Confederate trenches and took three hundred prisoners—but mostly the story was one of confusion and dreadful carnage.

Gibbon's division suffered a quite unnecessary martyrdom. A mere two hundred yards out from their own lines the men found themselves faced with a deep swamp that nobody had realized was there. Unable to get through this boggy area, the men milled in confusion around the edges, all the time being cut down by artillery and rifle fire. When Gibbon tried to reinforce his forward brigades the orders got jumbled and the relief troops went to the wrong place, where they were hit by Confederate artillery fire. There was no alternative but to retreat, and Gibbon pulled his men back, having suffered one thousand casualties. Many of the Federal soldiers dug scrape holes in the no-man's-land between the Union and Confederate trenches and kept up a fire on the Rebel lines. Men from Wright's corps were mown down as they approached what seemed to them a semicircle of Rebel trenches from which the fire was intense and was supplemented by artillery fire that hit their flanks. This was more than unsupported infantry could be expected to face and the wavering blue lines gave way.

The worst fate on this dreadful day was reserved for "Baldy" Smith's corps. The bulk of his assault troops had been fed through a shallow ravine toward the Rebel lines. But the Confederates merely concentrated on this narrow front and Smith's troopers faced a fire of volcanic proportions. The men bent forward as if walking through a blizzard, but in this part of the field the blizzard was of shot and bullets. Men fell not singly but in rows as if by tripwires. As one Confederate officer later told one of the New Hampshire men who made this doomed charge, "It seemed almost like murder to fire upon you." It was not murder, it was war. If there were murderers, they sat far behind the line of combat—and their names were George Meade and Ulysses Grant. In fact, to Meade, supposedly in control of the battle—if *control* is the right word for the chaos in the Union ranks—it seemed that things were going well. News was received that Hancock's men had seized part of the Confederate trench—a half-truth at least—and so Meade ordered Hancock to redouble his efforts, even though he knew that the attack had already failed. Wright and Smith were ordered to renew their attacks even though a simpleton could see that there was nowhere for them to go. On the other side of no-man's-land Lee exulted that he had no reserves—none at all—but needed none, for his defenses were completely invulnerable.

It was not until noon that Grant reached the front and spoke to his corps commanders. The picture could hardly be clearer now, and he told Meade, "The opinion of corps commanders not being sanguine of success in case an assault is ordered, you may direct a suspension of further advance for the present. Hold our most advanced positions and strengthen them." However one looked at it, Grant had suffered a shattering repulse, losing seven thousand casualties, most in the first thirty minutes—a butcher's bill to match any in the entire war. At first Grant was unaware of how heavy his casualties had been, but when he was told he said, "I regret this assault more than any one I have ever ordered," a hard admission for such an unemotional man.

Trenches had proved the master and would again. Union soldiers no longer criticized the Rebels for their lack of appetite for the offensive. The attritional struggle that now replaced the mobility of the earlier part of the war was grim and deadly, with none of the glamour that had attended Lee's earlier battles. This kind of warfare was beyond anyone's experience, and generals on neither side understood how to overcome the advantage that lay with the defender, safe behind earthworks and with entrenched artillery and massed musket fire. Frontal assaults were bound to be prohibitively expensive.

Grant had blundered at Cold Harbor because he had lost his patience. One of VI Corps's staff officers commented on the conduct of the battle: "its management would have shamed a cadet in his first year at West Point." Vitriolic Colonel Emory Upton said much the same in a letter to his sister:

I am disgusted with the generalship displayed. Our men have, in many instances, been foolishly and wantonly sacrificed. Assault after assault has been ordered upon the enemy's intrenchments, when they knew nothing about the strength or position of the enemy. Thousands of lives might have been spared by the exercise of a little skill, but, as it is, the courage of the poor men is expected to obviate all difficulties.... Some of our corps commanders are not fit to be corporals.[5]

But Grant knew that victory, though near, would not be easily bought, and the bloodbath at Cold Harbor was but a stage in the wearing away of the Confederate military machine. He had failed to destroy Lee's army as he had boasted at the outset. He had failed to sever Lee's communications with Richmond or to get between the Confederates and their capital. On the other hand, he had fought four battles against Lee without being forced to retreat and had held his position close to the Confederate capital, inflicting casualties on Lee's army that could not be afforded. In the thirty days of the campaign Grant's army had suffered 54,929 casualties against 39,000 suffered by the Army of North Virginia. But as a proportion of total strength Grant's losses—at 52 percent—were less than Lee's—at 59 percent. In the cruel logic of attrition, even Grant's blunder at Cold Harbor was justifiable.

The Battle of Manila Bay, 1898

THE EUROPEAN "SCRAMBLE FOR AFRICA" IN THE LATE NINE-teenth century did not pass unnoticed in the United States. American war hawks and jingoes like Henry Cabot Lodge and Theodore Roosevelt matched Britain's Cecil Rhodes and Joseph Chamberlain, and under the influence of naval theorist Alfred Thayer Mahan they began to appreciate the need for a powerful navy to support national interests, both in the Caribbean and in the Pacific. By the time Theodore Roosevelt became assistant secretary of the navy in 1897, American policy had abandoned isolationism in favor of a far more active foreign policy.

The Spanish colony of Cuba, situated scarcely a hundred miles from the coast of Florida, provided the issue that was to project the United States onto the world stage for the first time. The revolution that broke out in Cuba in 1895 was aimed at overthrowing the corrupt rule of Spain, and President Cleveland, although maintaining American neu-trality in the struggle, found it difficult to resist the calls by America's popular press for intervention. Under his suc-cessor, William McKinley, the United States moved closer to a direct confrontation with Spain. Theodore Roosevelt, as assistant secretary of the navy, prepared comprehensive plans for operations against Spain in the Caribbean, the Far East, and even in European waters. The basis for such plans was to be a powerful navy that—by 1898—contained five battleships, six monitors, twenty-nine cruisers and ten smaller gunboats. Although the main theater of war was bound to be in Cuba and on the seas around it, Roosevelt knew that Spain must be struck hard in the Far East, not-

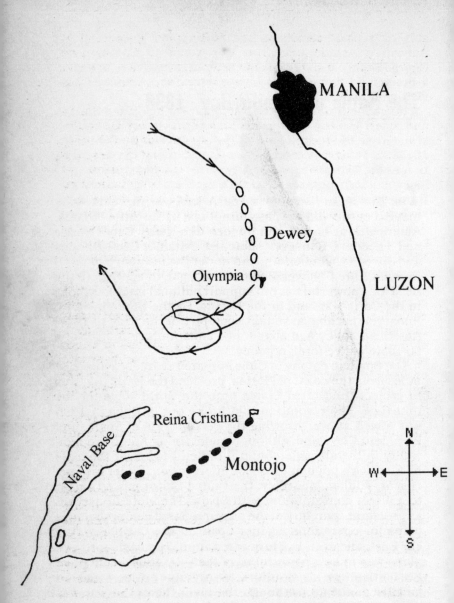

BATTLE OF MANILA BAY 1898

ably by a naval attack on the Philippines. Command of America's Asiatic squadron was given to Commodore George Dewey, a sixty-year-old veteran, who was to become a household name in his own country as a result of his victory at Manila Bay.

The incident that sparked war between the United States and Spain was the mysterious loss of the American battleship *Maine* to an explosion in Havana Harbor on February 15, 1898. Modern research has suggested that the destruction of the *Maine* was caused by an internal explosion and had absolutely nothing to do with the Spanish government. However, it was sufficient to provide McKinley with a convenient casus belli and the United States declared war on Spain on April 21, 1898. John Hay, America's ambassador to Britain, described his country's war against Spain in 1898 as a "splendid little war." Yet for the Spaniards the war was anything but splendid. Few countries have ever entered a war with as little apparent interest as did Spain in 1898. The prolonged struggle against the rebels in Cuba made the idea of war against the United States intensely unpopular in Spain itself, and it seems that Spain's decision to fight was based more on archaic notions of honor rather than on realistic strategy. As America's ambassador to Spain told President McKinley, "They know Cuba is lost but they will seek honorable defeat in war." As a basis for a war strategy this was incomprehensible.

Spain was quite aware that she had neither the army nor the navy to fight the United States. She was economically poor and had fallen far from the status of a great power, which she had held in the sixteenth and seventeenth centuries. Although she had large numbers of soldiers in both Cuba and the Philippines, they were poorly equipped and armed, had low morale and were led by incompetent officers. In order to fight a war in both the Caribbean and the Far East, Spain needed a powerful, modern navy. Instead she had just four armored cruisers, twelve old cruisers, five torpedo boats, three destroyers and some small gunboats. Even this diminutive force had to be split between the Caribbean and the Pacific. Nor were all of these units operational, for there was a dearth of trained sailors and most of the Spanish ships were seriously undermanned. Shortages of coal and munitions meant that fleet maneuvers were almost unknown and gunnery practice unheard of. In

Spain's primitive colonial ports there were no dockyard facilities, so ships damaged in action could not be repaired. Her admirals were imbued with a deep sense of despair and thought only in terms of personal honor and limiting their own casualties; victory was simply not possible.

At Manila, in particular, the fleet of Admiral Montojo consisted of what the Americans described as "old tubs not warships." Yet, once his government had opted for war it was incumbent on Montojo to make the best effort he could to resist the attack he knew the Americans would launch against him. However hopeless his situation seemed, he did have options, all of which he rejected in favor of an entirely passive defense.

While the Spaniards seemed enthralled by *mañana*, the Americans faced the challenge of war with energy. Commodore Dewey had taken command of the U.S. Asiatic Fleet stationed at Hong Kong in January 1898, and he immediately began preparations for an attack on the Philippines. He placed his ships on war footing and put his men through round-the-clock drills so that when the time came for action—and Dewey was certain that time could not long be postponed—everything would go smoothly. His main problems were shortages of coal and ammunition, yet by April he had chartered two British steamers to act as colliers, and when (on the twenty-first of that month) the cruiser *Baltimore* arrived from Honolulu with ammunition, he was able to bring his entire fleet up to 60 percent of maximum. After painting his ships battleship gray instead of the white usually sported by American ships in the Far East, he was now ready to fight. Ironically, when the signal for war came it was from a British source, the harbormaster at Hong Kong. As a neutral power, Britain requested Dewey to leave the harbor because his country was now at war with Spain. When the American ships left on April 24 they were saluted by the crews of the English ships stationed there, who wished them well. But as Dewey later remembered:

> In the Hong Kong Club it was not possible to get bets, even at heavy odds, that our expedition would be a success, and this in spite of a friendly predilection among the British in our favour. I was told, after our officers had been entertained at dinner by a British regiment, that the universal remark among our hosts

was to this effect: "A fine set of fellows, but unhappily we shall never see them again."[1]

As Dewey's four cruisers—*Olympia, Baltimore, Raleigh* and *Boston*—left Hong Kong with their attendant ships, they were sailing against an enemy whose preparations for war would have struck their American counterparts as shockingly inadequate. The fleet with which Spanish Admiral Montojo would defend the Philippines was archaic in ships, personnel and philosophy. Although he had some twenty-five vessels, few of them were fit to stand in line of battle against Dewey's powerful quartet of cruisers. Montojo's six cruisers were all smaller than Dewey's smallest, and several of them had iron hulls—and one, the *Castilla*, was made of wood. In both heavy guns and light weapons the Americans had an advantage, while the Spanish had no warheads to equip their torpedoes. In addition, Dewey's ships were larger, faster and more modern. Montojo's only possible advantage was that in any battle fought within Manila Bay, he could fight with the support of heavy shore-based guns, which could pose a very real threat to Dewey's ships. However, he chose not to do so, as we shall see.

After leaving Hong Kong, Dewey sailed north to recoal his squadron from a Chinese supplier quite prepared to imperil the neutrality of his country. There he received the following signal from U.S. Secretary of the Navy John D. Long:

War has commenced between the United States and Spain. Proceed at once to the Philippine Islands. Commence operations at once, particularly against the Spanish fleet. You must capture vessels or destroy. Use utmost endeavours.[2]

On the afternoon of April 27 Dewey began the six hundred-mile journey to Manila at a speed of eight knots. Leaving nothing to chance in the coming encounter, the Americans wrapped anchor chains around their ammunition hoists and draped nets over their boats and wooden objects on deck to limit splinters in the event of shell blasts.

Although the Spanish at Manila knew that Dewey was coming, and were well apprised of the strength of his

squadron, they made remarkably few preparations to meet
him. Incredibly, even after news had been received that the
Americans had been sighted, on April 30, Montojo insisted
on celebrating the birthday of one of his officers in the
admiral's house in Manila. Officers from throughout the
fleet were present at the party, and some returned to their
ships inebriated after the battle had already started, while
others—hung over the next morning—missed the action
altogether.

During the afternoon the American fleet reached Manila
Bay and Dewey sent the *Boston* and one of his gunboats,
the *Petrel*, to Subic Bay, where he felt it most likely that
Montojo would have positioned his ships. Montojo had
considered doing this and had sent orders for the harbor
to be fortified. To his chagrin he found out that his orders
had been overlooked and none of the work had been carried
out.

When Dewey heard that Montojo was not at Subic Bay
he called his captains aboard the flagship, the *Olympia*, and
made his plans for a battle to be fought inside Manila Bay.
Dewey had little up-to-date information about the shore
defenses in the bay and around the city of Manila itself,
but presumed they would be formidable. He therefore decided to enter the bay under cover of night, hoping to slip
by the shore batteries unnoticed. Just before midnight, and
with all lights extinguished, the American ships passed
silently under the Spanish guns. At one moment sparks
from the furnace of one of the American ships shot into
the air, causing a trigger-happy Spaniard to fire aimlessly
into the sea, but otherwise the Americans encountered no
resistance. Spanish soldiers on the island of Corregidor
later said that the American ships had been clearly visible
but that their officers had given no orders to open fire with
their eight-inch guns.

In fact, Spanish defeatism was to be Dewey's biggest ally
in the battle ahead. Montojo was so certain of defeat that
he had made two extraordinary decisions. In the first place,
he had decided to anchor his fleet at Cavite rather than under
the guns of Manila's fortifications. He apparently reached
this decision on the grounds that if he anchored in front
of the capital it was likely that stray American shells would
fall in the city, causing unnecessary civilian casualties. As
a humanitarian gesture it was admirable, but as a military

decision it was incredible. From Cavite the Spaniards would be able to bring only eight shore guns to bear on Dewey's ships instead of the thirty-nine available at Manila. In addition, Montojo was eager to save casualties among his own sailors, preferring to anchor in shallow water so that when his ships sank their crews would be able to reach shore easily. It is doubtful if such thoughts ever entered the head of a naval commander on any other occasion in history. Yet Montojo was no coward. He would fight the Americans to save his honor and the honor of his country. He would lose the battle but he would fight with what weapons he had, however flawed.

As dawn broke the Americans could make out the Spanish ships, standing sharply against the land with their white hulls. The water of the bay was like a millpond and a slight mist rose above the sea. Some of the Spanish shore batteries now opened fire—as did Montojo's ships—but their marksmanship was risible, with shells falling some miles from the American ships. For forty minutes the one-sided cannonade continued, with the Americans suffering no damage at all and conserving their own shells until they were well in range. At five-forty A.M. Dewey spoke quietly to Captain Gridley: "You may fire when ready, Gridley," and the *Olympia* opened fire with her main armament against Montojo's flagship, the *Reina Cristina*, closely followed by the rest of the American squadron. There were to be no heroics; what followed was "a military execution" carried out clinically and professionally. The Spanish fire continued, wild and inaccurate, and the American ships suffered no hits at this stage. Dewey led his squadron on a course parallel with Montojo's ships, firing broadsides as they went, before turning and closing the range to five thousand yards. In all, Dewey sailed five times back and forth parallel to Montojo, each time closing the range slightly until the two squadrons were only two thousand yards apart. At this latter range the Americans scored hit after hit on the main Spanish ships. Montojo's flagship, the *Reina Cristina*, received the concentrated fire of three American cruisers and was soon reduced to a blazing wreck. At one point, like a bull tormented beyond endurance in the ring, the Spanish cruiser turned bow-on to the American cruisers and tried to ram them. But as she limped toward them she was ripped to pieces by high-explosive shells. Her bridge was swept

away and her steering gear jammed, and only the flooding
of the magazine saved her from a catastrophic explosion.
With over half of her complement casualties, the wounded
Montojo transferred his flag to the *Isla de Cuba*.

The martyrdom of the flagship—described here by Lieutenant Ellicote of the *Baltimore*—had saved the rest of the
Spanish fleet for a while:

> Towards the end of the action the *Cristina* stood out
> as if unable to endure longer her constricted position,
> but the concentration of fire upon her was even greater
> than before, and she turned away like a steed bewil-
> dered in a storm. It was seen that she was on fire for-
> ward. Then a six-inch shell tore a jagged hole under
> her stern from which the smoke of another fire began
> to seep out. Right into this gaping wound another huge
> shell plunged, driving a fierce gust of flame and smoke
> out through her ports and skylights. Then came a jet
> of white steam from around her after smokestack high
> into the air, and she swayed onward upon an irregular
> course towards Cavite until aground under its walls.[3]

Once the *Reina Cristina* was destroyed the big guns of
the American cruisers turned inexorably on the rest of the
squadron, and the wooden cruiser *Castilla*—cruelly exposed in an age of armored steel hulls—was engulfed in
flames and scuttled by her own crew.

At this stage a curious event occurred that, had the Americans faced first-rate opponents, might have proved serious. Dewey was informed by Captain Gridley—incorrectly,
as it turned out—that his flagship had just 15 percent of her
ammunition left. Still unaware of how great a victory he
had won, the commodore ordered his squadron to withdraw from the vicinity of the Spanish ships. With the bay
almost totally obscured by smoke it was proving difficult
to know how the battle was going. Clearly three Spanish
ships were on fire, but so was the *Boston*, as far as Dewey
could tell. Should the American ships run out of ammunition they might easily fall prey to the Spanish shore batteries, even if Montojo's fleet was destroyed. One can
imagine Dewey's relief when it was discovered that the misleading message should have read that only 15 percent of
the ammunition had been used thus far. Yet Dewey did not

countermand his order to withdraw. It was time for breakfast, and he decided to rest his men, notably the engineers who had been stoking the furnaces in unbearable heat.

Dewey took the opportunity to hold a conference aboard the *Olympia* to check on damage to his ships and casualties. The reports were immensely reassuring. One man (Chief Engineer Randall of the *McCulloch*) had died of a heart attack—possibly as a result of the heat—but no one had succumbed to Spanish fire. The new gray paintwork had been scratched in places but the Americans had emerged largely unscathed. However, the American officers had been disappointed by their own inability to inflict damage on Montojo's ships. As one recounted later, "The gloom on the bridge of the *Olympia* was thicker than a London fog." In fact, it was only the smoke of battle that concealed from them the truth that the Spanish fleet was virtually destroyed. Nevertheless, the withdrawal of the American ships had so encouraged Montojo that he signaled Madrid that his fleet had succeeded in repelling the American attack.

At 11:16 A.M. the American fleet sailed into the harbor once again and recommenced the battering of the Spaniards. There was to be no escape now and Montojo ordered his captains to scuttle their ships after rescuing vital papers and having removed the breech blocks from their guns, so that the Americans could not refloat them later and use them again. So shallow was the water that when the *Ulloa* sank much of her superstructure remained above water and her crew found it easy to swim, wade and scramble ashore.

Dewey now sent a message to the Spanish shore batteries, threatening to bombard the city of Manila itself unless they ceased firing. The Spanish governor replied that the batteries would remain silent "unless it was evident that a disposition of the American ships to bombard the city was being made." This was as close to a truce as Dewey was likely to get. No thought had been given to what he would do once he had destroyed Montojo's ships, and he had no troops with him to effect a landing to capture Manila itself. All he could do was to blockade the city and hope that Filipino freedom fighters under Emilio Aguinaldo might force the Spanish to surrender.

With the action over, the Americans anchored close to the city of Manila itself. What followed was surreal even for this Alice in Wonderland war. Dewey wrote in his autobiography:

As the sun set on the evening of May 1, crowds of people gathered along the waterfront, gazing at the American squadron. They climbed on the ramparts of the very battery that had fired on us in the morning. The *Olympia's* band, for their benefit, played "La Paloma" and other Spanish airs, and while the sea breeze wafted the strains to their ears, the poor colonel of artillery who had commanded the battery, feeling himself dishonored by his disgraceful failure, shot himself through the head.[4]

In a more businesslike manner Dewey signaled to Secretary Long:

The squadron arrived at Manila Bay at daybreak this morning. Immediately engaged enemy and destroyed following vessels: *Reina Cristina, Don Juan de Austria, Don Antonio de Ulloa, Isla de Luzon, Isla de Cuba, General Lezo, Marques del Duero, El Cano, Velasco,* one transport, *Isla de Mindanao,* water battery at Cavite. I shall destroy Cavite arsenal dispensary. The squadron is uninjured. Few men are slightly wounded. I request the Department will send immediately from San Francisco fast steamer with ammunition. The only means of telegraphing is the American consul at Hongkong.

DEWEY[5]

The battle of Manila Bay had ended in a total victory for the American fleet. Yet rarely has a naval battle produced so one-sided a result. On the Spanish side ten ships were lost yet casualties were light (only 167 men were killed and 224 wounded)—a tribute to the cautious policy of Admiral Montojo—while the Americans suffered just seven men slightly wounded and little more than scratches to Dewey's warships. However, American marksmanship had been deplorable: of 5,859 shells fired by the American cruisers only 142 scored hits (2.45 percent), and the Spanish shooting had been so much worse that as few as 13 hits were registered on Dewey's vessels and more damage was caused to them by the concussion of their own eight-inch guns.

Was Montojo incompetent in the handling of his ships or was he merely a victim of years of neglect by a government that was no longer committed to the defense of its colonies? This is a moot point. Certainly the Spanish sailors fought bravely in a hopeless cause, yet Montojo made less attempt to win the battle than to save their lives. His decision to anchor in shallow water, away from the city of Manila, was a humanitarian gesture but was militarily unacceptable. The heavy shore batteries at Manila could have evened up the contest considerably and kept Dewey's cruisers at a far greater range so that their own highly inaccurate shooting would not have proved as decisive as it did. Montojo, of course, might have chosen to abandon his vessels and use his troops and guns to reinforce the land batteries. Or he might have met Dewey at sea, possibly under the guns of Corregidor, and fought a night battle against the superior American squadron. Failing this, he might have distributed his squadron throughout the hundreds of islands that comprise the Philippines. With far greater local knowledge than the Americans possessed, Montojo could have prolonged the naval campaign almost indefinitely and posed Dewey enormous fuel problems. But Montojo chose the worst possible option, assembling his fleet as if to facilitate Dewey's task and rejecting even the cover of the shore-based batteries. Every action Montojo took was token. He accepted defeat before a blow had been struck and fought back only to maintain personal and national pride. Whether Montojo or Spain's minister of marine was more to blame is difficult to decide. Montojo certainly made little attempt to prepare defensive positions at the entrance to Manila Bay, or even to see that the officers in charge of the shore batteries were vigilant: carousing at a party was hardly acceptable behavior for officers about to go into battle. As a result, Dewey's ships were able to enter the harbor unscathed and from that point onward a Spanish defeat was certain. Forced to maintain a blockade outside Manila Bay would soon have exhausted Dewey's coal supplies.

The Spanish government decided to court-martial Montojo in spite of an extraordinary witness for the defense: Commodore Dewey himself, with a testimonial by the American commander to the effect that the Spanish admiral had fought with great gallantry throughout the battle. Montojo was not slow to blame others and wrote in his own defense this explanation for the Spanish defeat: "The inefficiency of the ships composing the small Spanish squadron, the lack of all classes of personnel, especially of gun captains and seaman-gunners, the ineptitude of some of the provisionally engaged engineers, the want of quick-firers, the strong crews of the enemy, and the unprotected nature of the greater part of the Spanish ships, all contributed to make more decided the sacrifice which the squadron offered for its country."

One cannot help concluding with the thought that had Dewey commanded the Spanish squadron he would have made more of his admittedly limited material, while had Montojo commanded the U.S. ships he would not have dared to enter Manila Bay in darkness under the guns of the Spanish shore batteries. Courage is important in warfare, but willpower is often decisive.

France:
The Problem of Armored Warfare, 1940

A FEW MILES FROM THE BATTLEFIELD OF RAMILLIES, SCENE OF one of the Duke of Marlborough's greatest victories, stands the village of Merdorp, where, on May 13, 1940, the first major encounter between French tanks and German Panzers took place during the Second World War. Two of General Prioux's light mechanized divisions were pitted against the 3rd and 4th German Panzer divisions, backed up by Stuka dive-bombers. Although the encounter was by no means decisive, certain interesting conclusions could be drawn. Both sides suffered heavy losses and the Germans did not conceal their admiration for the quality of the French tanks, particularly the "unbelievable" armor of the medium SOMUA tank, which resisted all but the heaviest anti-tank guns. But what had also been apparent was the fact that the French tanks fought not in compact units, like their German counterparts, but usually singly or in loose formations, as if they lacked unified command. What the Germans did not know was that four out of every five French tanks carried no radio at all, and those that did had weak batteries that were constantly running down. French tank commanders usually found it impossible to communicate with other units in the heat of battle.

The clash at Merdorp was a purely chance encounter, for French and German tactics were totally different. To the Germans, the Panzer division was a sword, sharp as well as heavy, "to be used to slice through the enemy front and turn a tactical success into strategic victory." The Polish

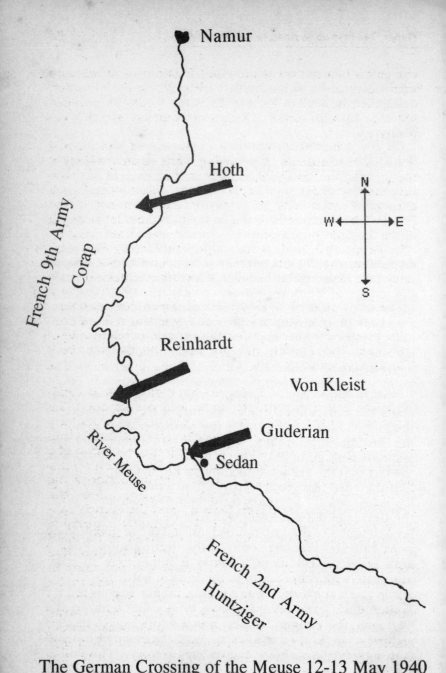

The German Crossing of the Meuse 12-13 May 1940

campaign had shown it enjoying freedom of movement, with other units subordinated to it. When the situation demanded it, several Panzer divisions would be grouped together into an armored corps of immense striking capacity.

On the other hand, France's commanders had no real doctrine of armored warfare, using tanks as an auxiliary of the infantry and as a mobile force to plug gaps in her continuous line of defense. Such outdated thinking and such misuse of technology reflected the incompetence of the French High Command. It was in the monumental strength of the Maginot Line alone that France placed her trust.

On February 6, 1940, Britain's General Alan Brooke commented on the complacency that he found in the French army as a result of its belief in concrete fortifications:

> The most dangerous aspect is the psychological one; a sense of false security, a feeling of sitting behind an impregnable fence; and should the fence perchance be broken, the French fighting spirit might well be brought crumbling with it.[1]

What Brooke was describing is what historian R. D. Challener has called "a national Maginot Line complex." The experience of the First World War, and most particularly the fighting around Verdun, became a part of the French psyche. The result was that the French made a fetish of a defense system in which, man for man, the French soldier would prove superior to the German. Yet, as Frederick the Great once observed, "experience is useless unless the right conclusions are drawn from it," and the French conclusion, erroneously, was that it was virtually impossible to rupture a continuous military front based on the kind of fortifications that had been built around Verdun, like Forts Douaumont and Vaux. Yet France was not alone in this conclusion, for though the Maginot Line was by far the most famous of the defensive lines built in the interwar period, Germany built the Westwall, Greece the Metaxas Line, Russia the Stalin Line and Finland the Mannerheim Line. The problem for France, however, was the effect that the Maginot Line seemed to have on not only the army but the population as a whole. It removed first the need and then the ability to keep pace with military developments in other countries. When Joffre visited the forts of Verdun in 1922, he encapsulated the theory of the continuous front in the words: "Let these lessons not be ignored." With this statement he was condemning the French military to carry the burden of the past into the rapidly changing technological world of the 1930s.

Rooted firmly in the past, the French army continued to believe that no offensive could be successful without a superiority of three to one in manpower, six to one in guns, and fifteen to one in ammunition. Yet these figures, based as they were on the experiences of the Western Front in 1914–18, were quite unrealistic. Faced by such logistics, the idea of the offensive became unacceptable. In 1921 a committee on the lessons of the war produced the *Instructions provisoire sur l'emploi tactique des grandes unites*, which emphasized the vital importance of industrial mobilization. The tactical expression of supremacy in *materiel de guerre* was to be seen in the artillery, which "destroyed and neutralized" while the infantry advanced and occupied. Thus firepower was considered superior to mobility, with tanks and aircraft, as expressions of the latter, becoming merely support weapons for the infantry. With the emphasis on *materiel de guerre* it became obvious that France's economic heartland—the coal, iron and industrial regions of the northeast, within easy reach of the German frontier—must be protected at all costs by a continuous front of fortifications.

The illusion of strength that the building of the Maginot Line gave France was supported by ostrichlike antics on the part of the High Command, which refused to acknowledge any examples of mobility and striking power from the First World War—such as Allenby's conquest of Palestine—and ignored theories of modern armored warfare, like those of Liddell Hart, Fuller, Guderian and de Gaulle.

General Andre Beaufre wrote of the influence of the Ecole de Guerre and general staff training on a generation of French officers: "Youth does not possess all the good qualities; but, on the other hand, experience can be a burden which may sometimes impede clear thinking." The French commanders of the inter-war period had all held command rank in the First World War and felt that the virtues that had brought victory in 1918 would be good enough in any future conflict. They therefore made the mistake of prepar-

ing to refight the war that had just ended and, more trag-
ically, preparing their students and the French nation as
a whole to believe that victory could be achieved in the
same way, thereby ossifying French military thinking for
a generation.

The failure of the tank to fulfill its potential in 1918 convinced the French commanders that its future was merely
as an adjunct to the infantry. The thousands of French
tanks left over from the First World War gave France a
feeling of artificial strength, which had the effect of dis-
couraging innovation in the area of armored warfare. There
seemed no need to modernize tank resources because the
tank had been shown so considerably inferior to the defensive fortifications that could be built. In 1921, French
general Philippe Pétain dismissed the role of the tank by
saying, "Tanks assist the advance of the infantry, by breaking static obstacles and active resistance put up by the
enemy." However, Pétain had no appreciation of what
might be possible as technical improvements, already
transforming the ordinary motor car, gave the tank so
much greater speed and maneuverability. In England, Basil
Liddell Hart was expounding his "expanding torrent" theory of tank warfare, with deep penetration by powerful
groups of fast tanks, backed by mobile self-propelled guns
and infantry in armored carriers.

Liddell Hart envisaged no battering of defenses along a
wide front but a deep penetration of a weak spot, with the
intention to create chaos deep in the enemy rear. To Liddell
Hart, the Maginot Line—from 1930 consuming much of the
French military budget—was an anachronism, as useful as
a baron's castle in the age of heavy siege guns.

In Germany, Colonel Heinz Guderian had taken up Liddell Hart's ideas as they appeared in "A New Model Army,"
published in the *Army Quarterly* in 1924, and had them
translated into German. Guderian had been lecturing on
mobility in warfare since the early years of the Weimar
Republic and was in the forefront of the German tank developments that the Treaty of Rapallo had enabled Germany to make inside Russian territory. Major General
Fuller's Haldane lectures of 1932 had a great impact on
Guderian, with their emphasis on the idea of independent
tank divisions allied to deep penetration, and the arrival
in Russia of sixty British tanks—including the Vickers me-

dium tank with a speed of fifteen to twenty miles per hour—
at last gave Guderian a practical example of what had previously only been a theoretical possibility. In 1934 he and
Lutz published the first German-language work on armored warfare, while the Austrian general Ludwig Ritter
von Eisensberger wrote *Der Kampfwagenskrieg*, which
was "a full-blooded advocacy on Fullerian lines of the tank
corps and tank army." It did not take long for the Germans
to create the first Panzer division in 1935, by which time
Guderian had developed his ideas further: "The armoured
divisions will no longer stop when the first objectives have
been reached; on the contrary, utilising their speed and
radius of action to the full they will do their utmost to
complete the breakthrough into the enemy lines of communication."

In his influential book *Achtung-Panzer!*, Guderian ex-
amined the successes and failures of Allied tank strategy
in the First World War, concluding that the Allies had failed
to attack in sufficient depth or support their breakthroughs with the use of mobile reserves. By failing to disrupt the enemy staff and reserves behind the front they left
themselves open to counterattack and thus the breaks in
the continuous front were sealed. Obviously if tanks were
to be linked to horse-drawn vehicles for fuel and supplies,
while their support infantry moved on foot, they were never
likely to make effective, deep penetrations. Moreover, they
must not be used in "penny packets" as had happened too
often in the past—notably on the Somme in 1916—but in
powerful concentrations supported by mobile firepower in
the form of dive-bombing planes rather than artillery bombardment. All this was to form the basis of German blitzkrieg warfare, and yet, incredibly, Guderian's book was
translated into neither English nor French, nor even studied by Allied military staff. By 1938 Guderian was the commander of mobile troops in Germany, and by reducing the
number of tanks in each division from 433 to 299 he was
able to create the nine Panzer divisions that faced France
in May 1940.

With hindsight it is easy to wonder how the French commanders in the late 1930s could have failed to foresee what
German tactics would be in 1940. It is true that they were
dominated by a doctrine that saw no strike function for
tanks and aircraft, yet it would be wrong to suggest that

no one in France was following developments in Germany. In February 1935, the Deuxieme Bureau informed the French High Command of the existence of the first Panzer division in Germany and more or less what its function was expected to be. Paul Reynaud and his young protégé, Charles de Gaulle, who challenged existing French views on armored warfare in his book *Vers L'Armée de Metier* and was struck off the promotion list for that year as a result, encountered opposition from most French military thinkers. Gamelin told de Gaulle, "Our doctrine is correct. You cannot hope to achieve real breakthroughs with tanks. The tank is not independent enough. It has to go ahead, but then must return for fuel and supplies."

De Gaulle encountered opposition at the tactical as well as the political level. He found that he needed to counter the argument that there was danger for France in too great a concentration on mechanized forces. France was particularly dependent on oil imports, which, in wartime, could be cut back, while the French arms industry was, by the 1930s, only slowly recovering after a period of comparative neglect. Nor could he easily dismiss the significant developments in anti-tank guns. Gamelin and Daladier based their opposition to the tank on what they had seen of the Spanish Civil War, in which they said that tanks had failed. To Gamelin the defeat of Franco at Guadalajara, in which he had used large numbers of Italian armored vehicles, showed the supremacy of the anti-tank gun. In the future, he believed, tanks would be useless unless they were supported by artillery and would need to be scattered among old-style infantry corps. Unfortunately for France, Gamelin had reached entirely the wrong conclusion.

The development of French tanks reflected a failure to understand the independent role that the tank was to have in the German army. The cavalry origins of the *Division Legere Mecanique* dictated that French tanks should emphasize a scouting and reconnaissance role, while the medium tank designed by Estienne was intended to support a breakthrough by the infantry so that its speed was linked to the speed of an infantryman. The doctrine behind this development of mechanized forces owed little to de Gaulle or indeed to the English military philosophers, but to a belief in "mobile defense," in which tanks would be used to "plug the gaps" in the continuous front. As such, French doctrine was hopelessly out of touch with contemporary awareness of the tactical possibilities of armored warfare.

In 1937 a new army instruction, "Tactical Employment of Major Units," was issued, framed by General Georges and signed by Daladier, containing the astounding opinion that technical progress had not appreciably modified, in a tactical sense, the essential rules laid down in previous directives, namely that the infantry was entrusted with the principal duty in battle, protected by its own guns, to conquer ground, occupy it, organize and hold it. This was no more than a nostalgic glance back to the glorious sacrifice of 1916 and reflected a total failure to understand how far technology had transformed warfare. German preoccupation with building light and medium bombers was a sign, to anyone who wished to read it, that her air force was envisaged as an offensive one, designed to operate in conjunction with the army. The Allies, typically, overlooked the tactical significance of the Stuka dive-bomber as a ground support weapon and concentrated their attention on the threat posed by the Heinkel He–111 medium bomber, which, it was feared, would devastate heavily populated areas, causing an expected 1.8 million casualties in six months in London alone.

So concerned was the French High Command with its own strategical appreciation of the situation in 1940 that it gave little thought to what the Germans might be planning themselves. To Gamelin the existence of the Maginot Line cut down the German options, leaving them with no choice but to reenact the Schlieffen Plan of 1914, which the French would counter by advancing into Belgium to meet them. Gamelin refused to listen to air force general Armengaud, who returned from Poland with an alarming account of how German tactics worked in practice:

> It would be mad not to draw an exact lesson from this pattern and not pay heed to this warning. The German system consists essentially of making a breach in the front with armour and aircraft, then to throw mechanised and motorized columns into the breach, to beat them down to right and left in order to keep on enlarging it, at the same time as armoured detachments, guided, protected and reinforced by aircraft, advance in front of the supporting divisions... in such a way

that the defence's manoeuvrability... is reduced to impotence.[2]

Armengaud warned Gamelin that he expected the Germans to strike the center of the French front and fan out behind using aircraft and mechanized troops. To Gamelin, however, the answer was simple: "We are not Poles, it could not happen here." For his advice Armengaud was relegated to an administrative post, while all the inspector general of tanks, General Keller, could say about the Polish experience was that it had changed nothing and that the role of the tank remained that of assisting the infantry.

The supreme irony of the fall of France was that the ultradefensive mentality of the Maginot Complex imposed on the French High Command a need to meet the German armies as far into Belgian territory as possible in order to save the sacred territory of France from a repeat of the dreadful attritional struggle of 1914–18. However, this necessitated a rapid, almost reckless, advance by the cream of the French army and the committal of much of its mobile reserve strength. It was not a static, passive French army that the Germans encountered but a force impelled by an urgency close to panic, whose morale was very brittle.

The Allied plan, "Instruction Number Eight," proposed that British and French forces should advance into Belgium to the Dyle Line, from Antwerp to the river Meuse, yet Gamelin, the commander-in-chief, wanted to extend this advance to Breda, almost twice as far from the French border as from the German. Georges, to whom Gamelin had entrusted the command of the northeastern sector, considered this unwise and, showing unerring prescience, commented:

The problem is dominated by the question of available forces... There is no doubt that our offensive manoeuvre in Belgium and Holland should be conducted with the caution of not allowing ourselves to commit the major part of our reserves in this part of the theatre, in face of a German action which could be nothing more than a diversion. For example, in the event of an attack in force breaking out in the centre, on our front between the Meuse and Moselle, we could be deprived of the necessary means for a counter-attack.[3]

Gamelin was undeterred and, on March 20, 1940, issued a new directive that involved the implementation of the Dyle Plan, with the addition of the Breda Variant, and this was agreed to by both the French and British governments. Instead of committing only ten French divisions with the BEF, Gamelin now proposed to use thirty French divisions, including two of the three new armored divisions, five of the seven motorized divisions and all three light mechanized divisions. The cream of the French army was going to be used in Belgium, with Giraud's 7th Army, originally planned to form part of Georges's mobile reserve, to be on the extreme left of the French front, nearest the sea. Far from being dominated by a purely defensive mentality, the French army was going to move at full speed into a trap that could have and should have been avoided.

The weakest elements in the French front, Corap's 9th Army and Huntziger's 2nd Army, would be left to hold the front along the Meuse, from where the river runs through the Ardennes, south of Namur, to Sedan and then to the Maginot Line. The removal of the 7th Army from the reserve destroyed France's capacity to launch an effective counterattack if the front was pierced at any point. Moreover, Gamelin's use of thirty divisions to back up the troops in the Maginot Line was the height of folly, for the battle would be lost before any of these troops could be effectively used. The entire French front would be only as strong as its weakest point and it was pitifully weak in the center, where Armengaud had warned that the Germans might well strike.

Along a hundred miles of the Ardennes, the line was held by just four light cavalry divisions, some still equipped with horses, and ten mediocre infantry divisions, behind whom there were no reserves at all. Facing them, across the Meuse, was Rundstedt with forty-five infantry and ten Panzer armored divisions. On the condition of Corap's 9th Army, General Brooke wrote:

> I can still see those troops now. Seldom have I seen anything more slovenly and badly turned out. Men unshaven, horses ungroomed, clothes and saddlery that did not fit, vehicles dirty, and complete lack of pride in themselves or their units. What shook me most, however, was the look in the men's faces, disgruntled

and insubordinate looks and, although ordered to give
"Eyes Left," hardly a man bothered to do so. After the
ceremony was over Corap invited me to visit some of
his defences in the Forte de St. Michel. There we found
a half-constructed and very poor anti-tank ditch with
no defences to cover it. By way of conversation I said
that I supposed he would cover this ditch with the fire
from anti-tank pillboxes. This question received the
reply: "Ah bah! on va les faire plus tard—allons, on va
dejeuner." [Ah bah! We'll take care of that later—let's
go have lunch.][4]

Hitler had already summed up the French army for himself:

Firstly I place a low value on the French Army's will to
fight. Every army is a mirror of its people. The French
people think only of peace and good living, and they
are torn apart in Parliamentary strife. Accordingly, the
Army, however brave and well-trained its officer corps
may be, does not show the combat determination expected of it. After the first setbacks, it will swiftly crack
up... [5]

What is so surprising is that Gamelin refused to see what
everyone else could see so clearly, that the center of the
French line, around Sedan, was shockingly weak. In March
1940, after a parliamentary inspection of the front, Deputy
Pierre Taittinger told Gamelin that in the Sedan sector
France risked disaster and added ominously, "These are
sinister battlefields for our arms." Gamelin's only response was to reinforce the area around Givet with a single
extra battalion and to begin the construction of a line of
maison fortes, built of masonry with a concrete ceiling and
quite incapable of resisting Stuka bombing or heavy shells.
   In any case, as the Germans could see, less than half
were completed by May 10. And those were lacking steel
doors or armored shields for the gun embrasures and were
equipped with sandbags as an alternative. At Sedan there
were no concrete installations for command posts or artillery and when work was begun on these in December
1939 the cold weather prevented the pouring of concrete,

as well as wrecking ten miles of slit trenches, which the
71st division had to remake.

To prevent the outflanking of the Maginot Line at Longwy,
Huntziger had placed his strongest divisions on the right
with his weaker ones on the left where they linked up with
Corap's weak divisions at Sedan. This was an unfortunate
mistake because it provided a soft center to the French
line, consisting of three B divisions at Sedan, the 55th,
71st and 53rd, of whom Grandsard commented, "Noncha-
lance was general; it was accompanied by the feeling that
France could not be beaten, that Germany would be beaten
without battle... the men are flabby and heavy... the men
are older, the training is mediocre." The 55th had only 20
regular officers out of 450, while the 71st, from Paris, was
of very poor quality, ill-disciplined and feebly led by the
ailing General Baudet. On May 10, over 7,000 of its men
were missing through illness or on leave. While the defenders along the Meuse lacked modern AA guns and anti-
tank weapons, the best equipment was in Belgium with the
1st and 7th armies. Too much weight was being attached
by Gamelin to the impenetrability of the Ardennes to protect this obvious weak point, which is difficult to understand in a commander whose belief in the continuous front
was sacrosanct.

Having spent so much money on the building of the Maginot Line, with the consequent cutbacks in other areas
of military spending, France had committed herself to a
lengthy war of attrition designed to blunt the offensive
strength of the German army. To leave the line at Sedan
so weakly protected was therefore the height of incompetence, equivalent to the householder fitting safety locks
on all his windows but leaving the front door open all night.

It was not as if the Ardennes had proved impenetrable
in the past. Alistair Horne points out that between the sixteenth and eighteenth centuries the Ardennes had been
penetrated on at least ten occasions by invasion forces,
while, astonishingly, during the 1938 French military maneuvers an attack by General Pretelat exactly paralleled
the German attack of May 1940. Using seven divisions, including four motorized and two armored, he broke through
the forests and completely overran the defenders. The results were so shocking that it was decided to suppress
them in order not to damage morale. The complacent Ga-

melin merely observed that it could never happen in a real war because reserves would have been available to parry the blow. The British Chief of the Imperial General Staff, General Ironside, added his weight to a growing body of opinion that believed that the Germans might try to attack through the Ardennes, but Gamelin refused to be convinced.

By 1940 aerial reconnaissance was playing an increasingly important part in military intelligence and the Germans had used it to observe the weaknesses of the Meuse defenses. Gamelin, on the other hand, had made no effort to detect the massive concentrations of German armor in the Ardennes. He had built up a scenario in his own mind and was unwilling to accept any unpalatable information that might challenge his decision to concentrate his forces in Belgium. The French military intelligence, the Deuxieme Bureau, was progressively building up a picture of German intentions that was quite different from that of Gamelin. From the end of March they had monitored a growing interest on the part of German intelligence in road conditions along the Sedan-Abbeville axis, which could only presage heavy military commitment to that area.

Moreover, French intelligence had managed to locate all the German Panzer divisions and the three motorized divisions, and all indications pointed to the Ardennes as their target. Any reader of Guderian's book, *Achtung-Panzer!*, would have realized the strong possibility that, with Guderian in charge of armored forces, a concentration on a weak point—like that at Sedan—was almost a certainty. From Swiss sources the French learned of the construction of eight military bridges across the Rhine between Bonn and Bingen, again indicating that the spearhead of the German attack would not be either in the south against the Maginot Line or in the north against Belgium. The French military attaché in Berne even informed the French commanders that he had strong evidence to suggest a German strike at Sedan, beginning some time between May 8 and May 10. However, with all this accumulation of evidence suggesting Sedan, Gamelin refused to alter his view that the main German strike would come in Belgium.

As the heavy German columns moved toward the French border on May 10 they presented a perfect target for air

attack. Admittedly, the reassuring presence of the Luftwaffe was overhead, but such dense concentrations of armored vehicles—Guderian's advanced units alone had ten
thousand—without room to maneuver on the narrow roads
would provide easy victims for Allied bombers. General von
Kleist's column was so long that when its van had reached
the Meuse its rear had scarcely crossed the Rhine. The
Ardennes provided the French with ideal country for de-
laying the German advance, with many gorges and small
villages that could have provided cover for determined
troops to fight rearguard actions. Yet little of the sort was
attempted, nor were the Germans much troubled from the
air.

Through administrative muddles the whole of *Group
d'Assaut* 1/54 failed to come into action during May 10 and
11, while the mass of Allied air strength was used in the
north to support Giraud at Breda, leaving only thirty-seven
planes in support of the 2nd and 9th armies. Even then the
British and French pilots committed to the Ardennes were
ordered to avoid bombing in built-up areas, which placed
a burden on pilots already heavily outnumbered by several
to one. The Germans could hardly believe their luck.

By the morning of May 11 General Georges was coming
to realize that the Germans were carrying out a strike in
the area of Sedan, so he ordered up the 2nd and 3rd armored divisions, the 3rd motorized, and the 14th, 36th and
87th infantry divisions to cover the threatened sector. However, this was not 1918 and the French were to be denied
the time they needed to assemble their reserves. Meanwhile, the Allied air effort continued to be concentrated in
the north, leaving Huntziger entirely without air support
until May 24.

The French commanders might have been "forged in the
fires of Verdun" in 1916 but for some their military education had ended there. At sixty-two, Corap was frankly out
of his depth in an age of armored warfare and rapid deployment and could not appreciate how fast the German
tank commanders could think and move. His time sched-
ules were those of an earlier war and he still believed that
the Germans would not attempt a crossing of the Meuse
until they had brought up their heavy guns to support their
tanks. All of this should take between four and six days.
The devastating effect of the Stuka dive-bombers acting in

support of the motorized divisions was something new to him, even though reports from Poland had been widely available of their effect on the morale of troops.

Nevertheless, Georges shared his view that matters would develop slowly "by reason of the poor rail and road communications." In contrast to the pedestrian pace of the French, the German armor had been instructed by von Kleist, "not to rest or relax; to move forward night and day, looking neither left nor right, always on the alert; the group must exploit its initial surprise and the enemy's confusion; take him everywhere unawares and have only one aim in mind: to get through."

By the evening of May 12, Guderian's troops had reached the Meuse and taken part of Sedan. It was on Huntziger's 2nd Army that the greatest blow would fall, particularly on the B divisions at Sedan, which were deficient in anti-tank guns, possessing no more than eight to each mile of front, and having quite inadequate blockhouses. In addition, by an amazing oversight, the 2nd Army had been equipped with fewer anti-tank mines than even those divisions sheltering behind the Maginot Line, which were unlikely to encounter German tanks at all. This oversight assumes greater significance when one considers the position of the 2nd Army as the hinge of the entire French front, which, should it be broken, might allow the British and French forces to the north to be cut off and encircled. The planning blunders of the French were now becoming apparent. The Ardennes had certainly not proved impenetrable, nor had it taken the Germans nine days to reach the Meuse; three had been enough.

Even now Gamelin was not convinced of the urgency of the attack at Sedan. Obsessed by the idea of a continuous front, he continued to direct his efforts to the north, content to plug any gaps in the Meuse front by committing units piecemeal. Even as late as May 13 Gamelin told Georges to direct cavalry units from Luxembourg to join the rear of the 1st Army in Belgium. Thinking in the time scales of 1918, Gamelin and the French commanders believed that, having completed a seventy-five-mile drive to the Meuse, Guderian's forces would need to halt, re-group and await artillery support. They were soon to learn how wrong they were.

Under Luftwaffe cover German sappers effected a cross-

ing of the Meuse in rubber dinghies, while the bridges on
the canal alongside the river were captured intact. By May
13, the situation was serious for the French, with the 1st
Panzer Division at Chemery three miles behind the French
lines and the 2nd and 10th Panzers advancing toward the
Meuse. Yet so far only German infantry were across the
river and the German armored divisions were in positions
to be counterattacked from the flanks. Now was the time
for the French armored divisions to strike. However, it was
becoming apparent that for whatever reason French morale was breaking and numbers of units were panicking,
particularly the gunners, who had hitherto held such a
high position of respect in the French army. Even though
there were no German forces within five miles, Colonel
Poncelet ordered his guns to be withdrawn, saying that
German tanks were arriving even as he left. Without both-
ering to verify these reports panic began to spread from
unit to unit.

By May 14 it was essential that a heavy counterattack be
launched if the German breakthrough at Sedan was to be
stopped. The pontoon bridges over the Meuse were attacked by British and French planes, though only three
were damaged and these were quickly repaired. With the
failure of the air force it was now the turn of the 3rd Armored Division.

The tank was the central weapon in the defeat of France
in 1940 and it is often assumed that the Germans owed
the ease of their victory to some overwhelming superiority
in modern armaments, tanks, anti-tank guns and aircraft.
If this were true there would be little point in charging the
French High Command with incompetence, other than
their failure to provide their nation with adequate resources to defend herself. However, this was by no means
the case. In May 1940, the French had more tanks, and
more powerful tanks at that, on the northeastern frontier
than the Germans. The failure of the French commanders
was in the misuse they made of equipment in many re-
spects superior to that of their enemy.

The occupation of Czechoslovakia in 1938–39 had
brought Germany control not only of the Skoda works in
Bohemia but also of a large number of Czech army tanks.
However, even with these the French armored strength outnumbered the German, and in the Type B. tank they had

the strongest tank on either side. R. H. S. Stolfi has conclusively shown that a numerical comparison between French and Czecho-German tank production up to May 10, 1940, was entirely favorable to the French in each category of tank. Viewed simply in terms of numbers and tonnage, it is clear that in the preparation of armored vehicles the French were by no means deficient. In fact, the Germans were taking a considerable risk in taking the offensive against an enemy with such armored strength. However, the advantage of surprise lay with the attacker, for it was unlikely that the defender would be able to concentrate all his armored strength at any one point in time to make his numerical superiority effective. In view of the French doctrine of a continuous front and the use of tanks to support infantry and plug gaps, it is easy to see how the Germans were able to achieve local supremacy in tanks and so seem to the defenders to be advancing in overwhelming numbers and strength.

According to Stolfi, the Germans employed 2,574 tanks on the northeastern front in May 1940, of which 627 were heavy PzKwIIIs and IVs, against the French force of 3,254. In any tank battle between these forces the advantage should have rested with the French, whose tanks had a better balance between armament and armor, though the German Panzers were faster on the road and more maneuverable. However, the French light mechanized divisions, equipped with SOMUA tanks—as fast or faster than the Panzers—were of equivalent strength to the Panzer divisions themselves and could have taken them on in tank-to-tank battle, as happened at Merdorp. Moreover, the superiority of the French anti-tank weapon was acknowledged by the Germans. Stolfi points out that the average French weapon was able to penetrate 47mm of armor protection at 400 meters, against the German weapon which could penetrate only 36 mm at a similar distance. In an action at Voncq on June 9, 1940, German anti-tank guns hit the FCM light tank of Sub-Lieutenant Bonnabaud forty-two times with armor-piercing 37-mm projectiles without making a single penetration. Why, given such advantages, was the French resistance so feeble?

The French army suffered from having to react so quickly to the German invasion of Belgium. It was forced to send its three light mechanized divisions north to join

combat with the Germans within forty-eight hours. Instead
of giving some credence to the numerous reports of German movement toward Sedan, Gamelin failed to be
swerved from a preconceived notion of enemy intentions
and committed himself too completely. As Stolfi states,
"Instead of coolly determining just how serious the danger
was around Sedan and co-ordinating attacks from both
north and south of the area against the German bridge-
heads, the French High Command dissipated its armour
in several hasty and ill co-ordinated attacks." The fate of
the 2nd and 3rd Armored Divisions reveals the incompetence of the French High Command in the utilization of its
armored resources.

The three armored divisions of the French army were
the strongest units that General Georges had at his disposal. The third division, under General Brocard, had two
battalions of Hotchkiss H–39 tanks and, although fewer
in number than the 10th Panzer Division, had greater
strength than the German unit—half of whose tanks were
light Mark I's and Mark II's not intended for tank-to-tank
combat. Unlike some units in the French army, morale
was high amongst the 3rd Armored, though it had not been
formed long and had only started divisional training on
May 1. It was in training at Rheims when it received its
orders to move on May 12, and had some forty miles to
cover through areas encumbered with refugees pushing
their possessions on carts or riding in horse-drawn wagons. Its journey was full of problems, caused by its lack
of engineers to repair the tanks and sappers to clear the
way for them, while the heavy B tanks had difficulty crossing the Aisne River. At one point the crush of refugees
was so great that the tanks had to force their way through
by crushing cars and wagons that obstructed their way.
The journey through a country filled with desperate refugees and deserters was not an experience to boost morale. As the tanks advanced, their crews heard wild tales
from the fugitives of masses of German tanks pursuing
them, exaggerated by fear in both size and quantity. Nevertheless, at 0600 on May 14, "full of spirit and eager to
have a go at the enemy," the 3rd Armored Division reached
Stonne and Brocard reported to General Flavigny, now
commanding the new XXI Corps. At once Brocard was
handed the following orders by Flavigny:

(a) Take up positions along the second line to the east of the Bar... and contain the bottom of the pocket created by the enemy...

(b) Having contained the enemy, counter-attack at the earliest in the direction of Maisoncelle-Bulson-Sedan...[6]

These orders were far from clear and as Colonel Goutard points out, the terms *containment* and *counter-attack* were mutually contradictory:

Containment is defensive and demands linear dispersion along a front; counter-attack is offensive and requires concentration in depth at one point.... How could one group fulfill these contradictory missions simultaneously, or even one after another? And when containment had been effected, the opportunity for counter-attack would be over; it would be too late. It was obvious that, with our mania for an unbroken front, the containing mission would have priority.[7]

Brocard informed Flavigny that in view of its thirty-mile night march his division would not be ready to go into action for some ten hours. Flavigny insisted that an attack should be launched at 1100 hours, but so slow was Brocard's preparation—particularly the refueling of the tanks—that his division was not deployed until nearly 1600 hours. However, Flavigny was already having second thoughts. He had not been impressed by what he had seen of Brocard's division and doubted its combat readiness. As an old tank commander himself, with First World War experience, his mind was already turning to thoughts of defending the second line and restoring the continuous front. At 1530 Flavigny came to a decision that was to have a marked effect on the future fortunes of France. He ordered the 3rd Armored Division to abandon its counterattack instruction and concentrate on containment.

A quarter of a century had passed since French tanks had last seen action and it showed. Coordination of tanks and aircraft was poor in comparison with that of the Germans and in any case their instructions were quite ridiculous in the face of the German blitzkrieg. Before counterattacking, the French decided that they must consolidate the line by plugging any gaps that had been forced. The result was that the 3rd Armored Division was ordered to disperse itself defensively along a twelve-mile front, from Omont to Stonne, to cover all tracks or possible points of penetration and form "corks," consisting of one B heavy tank with two Hotchkiss H–39s. This use of tanks in "penny packets," as part of a static defense, was a violation of everything the modern tank stood for. It was as if Fuller, Liddell Hart, de Gaulle and Guderian had never spoken or written a word on tank tactics. Colonel Le Goyet has pointed out that once consolidation became the French aim there was "a line, a few tanks but no 3rd Armoured Division. The steel lance was buried for ever, and so was the counter-attack." In the words of Alistair Horne, "It was a tragic error of judgement."

The fate of the French 2nd Armored Division was, if possible, even more of a tragic waste. Confusion is common in war but there are no second chances for those who squander their resources as did the French in these crucial few days in May. The 2nd Armored Division had only been formed in January 1940 and was commanded by General Bruche. On May 10 it had been located in Champagne, along with its sister divisions. Originally intended by Georges to reinforce the 2nd Army, along with the 3rd Armored, it was eventually ordered north with the 1st Armored on May 13, at a time when Guderian was crossing the Meuse. Because of the shortage of tank transporters, the 2nd Armored's tanks and other tracked vehicles were sent by train, while the wheeled transport of the division—mainly responsible for supplies and munitions—went by road. The earlier entrainment of the 1st Armored had already stretched the rail resources of the area to near breaking point and so Bruche's tanks were not taken aboard at Chalons station until the morning of May 15. The result was that with some vehicles traveling by road and others awaiting rail transport Bruche's division was scattered over a wide area. On the morning of May 14 Bruche arrived at Blanchard's 1st Army headquarters in person, only to be told that his division had been transferred to Corap's 9th Army. As if this was not bad enough, when Bruche's liaison officer contacted Corap on the fifteenth, explaining that the 2nd Armored would not be ready for battle for at least two days, he was told that the division had now been transferred to the "Army Detachment Touchon." Georges had already directed those of the 2nd Armored's vehicles traveling by road to move eastward to Signy-l'Abbaye, where they were to await the arrival of the tanks.

However, if the French were unable to make up their own minds, the Germans settled the matter for them when Reinhardt's Panzers overran Signy and drove a wedge right through the middle of Bruche's overextended division. Tractor-drawn guns and other artillery belonging to the 2nd Armored were destroyed on the road at Blanchefosse by the German tanks. Forced to move southward, the remains of the road column took refuge behind the Aisne at Rethel, while the tanks, unaware of the presence of German tanks, collided with some along the Liart-Rozoy road and were forced to escape northward, away from their own fueling lorries. By May 16 in Alistair Horne's words:

> ... almost all of General Bruche's armour lay scattered over a vast area between St. Quentin and Hirson on one side of Reinhardt's Panzer thrust, without any means of supply and having lost half its supporting artillery. On the other side, south of the Aisne, was General Bruche himself, with all the wheeled transport of the division, one gun battery, a company of H–39 light tanks, four solitary strayed 'B' tanks and two companies of Chasseurs. So the third and last of Georges' powerful "rooks" had simply broken up before it could even be committed to the battle.[8]

The French defeat was the result of many factors, not least of which was a willingness to allow the Germans to dictate how the battle should be fought. The Germans played to their strengths and the French let them. The German commanders could hardly believe their luck; everything that had been planned was working not only to schedule but often considerably ahead of it. With Guderian leading the assault on Sedan in person, there was never any question of "reining back" or "stopping to consolidate," it was speed and power all the way, allowing the Panzers to surprise and overwhelm the French defenders by the unexpected rate of their advance. Guderian took risks that would have been unthinkable in any earlier era but he was justified by the results. His combination of tanks and aircraft numbed the French defenders, sapped their morale and finally broke their spirit.

The collapse of the French army in 1940 was not a result of inferior equipment or even of a passive defensive mentality amongst the High Command. In fact, it was the overeager advance into Belgium that enabled Rundstedt to crack the "hinge" of the French line on the Meuse. The French commanders, particularly Georges and Gamelin, made serious mistakes, and their incompetence was most clearly seen in their misuse of the French armored divisions, which should have been able to blunt the Panzer advance and stabilize the front upon which the French relied. Their role was not to become a mere part of the line—a series of "plugs," as Flavigny used the 3rd Armored, to close up breakthroughs—but to be a mobile reserve to counterattack the German armored columns from the flanks, slow down the German advance and enable the French to mobilize their full resources. The French were not doomed to inevitable defeat in 1940, as so many writers suggest. Unlike the Germans, who needed a quick victory, the French had prepared themselves for a different kind of war. What they needed was time and this the Germans were determined to deny them.

Colonel Goutard has spoken of the lost opportunities of the French command, which was: "... overtaken by events every day, throwing divisions about like small change on a card table and ordering consolidation at points generally too close to the point of breakthrough. Most of its orders were based on inadequate or belated intelligence for want of proper liaison and a communications system suited to the speed of the Blitzkrieg, and it seemed impossible to carry them out from the very moment they were issued."

The French High Command was living in the past, unlike Guderian, Rommel, Manstein and even Hitler, and they had failed completely to understand the complexity of tank warfare. The idea of using tanks as auxiliaries to infantry was to deny them their true nature on the battlefield. To the French an armored division was essentially a defensive weapon, "a sort of blunt instrument to knock out any adversary who had put himself at a disadvantage," or to plug a gap in the defensive line. Linked as it was to the infantry, the armored division had no separate existence but became part of an army corps, without the means of reconnaissance, without anti-aircraft or anti-tank defense. It was left to the light cavalry divisions, with their self-propelled machine guns and light tanks, to fulfill their historical role of exploiting any success by pursuit and harassment.

The laggardly formation of the three armored divisions was a sign that the High Command, particularly Gamelin, was incompetent to direct the military fortunes of the French nation. Gamelin had earlier said, "When we want to form armoured divisions, we shall collect our tanks together and make them into units." What a man like Guderian would have made of this statement is not difficult to imagine. Divisions with such specialized functions needed time to gel together. According to General Dufieux, they were not only denied this time but were given no clear instructions of their operational roles.

They had been assembled by taking elements from many different places and consequently lacked the cohesion that the German Panzer divisions had in plenty. Even with their creation, some seventeen hundred French tanks were still left dispersed as independent battalions under infantry control. What use these would be against the concentrated offensive power of a whole Panzer division was to be revealed in May 1940, when the French armored weapon allowed itself to be destroyed piecemeal.

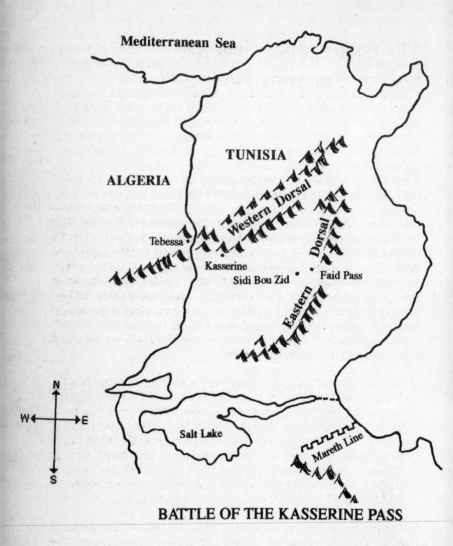

BATTLE OF THE KASSERINE PASS

The Battles of Sidi Bou Zid
and the Kasserine Pass, 1943

AMERICAN TROOPS IN TUNISIA IN THE EARLY MONTHS OF 1943 were inexperienced and suffered from the sort of overconfidence that often goes hand in hand with ignorance of what lies ahead. The fact that they were matched against the battle-hardened veterans of Field Marshal Erwin Rommel's Afrika Korps was their misfortune; that they were equipped with weapons and tanks that were like toys when compared to those of the Axis troops was their tragedy; that they were led by officers better suited to the static fighting of 1914–18 than to the mobile needs of a desert campaign was a disgrace. Only within this context can the battles of Sidi Bou Zid and the Kasserine Pass be understood. As General Lucian K. Truscott later wrote:

> American soldiers who survived the bitter months of January and February 1943 in Tunisia will never forget them—or forget Tunisia. For it was during this period in the deserts and the mountains...that American forces first crossed swords with veteran German legions and learned war from them in the hard way. These American soldiers, suffering from faults in leadership, from their own ignorance, from inferior equipment, reeled in defeat and yet rose to victory.[1]

Throughout the winter of 1942–43 American general Dwight D. Eisenhower's Allied forces in Tunisia held the Eastern Dorsal, a mountain range running from north to south for some two hundred miles. The northern sector of the line was held by British forces under Lieutenant General Kenneth Anderson, the center by General Juin's poorly equipped French XIX Corps, while in the south—in Eisenhower's eyes, the most vulnerable sector—was Major General Lloyd Fredendall's U.S. II Corps. East of the Dorsal were two German armies. The 5th Panzer Army—rushed by Hitler from the Eastern Front to counter the Allied *Torch* landings—was commanded by the tough but stolid Colonel General Jürgen von Arnim, who had already shown his fighting qualities by stopping Eisenhower's drive on Tunis in December. For the Tunisian battles von Arnim was joined by the brilliant Desert Fox, Erwin Rommel, with his Panzer Army Afrika. Rommel, however, was at a low point in his career, plagued by ill health and having just retreated fifteen hundred miles from Egypt pursued by General Bernard Montgomery's British Eighth Army. Rommel was always aware that while he was engaged in fighting the Americans there was the danger that Montgomery would enter Tunisia to his rear. To prevent surprise, Rommel had left troops in the old French fortifications in eastern Tunisia, known as the Mareth Line. Nevertheless, both von Arnim and Rommel knew that time was not on their side. They were both determined to break the confidence of the newly arrived American troops and instill in them and their commanders "an inferiority complex of no mean order."

Eisenhower fully appreciated the vital importance of holding the Eastern Dorsal until Montgomery's arrival, because then the Germans could be hit from both east and west simultaneously. On the other hand, should the Germans succeed in breaking through his lines, the passes of the Western Dorsal would then be exposed and after that the road was open to Algeria, with its glittering prize of Allied airfields and supply depots.

In February 1943, all was not well with the U.S. II Corps or with its commander, Lloyd Fredendall. In the words of British historian Charles Messenger:

> [Fredendall]... appeared to have modelled his image of a general in action on the theories of the motion picture industry. He was loud, outspoken and critical of both superiors and subordinates. His attitude was

overbearing, and he tended to speak in a Hollywood slang, which at times was almost impossible to understand.[2]

In his study of the Tunisian campaigns, *Crucible of Power*, Kenneth Macksey has been particularly critical of Fredendall, attributing much of the disappointing performance by American troops at the start of the campaign to him and to American commanders like him, who did not appreciate the kind of war they were being called upon to fight. As Macksey wrote:

> Formations and units are the mirror image of their leaders and Fredendall's showmanship became a facade for a man whose idea of leadership was anachronistic. Here was a General, senior in years and service but junior in appointment to Eisenhower, dearly wishing to emulate the commanders of the past and win glory for himself and his country. Fredendall's behaviour from the moment of his arrival in North Africa had been that of a g ilded commander from the First World War, in the lush set-up of his HQ in the best hotel in Oran to the startling isolation of his HQ in the field, far behind the line, served by a staff whose dress and manner in Oran aped the worst kind of snobbery and, in the field, deteriorated and became shabby.[3]

In February 1943 the Allied High Command received information that the Germans were planning to make an attack on their positions around Fondouk. To ensure that all was well in the American sector south of Fondouk, Eisenhower visited Fredendall's headquarters on February 13. There he found a frightening level of complacency throughout the whole command. Instead of ensuring good communications between headquarters and his front line troops, Fredendall had set up his HQ in a ravine seventy miles behind the front line and, apparently fearful that the Germans might still find it, had ordered his engineers to spend three weeks constructing deep shelters for himself and his staff. Eisenhower was horrified at his priorities, saying, "It was the only time during the war that I ever saw

a higher headquarters so concerned over its own safety
that it dug itself underground shelters." No proper defenses had been established and no minefields laid. Eisenhower was deeply disturbed:

> I found... a certain complacency, illustrated by an un-
> conscionable delay in perfecting defensive positions
> in the passes. Lack of training and experience on the
> part of commanders was responsible. At one point
> where mines were not yet planted the excuse was given
> that the defending infantry had been present in the
> area only two days. The commander explained, with an
> air of pride, that he had prepared a map for his mine
> defense and would start next day to put out the mines.
> Our experience in north Tunisia had been that the en-
> emy was able to prepare a strong defensive position
> ready to resist counter attack within two hours after
> his arrival on the spot.[4]

Fredendall, meanwhile, had made all his troop dispositions from maps spread out on the floor of his HQ, and
as a result of not taking proper account of the terrain his
men were spread dangerously thin at the front. The 1st
Armored Division, for example, was so dispersed as to
provide no useful opposition to the Germans at any point.
Fredendall's incompetence lay like a heavy hand across
U.S. II Corps.

But it was in his relations with his subordinates that
Fredendall caused most damage. His messages to them
were sometimes so obscure as to be almost meaningless.
One message to Brigadier General Robinett read:

> Move your command, that is, the walking boys, pop
> guns, Baker's outfit and the outfit which is the reverse
> of Baker's outfit and the big fellow to M, which is due
> north of where you are now, as soon as possible. Have
> your boss report to the French gentleman whose name
> begins with J at a place which begins with D which is
> five grid squares to the left of M.[5]

As Robinett reported later, it took him nearly as long as
the Germans (apparently) took to decipher Fredendall's

idiosyncratic code. But what did Eisenhower do about what he found at Fredendall's headquarters? The answer is nothing. Clearly the complacency did not end with Fredendall. Some of the blame for what occurred in February 1943 has to be laid at Eisenhower's door. It is interesting to note that in his own account of the visit to Fredendall—in his that in his own account of the visit to Fredendall—in his-book *Crusade in Europe*—he does not go on to mention that at the very moment that von Arnim was crushing American positions at Sidi Bou Zid on February 13, he was taking time out to visit some ancient ruins on his way back to headquarters.

When General Anderson pointed out the importance of the village of Sidi Bou Zid, at the head of the Faid Pass, Fredendall had ordered the 1st Armored Division's commander, Major General Orlando Ward, to occupy the hills surrounding the village, Djebel Lessouda in the north and Djebel Ksaira to the south, with two battalions from the 168th Infantry. In addition, Brigadier General McQuillan's Combat Command A was sent to hold Sidi Bou Zid itself. But the problem was that Fredendall was basing his dispositions on what he saw on his map in his underground shelter, seventy miles from Sidi Bou Zid. In the real world it just was not like that. Reconnaissance would have shown him that the hills were too big for the garrisons he was providing and too far from Sidi Bou Zid to be supported by McQuillan. Nor were they even self-supporting—they were two isolated pockets the Germans could surround and destroy at their leisure.

No sooner had Eisenhower completed his tour of inspection of Fredendall's headquarters on February 13—and while he was visiting ancient Carthage—the German attack—named *Fruhlsingwind* by its architect, von Arnim—burst on the unsuspecting Americans. Von Broich's 10th Panzer Division drove through the Eastern Dorsal by way of the Faid Pass. With a sandstorm covering their advance, and men on foot leading the Panzer and Tiger tanks forward, the Germans achieved total tactical surprise and pushed on toward the village of Sidi Bou Zid. Simultaneously, Hildebrandt's 21st Panzer Division broke through the mountains to the south of the village. McQuillan would either have to retreat with all speed to avoid being encircled, or else he would have to be re-inforced by major elements from Ward's division. As things stood he had absolutely no chance against two Panzer divisions. Incredibly, Fredendall did not suggest sending reinforcements. So sudden and decisive was the German attack that it seemed to remove his power to react.

In the poor visibility advanced American units in the Faid Pass were simply overrun. McQuillan ordered Lieutenant Colonel Hightower to counterattack but his tanks were massacred by the German Panzer IVs and Tigers, as well as the deadly 88-mm guns. From Djebel Ksaira, Colonel Thomas Drake, with his battalion of the 168th Infantry, could see that he was surrounded and completely cut off from any support. Below him on the plain he could also see that a general panic had overtaken the American ar-tillery and that many men were running away. He contacted McQuillan at Sidi Bou Zid to report the debacle, but McQuillan simply would not believe it. "You don't know what you're saying. They're just shifting their positions." But Drake was adamant: "Shifting positions, hell. I know panic when I see it."

American Honey tanks, armed with 37-mm guns, stood no chance against the heavier German tanks with their 75-mm and 88-mm cannons. The Americans watched in de-spair as their own shells ricocheted away from the thick army of the Panzer IVs and Tigers: not one German tank was damaged by an American that day. German air power dominated the battlefield, with Me−109Fs strafing the ground troops and Stukas terrifying the Americans with their wailing sirens. Even the American Sherman tanks were no match for the Germans, many being reduced to balls of fire that the GIs nicknamed, with macabre humor, the "Ronsons."

By evening McQuillan had been forced to abandon Sidi Bou Zid, leaving Fredendall's "islands of resistance" is-lands all right, but in a German sea. Two and a half thousand American infantry were trapped on the hills and Fredendall was planning a rescue mission the next day. In Macksey's words, "Fredendall still wanted to con-duct a kind of Red Indian warfare," and so he decided to send the cavalry to rescue the trapped settlers. For this difficult—if not suicidal—mission, Lieutenant Colo-

nel James D. Alger's 2nd Medium Tank Battalion of the
1st U.S. Armored Regiment was selected. Alger's force was
a hotchpotch, hastily assembled for the operation, with
some elements joining it just before the attack. Alger was
instructed by Orlando Ward to "move south and by fire
and maneuver destroy the enemy armored forces which
have threatened our hold on the Sbteila area...[and] to
aid the withdrawal of our forces in the vicinity of Djebel
Ksaira." Alger had no air cover at all and, denied any kind
of reconnaissance, was quite unaware that he was heading
straight for a hundred German tanks, which were supported by dive-bombers and heavy artillery. The American
Official History describes the start of Alger's heroic journey into the Valley of Death:

> Even through field glasses Sidi Bou Zid, about 13 miles
> distant, was a tiny spot of dark hued evergreens and
> white horses behind which rose the hazy slopes of
> Djebel Ksaira.... There was a considerable mirage. The
> dips and folds of the plain were for the most part grad-
> ual but several steepsided deeper wadis creased it in
> general from north to south.
>
> At 12:40 the attacking formation started over this
> expanse with great precision until its vehicles were
> reduced by distance to the size of insects and obscured
> by heavy dust. In the lead were the tanks...tank de-
> stroyers were grouped on each wing. The artillery and
> then the infantry in half tracks followed.... [6]

Alger first tried to retake Sidi Bou Zid and then pushed
on straight into a German trap. A German tank commander
described the progress of the fifty-four American Sher-
mans:

> We got to within 2000 metres of the enemy. It was
> simply incomprehensible to us, but he was staring
> straight ahead...and not one of the enemy tanks
> turned its turret towards us.
>
> ...scarcely had the first shells left our guns than the
> first three enemy tanks were on fire. They were burning
> ...There were at least fifteen burning tanks ahead of
> us and the most advanced of our tanks were already

making their way between the destroyed American
tanks to those in the rear...

...Later, when everything was over, only a single
enemy tank had escaped our guns to carry back this
day's report to its vanquished general.[7]

It had been a brave but futile gesture—not unlike an
American charge of the Light Brigade. But how Alger was
expected to rescue infantry trapped over thirteen miles
away by taking on two Panzer divisions, while overhead
Stukas dived and bombed him to oblivion, is hard to imagine. In all he lost fifty out of his fifty-four tanks and was
himself captured by the Germans. The movie was over—
there was to be no eleventh-hour rescue. Fredendall was
now forced to organize an airdrop telling the trapped infantry on the hills to try to break out and make their own
way back. That evening, February 15, Colonel Drake led his
sixteen hundred men down the slopes of Djebel Ksaira in
the darkness and tried to get them away across the plain,
but they were surrounded by German tanks and forced to
surrender. Major Robert Moore, commanding about nine
hundred men on Djebel Lessouda to the north, also tried
to get away under cover of night. Moore and three hundred
men made it, but the rest were captured or killed in the
attempt.

Fredendall had much to regret. In two days he had lost
two battalions of armor, two of infantry and two of artillery, and all at a minimal cost to the Germans. Eisenhower
felt there was no alternative now but to pull back the
American II Corps and the French XIX Corps to their north
about fifty miles to defend the Western Dorsal. As he
ruefully reflected:

Our soldiers are learning rapidly, and while I still believe that many of the lessons we are forced to learn
at the cost of lives could be learned at home, I assure
you that the troops that come out of this campaign are
going to be battle wise and tactically efficient.[8]

In spite of Eisenhower's optimistic words the American
retreat across Tunisia was a depressing experience in difficult desert conditions and under constant attack from
Axis tanks and dive-bombers. When Fredendall's II Corps

reached the Western Dorsal they turned to defy their attackers, determined to hold the Kasserine Pass, gateway
to the strategic Algerian town of Tebessa. Should Rommel
capture Tebessa he would have a free road to the Algerian
coast, disrupting the rear of the Allied positions to the
north. But the leadership of II Corps was disintegrating.
Morale had slumped and panic was never far from the surface. Fredendall, himself was at odds with his own commanders. According to historian Martin Blumenson,
Fredendall "hated Ward's guts." It was at this time of crisis,
when a show of unity was most important, that Fredendall
showed that he was too small a man to sink his differences
in the interests of the greater cause.

But the Americans were lucky that the Axis commanders
von Arnim and Rommel were also at daggers-drawn. Their
disagreement over strategy gave the Americans an unexpected two days' breathing space. Rommel appealed to
Field Marshal Kesselring in Rome to allow him to press his
attack against Fredendall, with the aim of taking Tebessa.
But von Arnim wanted to keep much of the German heavy
armor—notably, the sixty-ton Tiger tanks—for an operation of his own. Eventually Kesselring gave Rommel the
go-ahead. The delay had given Fredendall the chance to reform his shattered command, but yet again he had parceled
out his troops so thinly that they would be unable to hold
any of the five passes through which Rommel might choose
to advance.

In the Kasserine Pass, Fredendall had instructed the
26th Infantry Regiment commander, Colonel Alexander
Stark, to "pull a Stonewall Jackson." This was excellent
advice in principle, but what kind of bricks did Stark have
to build his wall with? The answer was "green as grass"
GIs and Colonel Anderson Moore's 19th Combat Engineer
Regiment, which had never been under fire before. It was
asking a lot of such men to stand against the battle-
hardened German troops who would be thrown against
them. And it was easy for Fredendall to give instructions
to "pull at Stonewall Jackson" when he was seventy miles
from the action—and twenty feet underground at that.

On February 19 the German Panzers, commanded by
Brigadier General Buelowius, tried to bulldoze their way
through Stark's defenses, but the Americans gamely held
them off with artillery, anti-tank and small arms fire. It

was not until the veteran Afrika Korps infantry got around
Stark's flanks and attacked him from the rear that the rot
set in. Stark's force panicked and cracked, and another
humiliating retreat began. On the road to Tebessa, a com-
pany of engineers panicked at what they assumed, in the
shadows, to be approaching German tanks. The panic
spread and soon an atmosphere of hysteria prevailed
among the American troops. Forward artillery observers
fled, declaring, "This place is too hot." As darkness fell
hundreds of men left their posts and began to run.
The Kasserine defenses were caving in. Reinforcements
of American infantry and eleven British tanks under
Lieutenant Colonel Gore were rushed in to hold the Germans for a while, but by the following afternoon Buelowius had broken through, knocking out the last British
tank in the process. According to the Official American
History:

> The valiant stands of Colonel Gore's detachment
> forced General Buelowius to commit his 1st Battalion
> 8th Panzer Regiment to force the breakthrough. The
> British fought until their last tank was destroyed. Cas-
> ualties were severe.[9]

At 4:30 P.M. on February 20 Allied resistance had cracked
and the Axis forces were pouring through the pass in force.
It seemed now that nothing could stop Rommel from breaking out into open country.

But Rommel, suffering from jaundice and desert sores,
was a prey to doubt. While he had not been impressed by
the American soldiers he had encountered so far, he knew
that they would get better with training and experience.
And what broke his spirit—and plunged him into despair—
was the seemingly limitless supplies the Allies had. How
could he maintain the fight against an enemy who could
replace everything—men, guns and tanks—he had lost?
Furthermore, at any moment he knew that General Montgomery's British Eighth Army would break through into
southern Tunisia. Could he afford to have his old enemy
operating in his rear? Eventually he felt he had no choice
and decided to pull back from western Tunisia. The Americans were to have the breathing space they needed to im-

prove. And Eisenhower made a start by replacing Fredendall, and in an inspired moment handed II Corps—beaten and humiliated—to a man who knew everything about inspiring men to fight: George Patton.

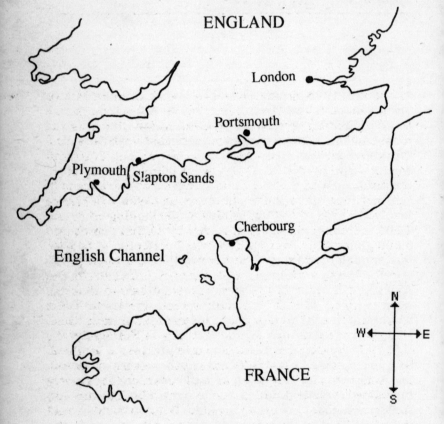

ENGLAND

London

Portsmouth

Plymouth Slapton Sands

Cherbourg

English Channel

FRANCE

Exercise Tiger 1944

Exercise Tiger, 1944

On June 6, 1944, American troops landed on the coast of France at Utah and Omaha beaches in Normandy. It was the culmination of months of training for what was the most complex military operation in the history of the world. The thousands of men—American, British and Commonwealth—who landed on D day were merely the tip of an operation so vast that the mind struggles to encompass it. The maritime operation to put these men ashore in France involved a total of 1,200 warships, 4,000 landing craft, and 1,600 merchant vessels, supported by 11,500 planes and 3,500 gliders. Not everything worked perfectly, of course, but enough worked well to ensure that the operation—Overlord—was a triumph for planners on both sides of the Atlantic. Yet some of the men who went ashore that day were carrying with them a dark secret, one few of them would find it easy to talk about for the rest of their lives.

In their preparations for the landings in Normandy, the U.S. VII Army Corps were stationed in the west of England. At a place named Slapton Sands, in the county of Devon, the Americans had found an area of coastline that closely resembled their destination—code-named Utah Beach—on the French coast north of Carentan. Slapton Sands could therefore be used to accustom the assault troops to the kind of terrain they would be encountering on D day. In the spring of 1944 a number of exercises were carried out, culminating in Exercise Tiger—a full-scale rehearsal for D day itself—to be carried out in late April. But the exercise turned out to be a disaster, and the true horror of Tiger was not simply that four times as many American lives were lost in this exercise than were lost to enemy fire at Utah Beach on D day itself, but that the American authorities chose to draw a veil over the events that occurred at Slapton Sands for over forty years. This disaster was the result of a series of shocking blunders by both American and British officers that could have shaken confidence in the Anglo-American alliance at this crucial moment of the war. To prevent this, a macabre cover-up was staged that prevented the truth of what happened at Slapton Sands on the night of April 27, 1944, from reaching the general public until just a few years ago.

The American troops stationed near Torbay in Devon included many very inexperienced soldiers. And during training exercises at Slapton one of General Dwight D. Eisenhower's aides, Harry C. Butcher, had noted about them:

> I am concerned over the absence of toughness and alertness of young American officers whom I saw on this trip. They seem to regard the war as one grand manoeuvre in which they are having a happy time. Many seem as green as growing corn. How will they act in battle and how will they look in three months time?
>
> A good many of the full colonels also give me a pain. They are fat, grey and oldish. Most of them wear the Rainbow Ribbon of the last war and are still fighting it...
>
> On the Navy's side, our crews are also green...I recall that in plain daylight, with a smooth sea with our LCI standing still, she nearly had her stern carried away by a landing craft fitted out as an anti-aircraft ship. We were missed only by inches—in clear daylight.[1]

This was far from reassuring, and the decision was taken—by Eisenhower himself—that in order to make exercises more realistic and to toughen up the men, live ammunition should be used on future exercises, notably in Exercise Tiger, planned for the end of April. This was a severe—but not unusual—step in preparing men for war. Fired over their heads or in front of their feet, live ammunition would provide the "taste" if not the consequences of real enemy fire. Obviously there would be mistakes and some men would be wounded, even killed, on such exercises. But the fundamental mistake that was made at Slapton was not to tell men that their ammunition was live. This was plainly a murderous error on someone's part and the results were all too predictable. Troops—careless and relaxed at first on what they thought were just exercises—were horrified to find that men were dying around them and that when they fired their rifles they were sometimes killing other American soldiers. Because of a breakdown in radio communications between ship and shore, neither side—defenders on shore nor attackers in the boats—were aware of the "live ammunition" ruling. It was against this background of tragedy and botched staff work that the early exercises—code-named Duck and Beaver—took place, and the date for the final exercise—Tiger—drew near.

The main purpose of Exercise Tiger is explained in this memorandum from SHAEF Headquarters (Supreme Headquarters Allied Expeditionary Force):

> Exercise Tiger will involve the concentration, marshalling and embarkation of troops in the Torbay-Plymouth area, and a short movement by sea under control of the US Navy, disembarkation with Naval and Air support at Slapton Sands, a beach assault using service ammunition, the securing of a beachhead and a rapid advance inland.[2]

It was intended that the men would be embarked from the same ports and in the same ships that they would use on D day itself and that everything would be as close as possible to the real thing. The one part of the "real thing" that they were not allowing for was the presence of an active enemy.

German E-boats—fast motor-torpedo boats—were a regular threat to Allied shipping in the English Channel and it was routine for the Royal Navy to keep a watch on the French port of Cherbourg, from where they were known to operate. The E-boats were fast and immensely maneuverable vessels, capable of a top speed of over forty knots and able to outrun any destroyer or corvette sent to intercept them. Each carried up to four torpedoes, as well as one 40-mm and three 20-mm guns. So potent a threat did these fast boats pose to troopship convoys that protection against them should have been a top priority in any exercise along the south coast of England. The level of protection that was provided for Exercise Tiger was so feeble that it defies comprehension.

Exercise Tiger began on the evening of April 26 when troops embarked on their LSTs and headed out to sea across Lyme Bay. It was known that E-boats were operating in that area and so the Royal Navy had placed an extra patrol of two destroyers and three MTBs across the bay, with another MTB watching Cherbourg for any sign that the E-boats were putting to sea. The first landings—by the 101st Airborne Division—began the next morning and passed without major incident. But the second invasion group— from the U.S. 4th Division—was not to be so fortunate. This second convoy suffered from just about every mishap that could have occurred to it. The Royal Navy had assigned as escorts for the convoy just two vessels, the corvette H.M.S. *Azalea* and the old destroyer H.M.S. *Scimitar*, a survivor from the First World War. Against the speed of modern E-boats these two ships would have had their work cut out in any case, but as fate would have it the *Scimitar* suffered some slight damage in a collision with an American LST and was given permission to go into dock for repairs without being immediately replaced. This blunder was to cost the lives of nearly one thousand American servicemen. The damage to the *Scimitar* was so slight that had it occurred in combat it would scarcely have been considered worthy of mention. Yet, although the ship was responsible for protecting a convoy of landing craft crowded with troops, it was still considered acceptable to undertake little more than routine repairs. This was a dreadful decision—and a black day for the Royal Navy, which between 1914 and 1918 had supervised the shipment of many millions of British and American servicemen from England to France without the loss of a single life to enemy action. Standards had slipped disastrously, and it was the American GIs who were going to pay.

The errors proliferated. Because of a typing error the American LSTs were operating on a different radio frequency from H.M.S. *Azalea*, as well as British navy headquarters on shore. Consequently when German E-boats were spotted after midnight on April 28 only the *Azalea* got the message, and its commander—assuming that the

LSTs had picked up the same message—made no effort to inform the American ships. This was an incredible oversight on his part and was to contribute in no small way to the disaster that was to follow.

But nobody was thinking about disaster as the troops boarded their landing ships at Plymouth at 9:45 A.M. on April 27. It was an exercise, after all, and however realistic they might try to make it there was one element they were not going to introduce and that was a real-life enemy. Commander B. J. Skahill was in charge of the LST group of convoy T-4, traveling in LST 515, and would lead the rest of the LSTs in a single column that would stretch across three miles of sea. It was a large area for a single corvette to protect. Skahill's group consisted of his LST, 515, followed by 496, 531 and 58, and off the coast at Brixham they would join up with three others: LSTs 499, 289 and 507. They would proceed at a speed of about four knots, at a distance between ships of about four hundred meters. Near the Eddystone Rocks, south of Plymouth, they were joined by their escort—alarmingly reduced to the single corvette H.M.S. *Azalea.*

The first sign of trouble was an outbreak of firing at about 1:30 A.M. on April 28, and the American naval crews went to action stations. In fact, they were about to be attacked by a flotilla of nine German E-boats based at Cherbourg, under the command of Lieutenant Günther Rabe, which had broken through the British patrols and now had the American troopships at its mercy. Rabe had left Cherbourg with his flotilla at 10:00 P.M on April 27 and had headed toward Lyme Bay, encountering no British covering ships, much to his surprise. To his astonishment he found his flotilla in visual contact with the American LSTs, strung out in an inviting way and without adequate protection. It was an opportunity of a lifetime for Rabe and his men.

What happened next is immensely confusing, pieced together as it has had to be from the reports of hundreds of men under fire at sea and in pitch darkness. When the firing began most of the soldiers thought it was just another element in the toughening-up process that had been a feature of the buildup to D day. The colorful tracers in the sky and the explosions were all part of the exercise. One officer told a soldier, "I guess they're trying to make it as real as possible." And then the torpedoes began to

strike and as men were pitched into the cold and oily sea
it soon became only too obvious that this was the real
thing. The temperature of the water that night—less than
45 degrees Fahrenheit—rendered many men unconscious
from shock when they hit the water or numbed them so
much that in minutes they had succumbed to exposure.

In the space of a few minutes after two A.M. explosions
rent the night as LSTs 507, 289 and 531 were hit by
torpedoes. At the head of the column, Skahill could only
look back at the confused horror behind him. The LSTs
were firing back, but at what? Submarines or MTBs? So
fast were the German vessels that no precise sighting
could be made and LST 496 strafed the decks of LST 511
by mistake, killing and wounding some of the men aboard.
It was like a scene from Dante's *Inferno*, with the night
illuminated by lines of yellow, blue and white tracer, and
explosions erupting all around, with red flames lapping
across the sea, now thoroughly covered in oil. To make
matters worse some men were already in the water,
screaming thinly amidst all the noise and soon slipping
beneath the cold surface of Lyme Bay. Inadequate training
added a new horror to this dreadful night: the life belts
actually drowned the men as they tried to use them. Each
soldier in the convoy had been equipped with an inflatable
life belt that would be inflated if either of two carbon dioxide
capsules was punctured. But the men had not been shown
how to wear them correctly. To compound the problem
the soldiers were heavily laden for the exercise and carried
backpacks. As a result they often wore the life belts
around their waist instead of under their armpits. The
result was that when they were in the water the life belt
made them top-heavy and forced their heads back under
water. Many bodies were later found, having been drowned
in this way—a criminal waste of life. Furthermore, most
soldiers later admitted that they had been given no "abandon ship" instructions or procedures to follow. When
disaster struck it was every man for himself. Lifeboats
could not be launched in many cases because their metal
bolts were rusted and they could not be lowered into the
sea. In at least one case soldiers shot the bolts away with
their rifles.

And the LSTs seemed to be entirely on their own, like
sheep bunching together against the attacks of predators.

Where was their escort? During this confused phase in the
fighting the LSTs received no message from H.M.S. *Azalea*
at all, and the commanders did not know whether to stay
together or scatter and try to make their way back to port.
LST 499 radioed a distress message to the effect that the
convoy had been attacked by submarines, but, although
the message was received and acted upon, there was no
chance that help could reach the LSTs in time. The Germans, in the meantime, returned to Cherbourg in triumph,
having suffered no losses themselves but having completely wrecked their target convoy, sinking two LSTs and
killing in the vicinity of one thousand American soldiers.

By the time the convoy leader, LST 515 with Skahill in
command, was able to return to the scene of action at the
rear of the convoy, there was little to do but lower boats
and attempt to rescue survivors. But where was the
Azalea? The commander of LST 289 later rightly complained:

> It will be observed that at no time were we given any
> apparent support from our escort or any other source,
> even though 33 minutes elapsed between the surface
> fire and the torpedo attack. It is to be hoped that future
> operations will avoid such futile sacrifices.[3]

Another American officer was very critical of the way the
convoy was organized. He felt that the speed adopted—four
knots—was far too slow and that the convoy commanders
should have been told that tracer fire and explosions were
not a part of the exercise, as many suspected, but were in
fact enemy fire. And why was such an inadequate escort
provided for such an important exercise where the lives of
thousands of troops were at risk? This officer summed up
his complaints by saying that he frankly had no idea what
to do in the event of an attack and felt that there had been
a catastrophic breakdown in communications between
those organizing the exercise and those taking part.
Should anything like this occur on D day itself then very
heavy casualties could be expected.

Exercise Tiger had been both a fiasco and a tragedy. But
who was responsible for what had gone wrong? The hunt
now began for culprits or, if necessary, scapegoats. On the
British side there was quite a case to answer. The Royal

Navy had been responsible for escorting Convoy T–4 with both the *Azalea* and the *Scimitar*—quite a thin cover in the first place—but to have allowed the latter to go into Plymouth dockyard for repairs was surely a terrible mistake. It was admitted by the Admiralty that *Scimitar* was perfectly seaworthy for calm sea conditions—which prevailed during the night of April 27—and therefore she should not have been allowed to forgo her duty. In any case, why was a replacement not made available? Apparently news of *Scimitar*'s docking did not reach naval headquarters at Plymouth until eleven P.M. on April 27. There, work overloads and shortage of staff—the perennial cries of the incompetent organization—were used to explain why no alternative vessel was sent to escort the convoy. There were a number of British destroyers in the vicinity that night, including H.M.S. *Onslow* and H.M.S. *Saladin*, but neither was close enough to cover the convoy in the event of a German attack. In any case, the corvette *Azalea* had instructions that in the event of an attack she was not to engage the enemy but to "close the coast," curious instructions in the context of what happened. Nevertheless, she was acting under the orders of American Rear Admiral D. P. Moon, who was the operational commander for Tiger, and he chose not to change her orders in spite of having already received warnings of E-boat action that night. When the German attack took place the convoy was some fifteen miles to the west of Portland Bill and *Azalea* confined her activity to escorting the six undamaged LSTs toward the shore before returning to escort the damaged LST, 289, along the coast to Dartmouth. By this time there was nothing that she could have done to help LSTs 507 and 531, which had both gone down.

What is inexplicable is how the operation was allowed to take place in the full knowledge that there was a potent E-boat threat in the area and that the Germans were actually at sea on the night of April 27. Rear Admiral Moon interviewed the commander of H.M.S. *Azalea*, Lieutenant Commander Geddes, the day after the disaster. Moon asked Geddes what were his reactions to seeing his fellow escort, *Scimitar*, leaving station and going into Plymouth for repairs. Geddes replied that he assumed that everything was in order and that some arrangement had been made by

Scimitar's commander for a replacement. Assumptions of this kind form an important part in the explanation of why Exercise Tiger came to grief. Geddes continued by saying that he took station at the head of the convoy off Brixham. The American ships were in an extraordinarily long single column, stretching across three miles of sea, with *Azalea* an additional mile ahead. In the event of an attack there was very little that the corvette could have done from her position to intercept the intruders. What is even more difficult to understand than the length of the convoy, the slow speed adopted and the position of the escort, is the fact that throughout the operation there was no radio communication between *Azalea* and the LSTs because they were operating on different wavelengths. For some reason Geddes chose not to bring his own radio wavelength into conformity with the American vessels. Once the attack had started, Geddes told Moon, he could not decide from which side the E-boats were operating. Had he chosen to go down the wrong side of the convoy—three miles at least in length—he would have been far too late to be effective.

Admiral Moon's frustration with Geddes can be seen in the following account of their exchange from Ken Small's book, *The Forgotten Dead*:

Admiral Moon asked him [Geddes] if he thought it was a little strange that he escorted the convoy with only one ship. He replied that he did. So the admiral asked whether he had made any protest against proceeding? "No, sir," replied the British officer...

"Did you arrange for radio communication circuits with the commanding officer or the convoy commander?"

"No, sir."

"Did the convoy commander make any arrangements with you before departing port as to radio communications?"

"No, sir, I joined the convoy in position after the convoy came out."

"Would it have been possible for you to have gotten together before and made arrangements?"

"Yes, sir, I think we could have made contact at the conference."[4]

Moon also interviewed Lieutenant Commander Shee, the officer commanding the *Scimitar*. He asked him about the extent of the damage to his vessel and was told that the *Scimitar* had suffered a hole "about two feet wide and two feet long...about twelve feet above the water line." According to Shee this would not have even reduced his top speed in good weather. Moon asked Shee why he had not sent him a dispatch about the damage and was told, "I didn't consider it serious enough to warrant and as I was returning to Plymouth I made the signal as a routine signal to inform them of the damage." So Shee did not consider it important enough to inform Moon that his ship would not be available to carry out its escort duties!

Yet there was no villain—or villainy—in accounting for the disaster that struck Exercise Tiger. It was human frailty—the small errors of many people—that combined to make simple mistakes appalling in their consequences. Moon reported his findings to Admiral Leatham at Plymouth and these were passed on to the naval commander of the Western Task Force, Admiral Kirk. But there was no remedy for the fact that 946 American lives had been lost in an unnecessary disaster.

While one group of military men was trying to uncover the reasons for the Tiger fiasco another group was charged with precisely the opposite task: to cover up as far as humanly possible this botched example of Anglo-American cooperation. It was difficult for anyone to look positively on the events of that April night, and so poor had combined operations been between the British and the Americans that if the news had broken that nearly a thousand American soldiers had been drowned in a fiasco, Anglo-American relations could have been harmed on the brink of the most important Allied operation of the war. Details of Tiger had to be kept hidden—the dead buried secretly, the wounded whisked away to Wales beyond any possibility of their talking to their fellow GIs. But most worrying of all for the planners at SHAEF was just how much the Germans had learned about Allied plans for D day. Included in Exercise Tiger had been about twenty American officers—known as BIGOTs—who were privy to the most detailed information about the timing of D day and the beaches chosen for the landings. This information would have proved so useful to the Germans that SHAEF seriously

considered postponing Operation Overlord or choosing
new sites for the invasion. However, SHAEF's fears were
unnecessary because by a quirk of fate all of the bodies of
the BIGOT officers were found and the Germans appear
never to have seriously considered taking prisoners from
the many men bobbing about in the water.

So much had gone wrong with Exercise Tiger that it
hardly seemed worthwhile to look for lessons. Surely it
could never happen again. Even after the presence of E-
boats in the vicinity of the convoy had been confirmed no
warning was given to the escort or to the LST commanders—a curious omission. Radar proved just as useless,
only confirming the presence of the E-boats when they
were already ten miles within radar range. And for all the
sightings by shore plotters indicating that E-boats were
operating in the east of Lyme Bay, convoy T-4 was still
allowed to sail straight into the path of the E-boats. And
when they encountered the German vessels they presented
such a sight as the Germans must have dreamed of, strung
out across the sea like a series of targets on a rifle range
and with just one escort vessel a mile ahead of them. Had
there been an escort vessel on both seaward bow and beam
the E-boats would have found their task very much harder.
Eventually Admiral Leatham accepted responsibility for
the inadequate escort cover and admitted that a second
naval vessel might have averted the disaster altogether.
This was true but should not be used as a mask to cover
all the other mistakes that combined to make Exercise
Tiger the most tragic—and the most avoidable—American
disaster studied in this book.

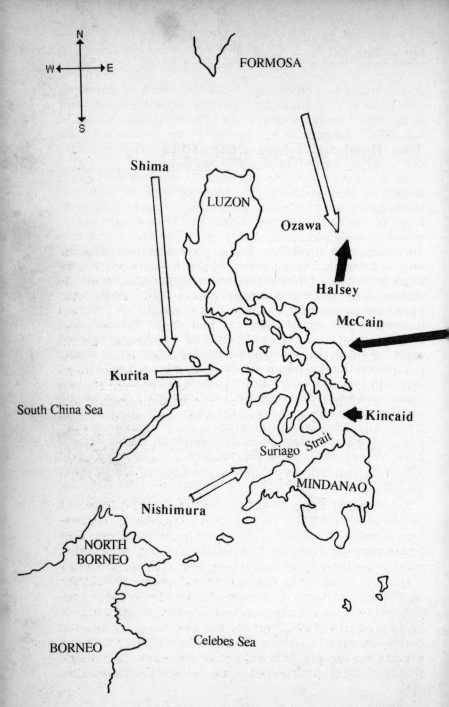

BATTLE OF LEYTE GULF 1944

The Battle of Leyte Gulf, 1944

JAPAN'S DEFEAT IN THE PACIFIC WAR WAS INEVITABLE FROM THE moment that her planes attacked the American Pacific Fleet at Pearl Harbor on December 7, 1941. The Japanese commander, Admiral Yamamoto, knew this. Yet as Japanese successes multiplied in the early months of 1942 his lone voice of warning was heard less often. The Japanese military hierarchy was indulging in a national "death-ride"—a *kamikaze* operation thirty months before a desperate navy would call on its young men to immolate themselves in the service of their nation. Japan entered the war on a wave of nationalism that so distorted the truth that it seemed for many months that the Japanese could walk on water and that men who had only months before been bank clerks in Tokyo were suddenly experienced jungle fighters in Malaya and, armed with bicycles instead of Panzer tanks, could overthrow the strongest naval base in the world at Singapore.

The western powers—Britain and the United States in particular—could not square these incredible achievements with their image of the small, underdeveloped Japanese male as cross-eyed, bespectacled and submissive, which was their racial stereotype. But this racial stereotyping was a two-way problem. To the Japanese the British were decadent lords or undernourished Dickensian caricatures, while the Americans were ill-disciplined and soft-living products of a corrupt society. The Japanese believed that neither the British nor the American fighting man was a match for the Japanese soldier, descendant of a Samurai tradition. Early victories in the war seemed to confirm this.

Yet the Japanese were not all samurais, nor were the Americans all ill-disciplined and soft. No war could be conducted successfully grounded on such misunderstanding of the enemy. It is probably true to say that American understanding of the Japanese was less easily achieved than that of the Germans, and this made it all the more difficult to assess how the Japanese might react. Yet the Japanese suffered severely from their inability to regard American servicemen as worthy opponents. The Japanese underestimation of American combat performance was an error not shared by German generals in Europe. Field Marshal Rommel wrote after his victory at the Kasserine Pass:

> Although it is true that the American troops could not yet be compared with the veteran troops of the [British] Eighth Army, yet they made up for their lack of experience by their far better and more plentiful equipment.[1]

The Japanese lacked Rommel's perception, refusing to allow that the Americans would improve with time. Their military traditions failed to educate them to the fact that militarism played little part in the history of the United States. Most American soldiers had—prior to call-up—been civilians, and it took some time for them to adapt to service life. They were not natural soldiers, but with good training and equipment they would soon surpass the Japanese, for all the latter's fanaticism and loyalty to archaic militaristic traditions.

Furthermore, Japanese feelings of technical superiority flew in the face of reality. American technological superiority in the field of radar was so vital an advantage that in a war fought across so wide an area as the Pacific Ocean, and in which ships rarely saw each other, it is not claiming too much to say that it was decisive. The pulverization of the Japanese battlecruiser *Kirishima* at Guadalcanal by the battleship *Washington*, equipped with radar-guided guns, illustrated this point very clearly.

The essential flaw in Japanese military thinking was the belief that she could fight a "total war" with the United States for control of the Pacific and much of Southeast Asia and survive, without in any way damaging America's potential to wage war. Japan was quite incapable of dimin-

ishing America's war production in the continental United
States by the sort of saturation bombing that the British
and Germans had inflicted on one another during 1940 and
1941. Without breaking America's capacity to wage war or
diminishing the morale of her people, the Japanese were
certain to lose an attritional struggle against a nation with
infinitely greater materials and technology. Thus Japan's
basic military blunder was to court war in any form against
the United States. However many local victories Japan
achieved on Pacific islands or however many ships her
airmen sank by temporary air superiority, she could not
escape the relentless logic of twentieth-century warfare:
that the captains of industry were the new masters of military campaigns. And in the attritional struggle that her
navy and fleet air arm faced in 1943 and 1944 she found that
she could not replace the elite airmen who fell in ever
greater numbers in their efforts to strike the American
aircraft carriers, now protected by impenetrable anti-
aircraft defenses. The Pacific war was a voracious monster
that consumed Japanese pilots at a greater rate than they
could be turned out by Japan's flying schools. In 1944 one
Japanese naval instructor explained: "The Navy was desperate for pilots, and the school was expanded almost
every month, with correspondingly lower entrance require-
ments... We were told to rush the men through, to forget
the finer points, just teach them how to fly and shoot... It
was a hopeless task."

And as the Japanese reduced their standards, the Americans increased theirs. The imbalance of power between
Japan and the United States increased as the latter became
geared to a war economy, to war production, and to the
application of technology and innovative research to war-
winning operations. Soon the training gap between Japanese and American pilots became unbridgeable and the
Japanese were eventually forced to rely on suicide raids
against American shipping.

By mid-1944 Japan was forced to fall back on a defensive
strategy based on a line drawn from the Kuriles and the
home islands in the north, through the Ryukus, Formosa
and the Philippines to the Dutch East Indies in the south.
While this line was maintained Japan could still draw on
the important raw materials of her conquests: 80 percent
of the world's rubber, for example, as well as tin, tungsten,

manganese, iron ore and—most vital of all—oil from the East Indies. But should the Americans sever communications between Japan and her southern conquests, by the reconquest of the Philippines, then the war would be lost. With a strong sense of Japan's vulnerability her military planners prepared for four separate *Sho* (victory) plans, the first of which covered the Philippines.

Sho I was little short of a *kamikaze* action fought by the entire Japanese navy. Accepting the probability of defeat and destruction, the Japanese nevertheless hoped to delay a successful American invasion of the Philippines by up to a year, during which time it might have been possible for Japan to rebuild her shattered economy.

The Japanese plan was overcomplex and involved four separate task forces. American knowledge of Japanese orders through SIGINT (signals intercept) enabled Admiral Nimitz at Honolulu to prepare his countermoves. The main Japanese strike force of five battleships commanded by Vice Admiral Kurita was to sail from Brunei Bay in North Borneo, on October 22, bound for the San Bernardino Strait, between the islands of Samar and Luzon. Kurita hoped to hit the invasion beaches at Leyte from the north, supplemented by Vice Admiral Nishimura's Task Force C and supported by Vice Admiral Shima's small Task Force D, which sailed from the Inland Sea of Japan. Shima's task was to cross Kurita's course, passing through the Suriago Strait between Leyte and Mindanao and catching Admiral Thomas Kincaid's 7th Fleet in a pincers movement. Knowing that Kincaid would be strongly supported by Halsey's 3rd Fleet, the Japanese planned to lure Halsey away to the north by sending Vice Admiral Ozawa's Mobile Strike Force of one heavy carrier, three light carriers and two hybrid battleship/carriers as a decoy or bait for the American 3rd Fleet. If everything went according to plan—a big if—then Kurita and Nishimura ought to have the opportunity to inflict a tremendous defeat on General MacArthur and Admiral Kincaid at Leyte. In fact, although the Japanese could not have known this, their decoy plan was just the sort of lure that might tempt the aggressive "Bull" Halsey, offering him the chance to destroy a primary enemy formation. But the Japanese were weak in the air; American air strikes on Formosa in the week before the Leyte campaign had resulted in the loss to the Japanese of many of their planes. This being so, the naval/air commander in the Philippines, Vice Admiral Fukudome, was given firm orders by Tokyo that his job was to provide an aerial umbrella for Kurita and Nishimura when their task forces arrived.

Japan's commander-in-chief of the combined fleet—successor to Yamamoto—was Admiral Toyoda, and the planning behind Sho I had been his. He was not optimistic of its success but felt that it was essential that the Imperial Navy should strike at the enemy one last time before the Philippines fell and the route to East Indian oil was cut off. After this catastrophe the Japanese navy would eventually become a helpless spectator in the struggle for its homeland. When Toyoda referred to Sho I as a decisive battle it was not with any great expectation of victory. He hoped to inflict enough damage on the Americans to justify the losses in ships that were virtually certain, and to buy time for Japan. Kurita's orders had been simple: "Hit the American transports, break up the invasion, and sink as many ships as you can." Ozawa—possibly Japan's most able commander—was given the near-suicidal job of luring Halsey away from Leyte, and few of his ships were expected to survive. This kind of fatalism—with its willingness to waste ships and their commanders—was a far cry from the western way of warfare. Even if Halsey had not specifically known that Ozawa's force was just a decoy—and he knew this through Nimitz's SIGINT intercepts—it did not take a Nelson to realize that Ozawa was on a voyage to nowhere and that the main Japanese strength must be concentrated elsewhere. After the war Ozawa confirmed his role as decoy to his American captors:

> A decoy, that was our first primary mission, to act as a decoy. My fleet could not very well give direct protection to Kurita's force because we were very weak, so I tried to attack as many American carriers as possible, and to be the decoy or target for your attack. I tried to let Kurita's fleet have little attack from you. The main mission was all sacrifice. An attack with a very weak force of planes comes under the heading of sacrifice of planes and ships.[2]

Not every Japanese commander supported *Sho* I, with its apparent waste of Japan's fleet. Admiral Kurita was forced to explain to his officers before sailing:

> I know that many of you are strongly opposed to this task. But the war situation is more critical than any of you can possibly know. Would it not be a shame to have the fleet remain intact while our nation perishes? I am willing to accept even this ultimate assignment to storm into Leyte Gulf.[3]

Kurita's speech had the effect he wanted and Japanese officers went about their tasks with all the finality of men who were about to die but with the determination to die well.

The *Sho* plan depended for its success on two factors Japan did not enjoy: surprise, which it was denied through American knowledge of Japanese codes; and aerial supremacy. With Japan failing to introduce new types of fighter planes she was increasingly outclassed by a new generation of American aircraft, and her hastily trained pilots were no match for the well-trained Americans. In this way *Sho* was doomed from the start. But the Japanese made their own task more difficult by self-deception. Although pilots often find it difficult to give an accurate estimate of enemy losses—for example the RAF exaggerated *Luftwaffe* losses during the Battle of Britain in 1940—it is important that inflated figures should not form the basis for future planning. The Japanese fell into the trap of believing their own propaganda. The result was that they thought that Admiral Halsey's 3rd Fleet had suffered very heavy losses from enemy air attack during the fighting off Formosa in the week before the battle of Leyte Gulf: no less than eleven aircraft carriers, two battleships, three cruisers and a destroyer had been sunk, while eight further carriers and two more battleships had been seriously damaged. Halsey's ships might as well have been a paper fleet in a rainstorm. The truth was rather different: in the fighting off Formosa, Halsey had suffered damage to one carrier and two cruisers. Yet uplifted by this staggering "victory" the Japanese undertook their *Sho* plan with renewed confidence.

The Japanese flight into a world of make-believe seemed to affect everyone from the emperor down. So horrified were the Japanese at the thought that the Americans might penetrate what they considered the "Essential Sea Area" around Japan that they simply tried to wish the Americans away. Apparently responsible Japanese authorities announced to a delirious nation that in the Formosa battles the Imperial Navy had destroyed "60 percent of America's effective naval strength," sinking over 500,000 tons of shipping and killing an estimated 26,000 American naval personnel. Emperor Hirohito joined the facade by announcing that fifty-three U.S. ships had been sunk, including sixteen aircraft carriers. Day by day the toll increased. Soon the Japanese "victory" off Formosa was claimed to be as great and crushing as Admiral Togo's victory over the Russians at Tsushima in 1905.

From early October, MacArthur's invasion fleet began assembling on the north coast of New Guinea. It was an enormous undertaking: 738 ships, including hundreds of amphibians and service vessels, all under the protection of Admiral Thomas Kincaid's 7th Fleet, consisting of Oldendorf's 6 old battleships, 18 light carriers and 8 cruisers. In order to ensure command of the skies during the invasion of Leyte a major air assault was launched against Japan's land-based air force on Formosa. For three days the planes from nine American carriers devastated ground installations and destroyed 807 Japanese planes. In the words of one Japanese commander, "Our fighters were nothing but so many eggs thrown against the wall of the indomitable enemy formation." Other air attacks were made on air bases in the Philippines and the East Indies, particularly on Mindanao and Luzon.

MacArthur's landings at Leyte Island began on October 20. By midnight on that day 132,000 men were ashore with 200,000 tons of supplies and equipment. Already *Sho* I was too late to catch the loaded transports and troopships before they disgorged their cargoes on the beaches. But the invasion sites were still vulnerable and would provide tempting targets for Kurita, with 151 LSTs, 221 LCTs, 79 LCIs and hundreds of transports and supply vessels of all kinds crammed together like sheep for safety.

Admiral Toyoda had received news that American ships were approaching Leyte on October 17 and had given the go-ahead for *Sho* I to begin. Kurita's main force left harbor at Singapore and headed for Brunei in North Borneo to refuel. On October 23—just seventeen hours after leaving Brunei—Kurita's force was sighted by two American submarines—*Darter* and *Dace*—near Palwan Island. Here was the verification that Nimitz needed: *Sho* I was under way. Kurita's anti-submarine precautions were so negligent at this stage that the Americans were able to punish him for it, *Darter* promptly torpedoing two cruisers—including Kurita's flagship, *Atago*—while *Dace* sank another. However fatalistic Kurita might have been, this was not what he had expected. Dumped into the sea while suffering from dengue fever was not a pleasant experience for a man of his age. Rescued by a destroyer and taken to the *Yamato* to recover, he must have felt that he now had a personal score to settle with the Americans. But how much the shock of his experiences affected his later performance we cannot be sure. Ill health and exposure for an old man are hardly recommendations for control in a battle as complex as Leyte Gulf.

Halsey responded to the news of Kurita's approach by deploying three of his carrier groups, under Rear Admirals Sherman, Brogan and Davison, to launch strikes against the main Japanese force. The next morning—on entering the Sibuyan Sea—Kurita's task force came under massed air attack and his new flagship, *Yamato*, was shaken by two bomb hits and took aboard two thousand tons of water, causing her to list temporarily. With the skies filled with American planes, Kurita was entitled to wonder where Fukudome's air umbrella had gone. Fukudome, in fact, was disobeying orders. Told by Toyoda to protect Kurita he had taken it upon himself to defend the main strike force by attacking the enemy at source. He had launched his two hundred land-based planes from Luzon against Halsey's American carriers. Still ignorant of the advance that radar and massed anti-aircraft fire gave the American ships, his planes were flying on a one-way mission. Fukudome sank the light carrier *Princeton* but paid the heavy price of losing most of his air fleet.

With Fukudome's air umbrella in flames off Luzon, Kurita was facing the assaults of hundreds of American planes of all kinds completely bereft of air cover. With only his anti-aircraft guns available, many American planes got through the heavy flak to score hits. The battleship *Musashi*—considered unsinkable—was hit by nineteen torpedoes and seventeen bombs and sank with almost all her crew—a symbol, if one was needed, of the closing of the age of battleships. At a time when—with the death of Yamamoto—Japan was turning away from the aircraft carriers toward the siren song of the battleship, the evidence was there for all to see. No battleship, unsupported by air cover, could survive carrier-based air attack.

With the approach of nightfall, Kurita, crippled but still with a powerful force of four battleships, six heavy cruisers, two light cruisers and ten destroyers, continued his voyage toward the San Bernardino Strait. Kurita may not have been feeling lucky, but two independent factors were about to help him and to lead Halsey into making a serious blunder. As we have already seen, pilots the world over are optimistic. From hundreds or even thousands of feet—and under constant ack-ack fire—it is difficult to assess the damage inflicted on ships zigzagging across a smoke-shrouded ocean. Near misses can seem to be fatal hits and the report that Halsey received of the air attacks on Kurita convinced him that the Japanese commander had received a severe drubbing. He reported to Nimitz that Kurita's ships "had been so heavily damaged in the Sibuyan Sea that they could no longer be considered a serious menace to Seventh Fleet." In addition, he had reports that Nishimura's Force C—the battleships *Fuso* and *Yamashiro* and the heavy cruiser *Mogami* with four destroyers—had been similarly mauled and that Kincaid would have no difficulty with what was left of them. But Halsey was badly mistaken. Under instructions from Toyoda in Tokyo that "all forces will dash to the attack," Nishimura was sailing on toward the Suriago Strait and Kurita was still bound for the San Bernardino Strait. Simultaneously with these overoptimistic battle reports, Halsey received the first report of Ozawa's fleet approaching from the north.

Nimitz, through his SIGINT intercepts, had presumably made it clear to Halsey that Ozawa's force was a decoy. Halsey need only have devoted a part of his immense force to driving Ozawa away. Yet, in the full knowledge that the Japanese wanted him to chase Ozawa with his entire fleet, and without certain knowledge that Kurita and Nishimura posed no threat to the landings at Leyte, Halsey ordered his entire fleet to turn north. Vice Admiral Willis Lee, commander of Halsey's battleships, actually suggested to his commander that he be allowed to remain behind at San

Bernardino with the battleships but with no air cover. He was convinced that Fukudome's air fleet was completely broken and felt that he faced no threat from the air. Surely it would be wiser to leave some kind of force in place in case Kurita did arrive? But Halsey turned down the offer. He wanted his battleships with him when he met Ozawa. "Bull" Halsey was looking for a decisive, killing victory over the Japanese. He knew that Ozawa would be helpless against his 3rd Fleet, whereas there was no certainty that Kurita would even arrive in the straits. By waiting for Kurita the chance to destroy Ozawa would be missed. Halsey was a fighting admiral who found all the waiting frustrating. He allowed his aggressive impulses to master his rational processes and made a decision that could have led to the worst American defeat of the war. Halsey compounded the felony by not even informing Kincaid that he was about to abandon him or telling Nimitz that he was about to imperil the whole Philippines campaign and endanger the progress of the war in the Pacific. Messages that did reach Nimitz were titled "for information," as if there was nothing that the commander-in-chief need know or could do about it if he did know. Kincaid only learned of what Halsey was doing by monitoring the 3rd Fleet's communications. In this way Kincaid made a misleading discovery—the existence of the phantom Task Force 34.

When Lee had discussed with Halsey the possibility of remaining behind in order, perhaps, to "field" Kurita should he break though into the straits, Halsey had spoken of creating a task force of battleships and carriers to be known as Task Force 34. But no action had been taken to create this force. When he heard the task force mentioned, Kincaid assumed that Halsey had already set it up with the intention of supplementing the 7th Fleet while the 3rd Fleet sailed north. Nimitz, not surprisingly, had reached the same conclusion and so neither he nor Kincaid was unduly worried to hear that Halsey was pursuing Ozawa. In any case, Kincaid had his own problems without worrying about Kurita—or Halsey. Nishimura's Task Force C was passing through Suriago Strait and would need to be attacked there.

It is surprising that in the normal round of communications Kincaid had not asked Halsey for details of Task Force 34, which he presumed was guarding the San Bernardino Strait. Yet in a sense, it was too obvious to need to be mentioned. Nobody in his right mind would have simply sailed off in pursuit of a decoy, leaving the invasion beaches open to enemy attack. Or would he?

As Nishimura approached Leyte Gulf from the Suriago Strait to the south Kincaid was preparing a reception committee. Rear Admiral Jesse Oldendorf, with a force of six battleships, four heavy cruisers and a host of destroyers and PT boats, had strung a fifteen-mile defensive line from Leyte to Hibuson Island. As Nishimura approached he was bound to be spotted early and brought to action by the battleships' big guns. Ironically, five of the American "battle-wagons" had been reincarnated for the occasion. Sunk at Pearl Harbor thirty months before, the crews of these old battleships were itching for a chance to settle scores with the Japanese. Nishimura must have realized that his chances of penetrating the American defensive cordon were nonexistent and yet he sailed on at full speed, with a display of fatalism that was to pervade Japanese thought throughout the whole campaign. Although Shima's task force was supposed to have effected a junction with him by this stage, Nishimura was not waiting for anybody and drove on into the mass of American torpedo boats crowding the straits. What happened next was predictable. First destroyers and PT boats attacked him with torpedoes and then the Mark 8 radar-guided guns of the American battleships *West Virginia*, *Tennessee* and *California* picked him up in the darkness and blasted him. Outnumbered and outperformed, the Japanese admiral seemed even bereft of common sense, failing to maneuver away from torpedoes and accepting destruction as if he welcomed it. Nishimura chose to stay at his post in the flaming battleship *Yamashiro* and died, with most of his crew, when his flagship was hit by two torpedoes from the destroyer *Newcomb*. As an American later commented, "Their strategy and intelligence seemed to be inversely proportional to their courage."

Yet to the north of Samar, Kurita had emerged unscathed from the San Bernardino Strait and found that the expected American covering force had gone. Instead, as he hurried south toward the unprotected invasion transports—unopposed for 150 miles—Kurita suddenly encountered resistance from an unexpected and unlikely source. Rear

Admiral Thomas Sprague with eighteen escort carriers—
affectionately called Woolworth carriers—and without a
single dive-bomber, now found himself between Kurita and
the success of his mission. At 0646 an escort carrier from
Sprague's group—nicknamed Taffy 3—made a sighting of
hostile ships approaching from the northwest. Sprague
was astonished. Where was Halsey? How had the Japanese
slipped past him? Kurita made his first sighting at about
the same time and soon realized that he had a group of
helpless carriers at his mercy. Sprague was now facing four
Japanese battleships, including the world's biggest, *Yamato*, with nine 18-inch guns. He responded quickly by
getting the 378 planes (Hellcats, Wildcats and Avengers)
from his eighteen carriers into the air and soon had the
Japanese zigzagging to avoid the American torpedo attacks. But without dive-bombers Sprague could do little
more than delay the inevitable. He sent out SOS requests
but Halsey was by now some 300 miles away. Even Oldendorf's battleships were 60 miles away. They might as well
have been on the moon. And yet now that his prey was
within his grasp Kurita seems to have lost his head. Perhaps the stress of the campaign so far—his own rescue
from the sea, his fever, the loss of the *Musashi*—caught
up with him. Certainly his handling of his ships in the next
few hours was atrocious. Instead of imposing order on his
squadron and forming a battle line, he issued the incredible
order "General attack," which sent every Japanese ship off
on its own, pursuing its own target and out of his control.
As Sprague wrote later, with charming understatement,
"The enemy was closing with disconcerting rapidity and
the volume and accuracy of fire was increasing." Faced with
total extinction, Sprague sent his destroyers into action,
firing torpedoes at the approaching behemoth—Kurita's
Yamato—until the shells from the battleships slammed
into the destroyers "like a puppy dog being smacked by a
truck." The American destroyer captains displayed great
gallantry, but first the *Johnston* was sunk by 14-inch
shells and then the *Hoel* went down in a welter of over forty
heavy shells. The escort carrier *Gambier Bay* was sunk by
four Japanese cruisers but then two of these "assassins"
were in turn sent to the bottom by the carrier's planes.

Yet uncertainty seemed to plague Kurita's every move.
Should he pursue the carriers and destroy them or turn

toward the invasion beaches at Leyte? Panic seems to have been close to the surface in the Japanese ships that day. Reports of false air attacks were frequent and information came in that Halsey's fleet had been sighted heading south— another false alarm. At 1236, having achieved little, Kurita appeared to give up, and headed back toward the San Bernardino Strait and safety. It had been a deplorable display by the Japanese commander. As one American wit observed from the bridge of an escort carrier, "Goddammit, boys, they're getting away."

Far to the north, Halsey had made contact with Ozawa and was preparing to destroy the decoy. There was little the Japanese admiral could do, as most of his planes had been sent to support Fukudome on Luzon and had been lost already. For ten hours Halsey's planes pounded Ozawa's ships, sinking all four carriers—the *Zuikaku*, *Chitose*, *Chiyoda* and *Zuiho*—though failing to finish the hybrid battleship-carriers, *Ise* and *Hyuga*. But if Halsey was enjoying this one-sided fight, he was not amused to receive the startling news that Kurita had slipped in behind him and was loose in the vicinity of Leyte Island. Kincaid's calls for assistance were answered when Halsey detached a carrier group to support him—even though these ships were refueling and could not reach him at best for four hours! At 1000 a message from Nimitz arrived that must have gone close to spoiling Halsey's day. The commander-in-chief was intrigued to know where Task Force 34 was, if there was such a force:

FROM CINCPAC ACTION COM THIRD FLEET INFO COMINCH CTF 77 X WHERE IS RPT WHERE IS TASK FORCE THIRTY-FOUR RR THE WORLD WONDERS.

He ordered Halsey to detach Lee and his six battleships— the *Iowa*, *New Jersey*, *Massachusetts*, *Washington*, *South Dakota* and *Alabama*—to return to the aid of Kincaid. Halsey felt torn. He was hoping still to finish off the hybrid battleships and Lee would be needed then. Yet the disgrace that would fall on his head if a disaster occurred to the 7th Fleet or MacArthur's invasion force would far outweigh the glory of two more Japanese "scalps." Even so, it took him a full hour to decide in his nation's interest rather than his own. It was too late for Lee to reach Kincaid in time to be of much assistance. Kurita must have succeeded or failed by now, and if the latter the credit would be Kincaid's. But Halsey was unrepentant and said later that he had regretted the decision to detach Lee as it enabled the *Ise* and *Hyuga* to escape.

Halsey's state of mind is not hard to understand at this moment and yet it is difficult to believe that a commander could have risen so high without being aware of his responsibilities within a hierarchical command structure. Halsey was playing war games with the lives of thousands of his compatriots who looked to him for protection, as well as with the national interest in the greatest of all wars. His behavior was more in keeping with the racial stereotype that the Japanese had of Americans—of ill-disciplined and gung-ho gunslingers, devoid of the martial virtues valued by military nations such as Germany and Japan. As American historian Samuel Morrison pointed out, had Halsey detached Lee when he was first informed of Kurita's presence, and had Lee sailed south at full speed, he would have been able to bring Kurita to battle during the night of October 25, when, with the advantage of his radar-guided guns, he could have achieved a total victory over the main Japanese task force. It is doubtful if Nimitz ever fully forgave Halsey's petulant and selfish display.

The Japanese plan had been a very bad one, doomed to failure from the start. Even had the Americans not had the advantages of SIGINT, there can be little doubt that their aerial superiority would have enabled them to form a clear idea of Japanese intentions. Certainly, because of Halsey's extraordinary decision, Kurita was presented with a chance to sink many of Sprague's escort carriers, or wreck the invasion fleet in Leyte Gulf, yet sooner or later he would have encountered the overwhelming firepower of the 3rd and 7th fleets. And Fukudome's decision to squander his planes in a doomed attack on the American carriers rather than use them as an umbrella for Kurita's fleet left him open to severe criticism. But to return to the overall architect of the plan, Admiral Toyoda, he stands accused of squandering Japan's remaining naval strength and thousands of Japanese lives in a futile operation that paid no attention to the strength and disposition of the enemy. In war there needs to be an equation that sets likely losses against potential gains, and in the case of the battle of Leyte Gulf it would appear that Toyoda had simply got his sums wrong. Japanese losses were enormous: three battleships, one fleet carrier, three light carriers, six heavy cruisers, four light cruisers and nine destroyers—a total of 305,000 tons or 45 percent of the total fleet. The American losses of one light carrier, two escort carriers, two destroyers and one escort vessel comprised just 2.8 percent of the fleet. It had truly been a *kamikaze* campaign.

Korea, 1950

AWAY FROM THE WORLD OF PIOUS HOPES, WHERE "AGE SHALL not wither them," there is no denying that old age is the enemy of the military commander. Faculties that were once sharp become atrophied, and weaknesses that were once merely dismissed as the follies of youth begin to exert a malign influence on ailing minds and bodies. And so it proved to be with five-star general Douglas MacArthur.

The outbreak of the Korean War in June 1950 drew from MacArthur a not untypical reaction. Seeing a last chance to boost a flagging ego, he remarked that the war was "Mars' last gift to an old warrior." If so then Mars had a malicious sense of humor. The Korean command was no gift of the gods; it was merely a final twist of fate—lifting MacArthur to the heights of his Inchon triumph before flinging him down in total ruin.

For ten months after June 1950 General MacArthur bestrode the Asian stage like a Titan. Ignoring both his political and military masters in Washington, he planned and fought a war in Korea that conflicted sharply with the perception of the war held by President Harry S Truman and his administration. Personifying his country—as no American general had since George Washington—and speaking for the greatest capitalist power and Guardian of the Free World, he fought not just to contain communism in Korea but to challenge and destroy it worldwide. For MacArthur there could be no limited war with communism, and once he had been appointed to command the forces of "right," his decisions became imbued with far greater significance than those made by "shady" politicians and their cronies in Washington. The tragedy for America was that her chosen hero had feet of clay. Many writers have drawn attention to his paranoia, which was "almost certifiable," according to biographer William Manchester. His hatred of Europe and Europeans was almost pathological, and his Asia-centric views gave him a distorted vision of the Cold War. His well-documented mental instability—mood swings ranging from suicidal depression to outbursts of irrational enthusiasm—robbed him of the sense of balance so necessary to a military commander. Few generals have earned so high a military reputation on such flimsy grounds. His failures in the Philippines in 1942 were disastrous and he deserved much of the blame for the humiliating American collapse there. Abandoning his doomed command at Bataan in 1942, he saved himself and his servants, justifying himself by saying that his own personal loss would have been a greater blow to his country than the loss of his men. One is forced to recall the unfortunate precedent of British general Charles Townshend at Kut in 1916, abandoning his men to the horrors of a death march across the Iraqi desert. Yet for all that his numerous critics did say against him no one could deny the enormous popularity MacArthur enjoyed in the United States and his symbolic value for the Allies during the Second World War.

The buildup of North Korean forces north of the 38th Parallel—the demarcation line separating Communist North Korea from South Korea—was known to American intelligence for some weeks before the North's "surprise" attack on June 25, 1950. The problem was that the intelligence was not correctly assessed. In Washington—as well as in MacArthur's command headquarters in Tokyo—it was not thought possible that the North's leader, Kim Il Sung, would dare invade the South without direct Russian or Chinese support. This was merely the first of many political miscalculations by the Americans that compounded the errors of their military leaders and made what began as a purely Korean struggle into a major war. President Truman in Washington and General MacArthur in Tokyo were as one—for perhaps the last time—in viewing the North Korean action as only the first step in a general Communist assault, in Asia as well as in Europe. In this way, they believed the Communist world was testing America's credibility as self-appointed Defender of the Free World, and an

American response was therefore essential. What this response should be required careful thought. Truman was not averse to becoming a "Cold War warrior," but he suffered at the outset from the mistaken belief that there was a single Communist philosophy and aim, and that it originated in Joseph Stalin's Moscow. The Americans had failed to appreciate the substantial differences that existed between Mao Zedong's China, with its peasant-based view of communism, and the totalitarian dictatorship that the Soviet Union had become under Stalin. The result was that many Americans felt, like Truman, that a strong reaction against North Korea and its Chinese backers would "bloody the nose" of Moscow. This was quite wrong, though Truman is hardly to blame because those who claimed to understand the problems of China and the Far East—and Douglas MacArthur was one of them—fed the president conflicting and ultimately inaccurate data. MacArthur proved a thoroughly unreliable source of intelligence, being unpredictable when his paranoia overwhelmed him. On some occasions he blew so hot in his confidence that he said that the Koreans and Chinese would crumble if he sent "a few Americans over there." At other times black despair struck and he faced the enemy as a potential suicide faces the pistol he is about to fire. And while Truman saw the war as an important opportunity to uphold American prestige and score a victory in the Cold War struggle against communism, MacArthur saw it as an opportunity—probably the last one—to catapult himself into the presidency.

From the start Douglas MacArthur badly underestimated the North Koreans—just as he had the Japanese in 1942—saying, "If Washington does not hobble me I can handle them with one hand tied behind my back." But words were easy. Already within two days of their invasion the Communists had driven the South Koreans back in disorder, taking the capital of Seoul and forcing Syngman Rhee to take flight. On hearing this news MacArthur panicked and began to talk of abandoning Korea and writing it off completely. According to his aides, he was "a dejected, completely despondent man." This sort of mood swing was to become a feature of MacArthur's personality in the months to come, and should have warned those around him that he was not fit for the responsibility of such a complex

command. Nevertheless, in spite of his known paranoia
and the fact that his age was against him, his reputation
was so great that there was never serious discussion of
choosing any other man for the command.

Yet the man was a magician who still cast a spell on
seasoned military experts in both Japan and the United
States. After a quick survey of the military situation on
June 29—with the Communists driving the South Koreans
in rout—MacArthur began to consider an amphibious
strike in the enemy's rear. This would involve a large-scale
commitment of American troops because the South Korean army was already broken. President Truman was prepared to accede to these demands but he wanted to make
it clear that there must be no question of getting involved
in war with the Soviet Union. He would support "any steps
we have to take to push the North Koreans behind the line
[the 38th Parallel]." However, his advisers told him that it
might be dangerous to limit the options available to the
military commander, particularly north of the demarcation
line. As a result Truman agreed that bombing north of the
line might be necessary, but only to hit supply lines and
airfields. If MacArthur were to cross the 38th Parallel it
could only be with the intention of reducing the North Korean threat to the South. On this basis, Truman authorized
the use of American ground troops on June 30 at Pusan
and also gave permission for tactical bombing north of the
38th Parallel. In fact, MacArthur had not waited for the
president's orders and had given the go-ahead himself.
This passed almost unnoticed but was the first pointer to
how president and general were to find their roles in conflict
during the war.

Under the fiction that the operation to save South Korea
was a UN one, MacArthur was appointed as overall commander of all UN forces—which had been drawn from fourteen countries. However, there was never any doubt that
he would be taking his orders directly from Truman and
not from the Security Council. The thirteen other countries
who committed troops to save South Korea soon learned
to their cost that they were merely a small part—and an
unconsidered one, at that—of an American Cold War adventure. All MacArthur's reports were to be forwarded to
the American Joint Chiefs of Staff JCS. As the only American five-star general—until Bradley was later elevated by

Truman—MacArthur outranked even his bosses at the Pentagon and he let them know it. It was not until July 8 that the UN formally accepted the American submission that MacArthur should be appointed commander of the UN forces in Korea, but once appointed he replied to Truman in words so effusive that the president must immediately have doubted their sincerity. MacArthur pledged his "complete personal loyalty to you [Truman] as well as an absolute devotion to your monumental struggle for peace and good will throughout the world." In fact, Truman was no fan of the great man. He described MacArthur as a "supreme egoist who regarded himself as something of a god." And yet in spite of his many reservations Truman still appointed MacArthur—by this stage more myth than man. Few Americans really knew MacArthur very well. Omar Bradley said of him, "He was awesomely brilliant; but as a leader he had several flaws: an obsession for self-glorification, almost no consideration of other men with whom he served, and a contempt for the judgement of his superiors." Bradley felt he was, like his Second World War contemporaries Montgomery and Patton, a megalomaniac. He had spent so long in the Far East building up his reputation "island-hopping" in the Pacific that his metal had never been tried as had Eisenhower's and Bradley's own against German generals of the quality of Erwin Rommel. Just how good Douglas MacArthur really was, nobody knew. It had been years since anyone had dared to doubt the legend, which was now bigger than the man inside and cocooned him from the real world.

The Second World War had been over for five years and America was no longer a nation equipped for war. Her troops were few and she was equipment-heavy. She would have to try to make her technological advantages offset her lack of fighting men. And the soldiers MacArthur did have stationed with him had grown fat, comfortable and complacent in the little bit of America they called Japan. It was hardly MacArthur's fault alone that American servicemen were poorly equipped and poorly trained in 1950, and yet he must bear some of the blame for the fact that his men were so consistently outfought in the early months of the Korean War. In the words of Colonel John Michaelis of the 27th Infantry:

In peacetime training, we've gone far too much falderal. We've put too much stress on Information and Education and not enough stress on rifle marksmanship and scouting and patrolling, and the organization of a defensive position. These kids of mine have all the guts in the world and I can count on them to fight. But when they started out, they couldn't shoot. They didn't know their weapons. They have not had enough training in plain, old-fashioned musketry. They'd spend a lot of time listening to lectures on the difference between communism and Americanism and not enough time crawling on their bellies on maneuvers with live ammunition singing over them. They'd been nursed and coddled, told to drive safely, to buy War Bonds, to give to the Red Cross, to avoid VD, to write home to mother—when somebody ought to have been telling them how to clear a machine gun when it jams.... The US Army is so damn roadbound that the soldiers have almost lost the use of their legs. Send out a patrol on a scouting mission and they load up in a three-quarter-ton truck and start riding down the highway.[1]

Quite simply, MacArthur was out of touch and did not appreciate the skills and toughness of the Communist soldiers. It was only as the realization began to sink in that he was up against a formidable opponent that he began to escalate his demands for men and equipment. Gone were the quips about defeating the North Koreans with one arm behind his back. The Americans were being drawn into a massive military commitment merely to save themselves from a humiliating defeat. By the end of July, MacArthur had 45,000 American ground troops and within four more weeks that number had swelled to 150,000. As the American buildup continued he had at least the reassurance of noting no similar Russian or Chinese support for Kim Il Sung's men.

As soon as MacArthur felt secure in holding the Pusan Perimeter he began planning the amphibious strike at Inchon that would destroy the enemy. Once this had been achieved he would "compose and unite Korea"—though it must be admitted that he had no authority from President Truman or from the United Nations for such an action. More worrying, however, was the general's first reference on July 9 to using the atomic bomb against Soviet supply routes to North Korea, notably the South Manchurian Railway. If anything was designed to give America's Cold War allies in Europe cold feet it was the mention of atomic weapons. It was crass for MacArthur to make such a loose reference to so important an issue. Once news reached Moscow and Beijing there was bound to be an increased fear of American intentions—and a consequent rise in tension in Europe as well as the Far East—while countries like Britain and France might begin to doubt the wisdom of supporting the United States in such an apparently mad venture.

Rumors began to abound in Washington about the emotional and mental state of General MacArthur. Many were merely scurrilous but there were enough to make Truman and the JCS wish they had not acted so hastily in selecting him. Truman actually sent aide Frank Lowe to report on the general's health, but Lowe appeared to find nothing out of the ordinary in MacArthur's physical or mental condition. But more worrying was the fact that MacArthur was becoming obsessive in his belief that the Communists intended to follow up their victory in mainland China by invading Chiang Kai-shek's stronghold on Taiwan. MacArthur's dream was to reverse Mao's victory in the Chinese civil war and aid Chiang to achieve a reconquest of his country. But this flew in the face of reality, as did so many of his ideas. He failed to realize that the discredited Guomindang had no power base left in China and that Mao's regime rested on the support of China's teeming millions of peasants, who hoped to benefit from the reforms in land ownership that Mao promised. Nevertheless, MacArthur was hoping for a chance to fight the Communist Chinese, with or without the support of Chiang's Nationalist soldiers.

MacArthur's plan for an amphibious landing at Inchon was his masterpiece. He assured X Corps's commander, Lieutenant General Edward Almond: "We'll all be home by Christmas." It sounded good—it always did—but it had taken the men of 1914–18 almost five Christmases to reach home, and for some Americans in Korea the wait would be as long or even longer. In fact, Inchon was so risky a mission that it was doubted by almost everyone who heard the planning. But MacArthur had no doubts. From his lofty perch he declared that the "fate of Europe" would be decided in Asia—in fact, at Inchon in Korea. Inchon was a Napoleonic conception, daring and decisive, and though writers since have diminished its stature as an operation by pointing out that Communist resistance was feeble, this does scant justice to the daring of a man of seventy years of age. Yet in a sense the victory at Inchon was counterproductive. It seemed, on the one hand, to finally sever the link with reality that bound MacArthur to his colleagues in Korea and to the politicians in Washington. In addition, it filled MacArthur's critics with self-doubt. Perhaps the man was right after all. So great was the general's reputation after Inchon that everyone feared to question any of his decisions. In the words of General Lawton Collins, MacArthur was "like a Greek hero of old, [marching] to an inexorable and unkind fate." MacArthur was in danger of hubris.

MacArthur's victory at Inchon was sufficient in itself to force the North Koreans beyond the 38th Parallel and out of South Korea. This was what the UN had resolved to do and in Washington diplomats began to discuss the chances of a negotiated settlement. But party politics at home made it difficult for President Truman to hold back now that MacArthur had gained the upper hand. Would the president's Republican critics in Congress allow him to look for a diplomatic solution now that the Communists were on the run? Pressures from this direction as well as the natural desire to make the most of the situation put backbone into Truman and he and his secretary of state, Dean Acheson, now planned a unified Korea under Syngman Rhee. Neither the Russians nor the Chinese had shown the slightest inclination to join in the fighting and this encouraged the Americans to believe that they had a free hand in Korea. Again Truman was ignoring intelligence warnings that the reason the Communist powers had not reacted so far was that the fighting had been confined to South Korea. The CIA warned the president that if an attempt was made to push up to the Chinese border there would almost certainly be a Chinese military response. But success sometimes breeds complacency. And the ease with which MacArthur had rolled the North Koreans back in his September offensive made a crossing of the 38th Parallel a mere incidental. At this stage some of the clouding of judgment that permanently afflicted MacArthur seems to have affected Truman also. Without a full appreciation of likely Soviet or Chinese reactions, he ordered the JCS on September 27 to authorize MacArthur to cross the 38th Parallel to destroy the remaining North Korean military units. For a general acting under the umbrella of UN resolutions, MacArthur would be violating fundamental UN principles by invading an independent country. But the Americans were on the roll and were not prepared to look too closely into the legality of their actions. This was war and they had the enemy down. Now they were going to finish him off. Truman covered himself with a fig leaf—a small and flimsy one—by telling MacArthur that only Korean troops should be allowed to enter the provinces bordering China. Defense Secretary George Marshall—never a friend of MacArthur's—nevertheless tried to reassure him by saying "We want you to feel unhampered strategically and tactically to proceed north of the 38th Parallel." This was another mistake. Marshall might have been trying to be helpful, but MacArthur was not a man to need allowances. Telling him that the president did not want to hamper him was tantamount to saying that he had a free hand. MacArthur summed up his new role by saying that he had "all of Korea open for our military operations unless and until the enemy capitulates." Driven by a veritable bloodlust, MacArthur became—in the words of a British Foreign Office official—"pretty dangerous." But who was facing the greater danger? Within a few weeks it would not be at all clear.

Observers in Beijing had anxiously watched the American reaction to the North Korean invasion. Now that the Americans were crossing the 38th Parallel alarm bells began to sound. Was this a prelude to an assault on China itself, from Korea into Manchuria and from Taiwan onto the mainland? The Americans would have to be met in Korea, "where the risks and consequences were more manageable." By using North Korea as a buffer zone China would prevent war from striking her own frontier provinces. Mao reasoned that the Americans were guilty of misjudging China's attitude to their aggression. If he could demonstrate to the Americans by a short, sharp reverse what the likely costs of a war with China would be, he believed they would see reason and agree to a negotiated settlement of the Korean question. But Mao did not know who was really making policy for the Americans, Truman or MacArthur. On October 3 the Chinese used the channel of the Indian ambassador to Beijing, K. M. Pannikar, to make it clear that if the Americans did proceed into North Korea they would "encounter Chinese resistance." And to substantiate this threat they moved upwards of half a million men into Manchuria, all of which the Americans knew through their intelligence services. But "whom the Gods wish to destroy they first make mad." MacArthur was running hot again and simply dismissed these reports as "pure bluff." With sheer bravado he declared that he "had plenty of troops to deal adequately with the Chinese and even with the Russians if they should prove so foolish as to enter the arena at this stage." The Chinese, he said, "had neither troops, nor equipment, nor air power to take him on..." American contempt for China's military potential was built on the merest racial stereotype. In MacArthur's mind he could not understand why the Chinese would risk defeat just to save North Korea. After all, the United States had no designs on China itself. But how could the Chinese know this, particularly in view of MacArthur's wild comments about using Nationalist Chinese troops from Taiwan and even the atomic bomb in Manchuria?

On October 7 the United Nations passed a resolution calling on North Korea to surrender and authorizing MacArthur to cross the 38th Parallel. Korea was now to be unified by force. At this news Mao Zedong immediately sent troops into North Korea. For once the American intelligence services failed to pick up the movements of the Chinese, although it hardly mattered anyway as MacArthur would have dismissed their reports. But as nemesis approached, MacArthur began to disintegrate. So confident was he that he divided his invasion forces, sending the U.S. Eighth Army up the west side of Korea to take Pyongyang, while he detached X Corps to make an amphibious landing at Wonsan. It was a follow-up to his great success of July— "son of Inchon"—but this time the gods had deserted him. All that remained was tragedy.

Before American troops crossed into North Korea, Truman had reached the decision that he should meet his commander face-to-face on the Pacific island of Wake, conveniently located halfway between Tokyo and Honolulu.

Truman had never met the great man before and, as he said, MacArthur had lived so long in the Far East that he might "have lost some of his contacts with the country [America] and its people." But not all of the president's advisers agreed that the meeting was a wise move. In fact, Acheson, Marshall and the JCS—with the exception of Omar Bradley—found more pressing engagements when the Wake meeting was arranged. Acheson in particular was biting: "While General MacArthur had many of the attributes of a foreign sovereign ... it did not seem wise to recognize him as such." In the end Truman took with him Dean Rusk, Averell Harriman and a planeful of reporters. At their first meeting, on October 15, the president found MacArthur full of confidence, talking about a quick end to the war, with formal fighting finished in time for Thanksgiving. The Eighth Army, MacArthur added, would be back in Japan for Christmas and other troops available to transfer to Europe. He led Truman to believe that all was well and the war would soon be over. When asked if there was any likelihood of Soviet or Chinese intervention, he told the president:

Very little. Had they interfered in the first or second months it would have been decisive. We are no longer fearful of their intervention. We no longer stand cap in hand. The Chinese have 300,000 men in Manchuria. Of these probably not more than 100,000 to 125,000 are distributed along the Yalu River. They have no air force. Now that we have bases for our air force in Korea, if the Chinese tried to get down to Pyongyang there would be the greatest slaughter.[2]

In any case, he quipped, had the Russians tried to bomb us they almost certainly would have bombed the Chinese by mistake. Before he left Wake Truman decorated the general with his fifth Distinguished Service Medal and told pressmen that the meeting had been a great success and that there was "complete unity in the aims and conduct of our foreign policy." If Truman was trying to mislead the media he was about to be punished for it. The Wake Island meeting had been a big mistake on the president's part and had only served to convince MacArthur that Truman was a conniving politician, in no way the equal of FDR, and that he could expect little support from him in the coming struggle. On the other hand, Truman returned home convinced that there was no danger of either Chinese or Soviet intervention in Korea.

Behind the rhetoric, the JCS, notably Bradley, was convinced that MacArthur was not presenting a true picture. The Joint Chiefs thought that the division of the forces—Eighth Army and X Corps—had been precipitate and that the amphibious landing at Wonsan was merely a vain gesture. So absurd was the latter plan that, according to Bradley, had a major at staff school proposed it he "would have been laughed out of the classroom." But nothing deterred MacArthur, and on October 20 he again went on record as saying that the war was "definitely coming to an end."

Overconfidence made MacArthur careless and he ignored the JCS order not to allow American troops to operate in regions bordering China or Russia. He simply insisted on using "any and all ground forces" available to him. When they heard that he was ignoring their directive the JCS requested clarification from the commander-in-chief only to be told that his South Korean troops were inadequate to the task. He also reminded them that Defense Secretary George Marshall had told him that his operations should be unhampered and that, in any case, the whole issue had been covered in his meeting with Truman at Wake. This was enough to persuade the JCS to tamely drop the matter; it was also enough to light the fuse for the next stage of the war. MacArthur's intelligence was quite appalling at this time, informing him—and Washington—that some 15,000 to 20,000 Chinese troops had crossed the Yalu River when the correct number was in excess of 200,000!

Chinese strategy at the opening of their attack is difficult to accurately assess. Their commander, Peng Dehuai, claimed that his initial intervention was merely a ruse to present MacArthur with an illustration of Chinese weakness and to draw him deeper into "our areas." Other interpretations—perhaps more convincing in view of China's later tactics in the Himalayan war against India—see China's initial attacks as merely a demonstration of her power and their sudden cessation on November 6 as designed to give the Americans a chance to reconsider their options before a full-scale conflict became necessary. Whatever the truth, MacArthur clearly suffered one of his extreme mood swings, calling on his air force to destroy "every means of communication" between his front lines and the Yalu River. Crews were to be flown to exhaustion and there was a clear air of panic at his headquarters. He made no effort to inform Washington of his decision to bomb bridges inside China and news only reached Truman via air force chief Hoyt Vandenberg. Immediately crisis talks were called. An escalation of the war to involve bombing inside China was certain to alienate America's NATO allies in Europe, notably the British, and this was too high a price to pay. Truman instructed MacArthur that there must be no bombing within five miles of the Chinese border. This was a serious rebuff for MacArthur and he responded by threatening to resign. In a display of theatricality disgraceful in a commander in a desperate war situation he allowed himself to be talked out of resignation only by the untiring efforts of one of his aides. Employing the tactics of a spoiled child he berated the JCS, claiming that Chinese troops and equipment were pouring across the Yalu River bridges and threatening to destroy his entire command. Only air attacks on the bridges would be good enough, otherwise a high price would be paid "in American blood."

Omar Bradley later admitted that the JCS should have acted immediately to order MacArthur south to a more defensible position. "Right then," he wrote, "that night the JCS should have taken the firmest control of the Korean War and dealt with MacArthur bluntly." But the JCS feared more of his histrionics and, in all probability, a dramatic resignation, which would have hit American troop morale at a crucial moment. Instead they gave MacArthur the go-ahead for his bombing raids on the Yalu bridges, though his planes knocked out just four of the twelve bridges available to the Chinese. But before the Americans could fully digest what had happened to them the Chinese suddenly broke off their attacks and melted away to the north. The Americans were bloodied but essentially intact. For three weeks peace descended on the battlefields of Korea. But what were the Chinese playing at now? Dean Acheson, for one, guessed the significance of this mysterious Chinese maneuver. In his eyes, the Chinese were giving the United States the "last chance to halt the march to disaster in Korea."

MacArthur would not believe the evidence of his own

eyes, namely that the Chinese had defeated his forces only
to withdraw on the point of victory. Instead he continued
to express his confidence in being able to handle the Chinese and they in turn noted that Washington continued to
follow the decisions taken by MacArthur in Tokyo. Clearly
their warning had not been heeded and so they would have
to face up to American aggression and prevent attempts to
encircle them from both Korea and Taiwan.

If MacArthur was supremely confident of victory in Korea—claiming that his bombing raids had turned parts of
Korea into a desert—the JCS in Washington were getting
cold feet. If the commander's offensive to the Yalu was
successful then he might be difficult to stop from continuing into China itself. However, if his offensive failed then
America might be forced into attacking China in order to
extricate him from trouble. It seemed to be a no-win situation. The JCS saw the only sensible move to be a withdrawal to the 38th Parallel after clearing the border regions
of hostile troops. But for MacArthur this was unthinkable.
In the words of his deputy, Matthew Ridgway, MacArthur
saw himself as "the swordsman who would slay the Communist dragon."

On November 25, 1950, the Korean War took on a new
and much more desperate character. A massive Communist counterattack—comprising some 300,000 Chinese
and 65,000 North Korean troops—swept away MacArthur's
preparations for a war-winning offensive. Within two days
UN forces had suffered 11,000 casualties and were in danger of a total debacle. Far from facing elite Chinese troops,
the Americans were swept back by a hurriedly assembled
army of press-ganged peasants and recently released
Guomindang prisoners. It was a thoroughly unconvincing
performance by an American army not heavily outnumbered, as was later claimed, but fighting an enemy deficient
in heavy equipment and armed only with a fanatical courage and endurance that put the Americans to shame.
MacArthur was first shaken and then plunged into despair.
His men were being whipped by an enemy for whom he had
nothing but contempt.

Facing unexpected failure in a campaign he had hoped
would open a road for him to the White House, a "trigger-
happy" MacArthur looked for excuses and found them in
Washington's refusal to allow him to bomb the root of the

problem—China itself. He now returned to two of his fa-
vorite ideas, using Chinese Nationalist troops from Taiwan
in Korea, and the use of atomic bombs. He went on record
as saying that one or both of these would be needed if the
United States was to avoid losing the war and perhaps all
Asia with it. His vision was apocalyptic but it was also the
product of a disturbed mind. A British general met Mac-
Arthur at this time:

> He appeared to be much older than his 70 years...
> Signs of nerves and strain were apparent... When he
> emphasised the combined efforts and successes of all
> front-line troops in standing shoulder to shoulder, and
> dying if necessary in their fight against communism,
> it occurred to me that he could not have been fully in
> the picture. I cannot believe he would have made these
> comments in such a way if he had been in full posses-
> sion of facts which I would inevitably learn later, that
> some Americans had been far from staunch. It oc-
> curred to me then, and was emphasised later, that the
> war in Korea is reproduced in Tokyo with certain omis-
> sions of the more unpalatable facts.[3]

By this stage President Truman was thoroughly alarmed
at the pronouncements of his commander in Korea. He
knew that he would have no support from his European
allies for the use of atomic weapons in Korea. In the view
of his advisers it was the wrong war, in the wrong place,
and against the wrong enemy. Only Soviet Russia could
benefit if the United States wasted her strength against the
limitless human resources of Communist China. As usual
the Americans were assuming a unity of interests between
Moscow and Beijing that simply did not exist. Stalin had
almost as much to gain from a humiliation of Maoist China
as he had from the failure of the United States. Blows
against the Communist Chinese would do no harm at all
to Stalin's monolithic state.

The more MacArthur pressed for the atomic option the
more Truman took fright. Already the Europeans—notably
the British—"were in a virtual state of panic." They believed that the United States was failing them by making a
stand on an issue that was not vital to the security of Europe. They did not agree with MacArthur that the battle of

Europe would be fought in Asia. This theory was just another of the general's unbalanced judgments, revealing a profound ignorance of the realities of the European situation. Britain pressed Truman to exert his authority over his commander in Korea to prevent the irrevocable, war-threatening blunder he might make at any time. In the opinion of Omar Bradley, MacArthur's latest pronouncements on the use of Nationalist troops and/or atomic bombs showed that "he was monumentally stupid, had gone mad, or had rejected JCS and administration policy to keep the war localized and was willing to risk an all-out war with China, regardless of consequences."

While the leaders squabbled, the American troops on the ground suffered a series of stunning reverses, indicative as much of poor leadership and low morale as of superior fighting ability on the part of the Chinese. By December 3 the JCS was in despair, afraid to issue orders to MacArthur for fear that he would simply ignore them. Clearly there was a failure of leadership in these desperate days. Truman and his advisers in Washington had got the right to sack MacArthur but they feared that an action so decisive would create severe shocks that could threaten the entire administration and perhaps lead to a total American collapse in Korea. Truman feared to extend the war into China, yet perhaps for him this was the least dangerous option. He could either back MacArthur or sack him. Would backing him be any more damaging than sacking him? When Prime Minister Attlee of Great Britain arrived in Washington in December he found to his horror that Truman was seriously considering following up MacArthur's suggestion to extend the war against China to involve "economic blockade and stimulating internal trouble in China." Attlee was so alarmed at the possibilities of escalating the war that he made it clear to Truman that if he should extend the war against China Britain would remove her support for America, and this action would be repeated by many European and Commonwealth states. Eventually Truman agreed that the priority should remain the preservation of South Korea, not the unification of the country—which was the purpose of the original UN action—and that in the event that America considered extending the war to China or using the atomic bomb, no action would be taken until London had been consulted.

In January 1951—to the chagrin of MacArthur himself, whose Inchon triumph had liberated the capital six months earlier—Seoul fell to the Communists. It was a symbolic victory rather than one of great military significance. Most of the American troops had already fallen back deep into South Korea to prepare for the expected Chinese offensive, which aimed at driving them into the sea. In this crisis the JCS discussed the possibility of a Korean Dunkirk, with American troops being taken off by the navy from Pusan. But MacArthur was thinking less of damage limitation than of escalation. He talked of using up to twenty-six atomic bombs, with four bombs to drive back invasion forces and four more to destroy enemy air power in Manchuria. He was clearly planning to fight the battle of Armageddon. When the JCS suggested fall-back positions in the south, MacArthur spoke of direct action against China instead, to save the whole of Asia from being engulfed by the Communists. It was clear to everyone by now that MacArthur would not be satisfied until he had dragged the United States into a full-scale war with China. To Omar Bradley this smacked of MacArthur's wanting to get his revenge on the Communist generals who had made a fool of him.

MacArthur's grip on reality became less secure day by day. Fortunately the new American Eighth Army commander, Matthew Ridgway, was rejuvenating the fighting spirit of his men so that, at least on the ground, the situation looked more hopeful for the Americans in the early part of 1951. However, the commander-in-chief had thought up a new plan with which to win victory over the Chinese. To readers in the 1990s this scenario could have been scripted by one of Hitler's least reputable scientists. It consisted of "massive air attacks" against North Korea and the laying of a field of radioactive waste to prevent Chinese troops from entering Korea from Manchuria. The long-term consequences of this deliberate desertification by nuclear waste seemed never to have occurred to him. In his last years MacArthur became an exponent of atomic warfare and later tried to persuade President Eisenhower to use "a belt of radioactive cobalt" on the Sino-Korean border prior to an invasion of China by Chiang Kai-shek's Nationalists. On another occasion he admitted to reporters that he had wanted to drop as many as fifty atomic bombs in Manchuria.

The alarming decline in MacArthur's mental condition went hand in hand with ever larger fantasies. From mere victory in the war, MacArthur had moved ahead to thinking of not only the defeat of Communist China but the end of communism itself. He hoped to earn himself a place in history as the man who had turned back and destroyed the peril from the East. Convinced—for no good reason—that the Chinese peasants would welcome back the corrupt and tyrannical rule of the Guomindang, he continued to believe that the Nationalists were destined to retake the mainland. Matthew Ridgway was disturbed by the mental state of his chief and believed that MacArthur's war aims went even beyond the defeat of China to a war to the finish with the Soviet Union.

During March peace feelers were put out by both sides but these only brought forth from MacArthur one of his most intemperate outbursts. On March 24 he warned the Chinese that only the acceptance of peace could save them from destruction, and should they fail to accept the UN's terms he would have no alternative but to extend military operations to China's coastal and inland bases, thus ensuring her military collapse. The terms he would offer China included no change in the status of Korea, Taiwan or the matter of the Security Council seat in the United Nations. Furthermore, to even achieve this the "defeated" Chinese commander-in-chief would have to come "cap in hand" to meet the American field commanders. MacArthur later tried to say that this was merely a routine communiqué but it was obvious to everyone that he had gone too far this time. Panicking, MacArthur then accused Truman and his advisers of a plot to hand over Taiwan to Red China. He obviously hoped to swing American public opinion to his side and stop any chance of the peace initiative. But he was operating in "cloud cuckoo land" by then. The thirteen other members of the United Nations armed forces, with Britain at their head, were alarmed by this clear evidence that Truman had no control of his commander in Korea. The JCS was convinced now that at whatever cost to the war effort MacArthur had to go. This was music to Truman's ears. He had been absolutely furious at the way MacArthur had openly defied his presidential authority. As he said, "It was an act totally disregarding all directives to abstain from any declaration on foreign policy. It was in

open defiance of my orders as President and as commander-in-chief." He now looked for a way to relieve the
general of his command.

America's allies were distressed by the lack of unity
among the American leaders. Britain had lost faith in
MacArthur and indirectly in Truman as well. The British
Chief of the Imperial General Staff, Sir William Slim, was
convinced that nothing but removal could prevent Mac-
Arthur from fighting a war with China. Slim warned that it
was not even safe anymore to rely on the judgment of the
American JCS, as "they were scared of MacArthur" and
were easily manipulated by him. Truman heard from the
British that their principal problem in Korea was Mac-
Arthur and that they would not support him in a war
against China. As they told the president, the general had
publicly shown that his policy was not the policy of the
American government and that it would, nevertheless, pre-
vail. Faced with this ultimatum from his allies, Truman
realized that the time had come to act.

On April 8 the JCS officially informed the president that
it was its view that MacArthur should be relieved of his
command. He had been guilty of insubordination and of
following a policy hostile to the wishes and orders of the
government in Washington. It was clear that no country
could continue for long with two foreign policies: one pro-
mulgated by an army commander, however senior, and the
other by the elected president and his government. Truman
had a more than adequate replacement for MacArthur in
Matthew Ridgway, and on April 11, 1951, the deed was done.
Truman issued the following statement to the press:

> With deep regret I have concluded that General of the
> Army Douglas MacArthur is unable to give his whole-
> hearted support to the policies of the United States
> government and of the United Nations in matters per-
> taining to his official duties. In view of the specific
> responsibility imposed on me by the Constitution of
> the United States, and of the added responsibility
> which has been entrusted to me by the United Nations,
> I have decided that I must make a change of command
> in the Far East. I have, therefore, relieved General
> MacArthur of his commands, and have designated

Lieutenant General Matthew B. Ridgway as his successor.

Full and vigorous debate on matters of national policy is a vital element in the constitutional system of our free democracy. It is fundamental, however, that military commanders must be governed by the policies and directives issued to them in the manner provided by our laws and Constitution. In time of crisis, this consideration is particularly compelling.

General MacArthur's place in history is fully established. The nation owes him a debt of gratitude for the distinguished and exceptional service which he has rendered his country in posts of great responsibility. For that reason I repeat my regret at the necessity for the action I feel compelled to take in his case.[4]

MacArthur's fall was not entirely unexpected but it provoked intensely partisan views in the United States. Truman's decision was seen in some quarters as being determined by America's European allies, particularly Britain, who disapproved so strongly of his belligerence and his apparent willingness to use the nuclear option. Far fewer Americans were afraid of his threat to use atomic bombs. One Korean veteran wrote later:

I favored using the bomb in one unoccupied area—say, the Punchbowl. Pop it off. Say to the Communists: "Come off of this stuff and get out." The Korean War was our first real national vacillation, the first evidence of the great decline in our will as a nation to make a real hard decision.[5]

Another veteran, Colonel Paul Freeman, said: "We should have knocked the Chinese out, whatever it took. My senior officers were certainly in favor of using atomic weapons. But some of the European nations were scared we were going to start something." MacArthur certainly wanted to start something. And George Marshall and Omar Bradley knew that it was something that was better not started. In Matthew Ridgway they had a better man, a younger man and a sounder commander. Ridgway was no fan of MacArthur's posturing and ridiculous fantasies. He got on with the job of saving America's face and ensuring that his side did not lose the war. He did not like to see the great man go without dignity but as he saw it MacArthur was a liability, capable of setting off The Third World War and seeing Europe overrun by the Soviets.

If Americans were divided over the fall of MacArthur, Europe and Asia rejoiced. The British ambassador in Tokyo wrote of "his tremendous relief" at the news, while a colleague in Paris echoed his comments, adding: "The United States Administration had almost lost control." One Pakistani newspaper spoke for many when it said, "Truman has earned the gratitude of all peace-loving peoples everywhere by eliminating the greatest single opposition to peaceful efforts and policies in the Far East."

The fall of MacArthur was the stuff of tragedy. A great man, now oppressed by age, saw a last chance to achieve perhaps a lifetime goal—the White House. Fate had placed him in control of American forces in Japan at a time when the free world faced a challenge from Communist expansion in Korea. Given supreme command—not just of American troops but of the entire UN operation—he believed he saw more clearly than the narrow-minded politicians in Washington, ever eager to please an electorate in an election year, that the survival of the free world was in the balance. Fate had ordained that he should have been called to combat the Communist threat. But his judgment had gone and he was quite unable to handle the stress of commanding so vast an operation. Nor could he understand the motives of the Chinese, who saw him as the potential aggressor and feared that he would carry the war into Manchuria with the intention of overthrowing the Communist regime in Beijing. Their response was defensive, not aggressive. They warned both Truman and MacArthur that if American troops approached their borders they would feel obliged to respond. But MacArthur simply disregarded instructions from Washington to keep away from the Yalu River, either because he misjudged the situation or because he deliberately wished to provoke the Chinese into retaliating. In either case he proved that as UN commander he was a dangerous liability. It is difficult to disagree with the judgment of British historian Max Hastings that "it was fortunate that his removal was achieved before he could inflict a historic military, moral or political disaster upon the West's cause."

Vietnam: The Media War, 1968

IN MODERN WARFARE THE ROLE OF THE MEDIA IS VITAL. DEMOC-
racies constantly face the challenge of balancing censor-
ship in the national interest with the need to keep a free
people in touch with developments at the front.

With the proliferation of the television as the main news
medium in the modern world—by 1968 there were over 100
million sets in the United States—the problem of just how
much freedom TV editors should be allowed in showing
military material to their viewers is a vital consideration
for any government. Wrongly used television can become
a potent weapon for the enemy, yet can a democratic government justify using it as an agent of its own propaganda?
In the Vietnam War this problem was never successfully
resolved and television coverage of the war contributed to
public alienation and ultimately to national defeat.

Historians of America's long struggle in Vietnam point
to the night of February 27, 1968, as a turning point in the
war. On that night the United States underwent a devastating defeat yet suffered scarcely any casualties. It was a
defeat to rank with the most embarrassing in American
history even though it took place on a battlefield no larger
than an average television screen. It was a battle that involved millions of Americans but was fought in their living
rooms, thousands of miles away from the battlefields of
Vietnam. Commanding the offensive for the American people was veteran broadcaster Walter Cronkite and opposing
him was the entire American military machine. It was a
civil war and it was fought in the "hearts and minds" of
ordinary American citizens. At the end of the battle the

American troops and their commanders were in tatters, their positions shot away by their savage exposure to the awesome power of television.

On that evening Walter Cronkite spoke of the Tet offensive, which had been launched by the Communist Vietnamese throughout South Vietnam on January 31, 1968. As he spoke the television pictures showed scenes of absolute destruction in and around Saigon—supposedly safely held by the Americans—and Cronkite contrasted the pictures with official American claims of success and unofficial evidence of disaster. He made it clear that military leaders were misleading the American people and that the war was far from being won. Cronkite concluded his piece with these words:

> We have been too often disappointed by the optimism of the American leaders... To say that we are closer to victory today is to believe, in the face of the evidence, the optimists who have been wrong in the past... To say that we are mired in stalemate seems the only realistic, yet unsatisfactory conclusion... It is increasingly clear to this reporter that the only rational way out will be to negotiate, not as victors, but as an honorable people who lived up to their pledge to defend democracy, and did the best they could.[1]

These fine words—deeply felt by an honorable and widely respected broadcaster—were nevertheless a knife planted firmly in the back of the American soldiers fighting in unprecedentedly difficult conditions against a foe few of them could recognize. Cronkite was showing the people back home something that had never been seen by previous generations—the full horror of war, brought into their own living rooms in small-town America. The horrors were no different from those in previous wars. Soldiers throughout history had seen them and come to accept them as part of their life. But twentieth-century Americans had never been exposed to them before and the shock was enormous. Had the murderous stalemate on the Western Front in 1914–18 been beamed nightly into civilian homes in London, Paris and Berlin, the war would have been brought to an end in an overwhelming tide of civilian disgust. In the butchered corpses of Verdun and Passchendaele—just as in the dead of Saigon—there was none of the "chivalry of war" that had been doled out for home consumption. In 1968 American viewers were shocked from their complacency and began to ask not just if the war could be won but whether it was worth winning. In the two months that followed the Tet offensive more than one in five Americans changed from supporting the war to opposing it and President Lyndon Johnson's popularity rating dived.

The American media—press and television—played a very significant part in the Tet offensive. Yet—as had happened in some earlier wars—in their search for a good story they failed to realize that their action was helping the cause of America's enemy. In their concern for telling the truth and revealing the skeletons in the war chests, they were doing a disservice to the American fighting man. Their reports sent back from the front revealed that the Vietnam War was not proceeding along the calm, ordered lines suggested by General Westmoreland. Far from it—as the bodies in the American embassy compound in Saigon showed. Yet the assault that the media launched against the American military was every bit as deadly as any launched by the Communist Vietnamese. They were undermining civilian morale at home and turning the Vietnam War into an unwinnable struggle for the United States.

The Vietnam War was the first television war. Before February 27, 1968, television had presented the American people with a familiar, almost comforting, view of the struggle. It was war at a distance. In the words of American historian Stanley Karnow:

> Columns of troops, disgorged from hovering helicopters, cut through dense jungles or plodded across muddy rice fields towards faraway villages, occasionally stumbling into mines or booby traps, or drawing fire from hidden guerrillas. Artillery shelled distant targets from lonely bases, and aircraft bombed the vast countryside, billows of flame and smoke rising in their wake. The screen often portrayed human agony in scenes of the wounded and dying on both sides, and the ordeal of civilians trapped by the combat. But mostly it transmitted the gruelling reality of the struggle—remote, repetitious, monotonous—punctuated periodically by moments of horror.[2]

It was war at long distance, with binoculars reversed. Then, on January 31, all this changed in a single night as the Tet offensive began. Now the American people were to have war presented through zoom lenses. On that night, throughout South Vietnam, 70,000 Communist soldiers (Vietcong and North Vietnamese regulars) attacked a hundred cities and towns, including Saigon. The intensity of the offensive was unprecedented. The war moved at a single leap from the countryside to the supposedly safe urban areas. Preconception fell victim to the Tet offensive, but it was Truth—so often the first casualty of war—that simply refused to die.

The Communists staged their most dramatic televised "coup" at the U.S. embassy in Saigon. Complacency had led the Americans to leave the security of the Saigon area in the hands of the South Vietnamese, who proved to be very slack. Vietcong groups moved weapons and ammunition into Saigon concealed under truckloads of rice and tomatoes. A bicycle repair shop provided a haven for the stores until they were needed, though termites ate through the wooden stocks of their guns and they were forced to improvise new handles. American security was no more efficient than that of the South Vietnamese army (ARVN): once inside the city the Communists were guided by a chauffeur from the U.S. mission armed with a Russian machine gun but affectionately known as Satchmo. At about three A.M. on January 31, the Communists arrived outside the U.S. embassy on Thong Nhut Boulevard—nineteen members of the C-10 Saigon Sapper Battalion loaded into a small Peugeot truck and a taxicab. The VC encountered four South Vietnamese policemen who simply fled. Then, blasting a hole in the outer compound wall, they rushed in, firing as they came. In an exchange of fire with American military police the two Vietcong leaders were shot but not before five Americans had been killed.

While the struggle continued for control of the embassy compound, the news was reaching America. The Associated Press reported: "The Vietcong seized part of the U.S. Embassy in Saigon early Wednesday... Communist commandos penetrated the supposedly attack-proof building in the climax of a combined artillery and guerrilla assault that brought limited warfare to Saigon itself." With the enemy inside the compound and several American officials trapped in the building, the U.S. commanders took their time, not realizing that the world's television was now concentrating its attention on this single point on the planet and was waiting to see what the Americans were going to do to evict the enemy. It was not until five A.M. that a helicopter with airborne soldiers was ordered to land on the embassy roof, but, embarrassingly, it was driven off by fire from the surviving Vietcong. At daybreak—and before the helicopter could return—U.S. military police killed the surviving guerrillas. It was one of the most important actions—for its size—in military history, with consequences few could guess.

Afternoon newspapers in America carried graphic headlines, while television stations began conveying the pictures of the battle-torn city of Saigon to millions of homes. Far from the peace and security the American presence in Vietnam was assumed to have brought to life in the Vietnamese capital, television viewers now saw every sign of war. In full color there were scenes of terrible devastation and chaos, smoke-filled skies, bodies of dead and wounded littering the streets and the constant sounds of firing and explosions. American soldiers were seen in action at close quarters with the enemy, firing small arms at tiny figures sheltering within the compound walls. The fighting lasted for six hours before the embassy compound was declared "liberated." But how had any of this been possible within the heart of Saigon?

When he spoke to reporters General Westmoreland seemed almost relaxed. But as the *Washington Post* wrote: "The reporters could hardly believe their ears. Westmoreland was standing in the ruins and saying everything was great." No one believed him and his words were clear proof that he had been deeply shocked by the experience. He spoke of enemy "deceitfulness" in breaking the New Year truce and that their "aim had been to create maximum consternation," as if this was a novel departure for an enemy in wartime. Yet however reassuring his words were meant to be, the visual evidence gave the lie to everything he said. Behind him was chaos and carnage on a grand scale. This was no isolated raid but just a small part of a countrywide offensive by thousands of well-trained and well-led Communist troops. America's claim that the war was under control had been shown to be hollow. West-

moreland's own headquarters at Saigon's airport had been
attacked as part of a systematic attempt to undermine the
entire structure of American power in the south. It was a
considerable shock to the American military command
that the Communists were capable of launching such an
offensive. But, impressive as the Tet offensive was as a
publicity exercise, it was militarily unsound. The Vietnamese had spread themselves so thinly over the whole country
that they had ensured defeat everywhere rather than concentrating their efforts on winning decisively somewhere.
General Tran Do later wrote:

> In all honesty, we didn't achieve our main objective,
> which was to spur uprisings throughout the south.
> Still, we inflicted heavy casualties on the Americans and
> their puppets, and that was a big gain for us. As for
> making an impact in the United States, it had not been
> our intention—but it turned out to be a fortunate re-
> sult.[3]

So fiercely did the Communists pursue their goals that
their casualties were very heavy indeed. Nevertheless, the
sheer scale of the operation astonished the Americans,
who had never for a moment believed that their enemies
could operate on such a large scale. One American remarked that the lights on his map of Saigon were acting
like those on a pinball machine, so rapid and widespread
were the VC raids in the city. The television cameramen
had a field day. No sooner had the excitement of the embassy siege dropped than there were other skirmishes
sprouting up all around the city. Attacks on the presidential palace were repelled but in the heavy fighting there
some American soldiers lost their lives in full view of their
folks at home.

In the television coverage of the Vietnam War one incident stands out that, in its impact on the American home
audience, had a greater influence in boosting the anti-war
movement than perhaps anything else. General Nguyen
Ngoc Loan—chief of South Vietnam's police—carried out
a public execution of a suspected Vietcong in full view of
an American reporter with his Vietnamese cameraman.
Within hours the film was being shown on American television by NBC. In full color the police chief was shown

holding a gun to the prisoner's head and firing, sending a spray of blood and brains spurting across the street. West-moreland's bland words that the situation remained normal were drowned in the hostile media backlash. Across America, newspapers carried photographs of the grisly execution and writers questioned what kind of allies America had in Vietnam and what kind of war was it anyway?

The Communist attack on the American embassy in Saigon had been intended for home consumption rather than for powerful propaganda in the United States. In that respect, American television was the unwitting ally of the Communists, and an ally whose impact could scarcely be measured. General Giap had hoped to show the South Vietnamese people that the Americans were not as strong as they claimed, nor was their hold on the country as complete as everyone believed. If the Vietcong could actually pierce the defenses of the American embassy in the capital then clearly nowhere was safe. Ironically, Giap's original plan failed. But through the assistance of the American media the Tet offensive was rescued from total failure and turned into a potentially war-winning propaganda coup.

President Johnson was convinced by his advisers that the attack on the embassy was part of a Communist ploy to enter American homes through their television sets. This raised the whole question of media coverage of the war. Was it un-American to report incidents that might give comfort to America's enemies? And if so, was freedom of the press to be suspended during wartime?

The media backlash that followed the Tet offensive was of extraordinary intensity. After all, the Americans had won a crushing victory over the Communists. Having suffered four thousand casualties themselves, and with the ARVN allies having suffered perhaps six thousand more, the American forces had killed up to fifty-thousand Vietcong and North Vietnamese soldiers. It was the sort of victory that in other contexts might have been thought to match the Communist triumph at Dien Bien Phu in 1954. Yet—incredibly—most Americans believed they had been beaten. Many Americans felt that the victory should have been decisive, yet as one American soldier wrote, "To our complete bewilderment in the weeks that followed, nobody ever publicized this feat of battlefield triumph. Instead, we read that we had been defeated." And in a sense the Americans had won a battle but lost a war. The wounds were self-inflicted. Men with cameras and microphones had fought more effectively for General Giap than any of his fighters with their Russian automatic weapons. The Communists had enjoyed a propaganda triumph in spite of themselves. The planner of the embassy raid—entirely missing the point—criticized his men for a poorly executed operation. Only later did he come to realize that this single incident—"in many ways...a microcosm of the entire war"—was in fact the decisive moment of the whole struggle.

The Tet offensive caught the Americans at a period of political irresolution and confronted them with a stark choice—either escalate the conflict in search of an elusive victory or accept the necessity of looking for a diplomatic settlement. With the enormous boost to the anti-war movement in America provided by TV coverage of the embassy siege, President Johnson was unwilling to make this choice. Haunted by the pictures he had seen of the fighting in Saigon, Johnson decided to withdraw from the presidential race and not seek reelection. Constantly fed soothing intelligence about the way the war was going, he simply could not cope with the truth, that the enemy he had assumed to be beaten was capable of attacking the U.S. embassy in Saigon. Once he had absorbed the full enormity of the crisis he began a damage-limitation exercise, instructing Westmoreland to brief the press correspondents in Vietnam "to reassure the public here that you have the situation under control." But it just was not true, as anyone could tell from the TV pictures flooding nightly into their homes. Art Buchwald satirically suggested a caption for his column on the lines of General George Armstrong Custer announcing that the battle of Little Big Horn "had just turned the corner." Other papers put it more bluntly. Americans should brace themselves for news that the war was lost. And then came Cronkite—the voice of Middle America—delivering his verdict on February 27. It was the final straw for a shattered president whose popularity had slumped.

A rattled Dean Rusk challenged reporters: "Whose side are you on? Now, I'm secretary of state of the United States and I'm on our side! None of your papers or your broadcasting apparatuses are worth a damn unless the United

States succeeds. They are trivial compared to that question. So I don't know why people have to be probing for things that one can bitch about, when there are two thousand stories on the same day about things that are more constructive." Without realizing it, Rusk was asking the decisive question—the one that governments of every democracy need to ask in wartime—but he was too angry to wait for an answer. In a free society should the media be muzzled in wartime? An affirmative answer may raise the question of what sort of society a nation's soldiers are fighting for. If a negative answer is given then politicians can hardly be expected to escape from the truth, particularly if responsible newsmen feel that it is in the national interest that the truth should be revealed. The effects of the television coverage of the embassy fighting in Saigon is seen in this comment by one of the president's aides, Harry McPherson:

> I watched the invasion of the American embassy compound, and the terrible sight of General Loan killing the Vietcong captive. You get a sense of the awfulness, the endlessness, of the war—and, though it sounds naive, the unethical quality of a war in which a prisoner is shot at point-blank range. I put aside the confidential cables. I was more persuaded by the tube and by the newspapers. I was fed up with the optimism that seemed to flow without stopping from Saigon.[4]

Lyndon Johnson was not the only casualty of Tet. General Westmoreland, speaking smoothly but unconvincingly in the ruins of Saigon on January 31, was "kicked upstairs" and left Vietnam to take up his new position as army chief of staff. Westmoreland had been responsible for much of the optimism that had so annoyed Harry McPherson. Yet the shock of the Tet offensive had been terrible for him and he was a broken man, dispirited and deeply shaken that the Communists could have organized such an attack when he had believed them beaten. Under his successor, General Creighton, the United States began to scale down its commitment to the war and introduced its ill-fated "Vietnamization" policy, which was to eventually lead to Communist victory in 1975.

The Americans had misread the significance of the Tet

offensive, seeing in it an opportunity to inflict stunning casualties on an overextended enemy. Yet, in spite of winning a clear battlefield victory, America had suffered a political defeat. Both in the United States—where the citizens were shocked to find themselves allies of a man like General Loan—and in South Vietnam—where they still hoped to win the support of a people they despised and frequently killed in error—the American generals had lost the battle for "hearts and minds." They had been "tried" by television and found wanting. Their words were no longer believed by a nation rudely awoken to the sordid realities of the Vietnam War and now eager to see it ended.

The Iranian Hostages, 1980

ON APRIL 25, 1980, AMERICAN TELEVISION AUDIENCES WERE treated to a spectacle so gruesome that it might more readily have found a place in a horror novel by Stephen King. Against a desert background of wrecked helicopters and planes, many twisted by fire but still dimly showing American markings, a dark robed Muslim holy man—the Ayatollah Khalkali—was picking over the remains of a dead American serviceman, holding up to the greedy cameras first a forearm and then a charred skull. The shockwaves felt throughout the civilized world by this ghoulish behavior were tempered by the realization that the Americans had brought this humiliation upon themselves. What were their men and planes doing inside Iran anyway? The answer, which a shocked President Jimmy Carter told the world on April 25, 1980, was that they had been part of— for its size—probably the most complex military operation of all time—and that their mission had been to rescue American hostages from Teheran. Planned as a surgical strike, the plan had misfired, with the startling results all too clear to see. But had the plan been bungled or was it just so ambitious that failure was certain?

On Sunday November 4, 1979, the American embassy in Teheran was attacked and overrun by three thousand revolutionary followers of the Ayatollah Khomeini. They took prisoner sixty-six Americans and held them hostage in a bid to force the U.S.A.—the "Great Satan"—to hand over the deposed shah, then in exile in Egypt, so that he could be put on trial in Iran. The civilian government in Iran was quite unable to secure the release of the hostages and with

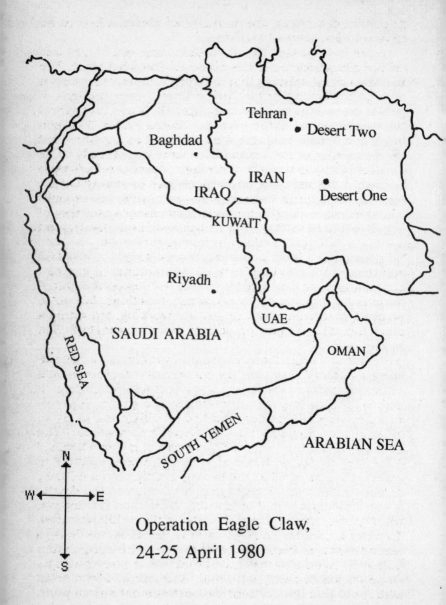

Operation Eagle Claw,
24-25 April 1980

Khomeini describing the militants as national heroes no easy solution seemed available.

As the days passed the news that came out of Iran was deeply disturbing, as it was no doubt intended to be. The militants were insisting that the American hostages be put on trial for spying or for "war crimes"; even the idea of public executions was mooted. After all, it was just part of the psychological battle with the United States. Thirteen black and female hostages were released as a gesture but the remainder of the white males were now clearly to be used as pawns in a political struggle. American flags were burned in the streets, along with effigies of Jimmy Carter. And—as during the Vietnam War—all of this was brought into the homes of ordinary American citizens courtesy of television. In the struggle for hearts and minds, the Iranian militants had won the opening round with ease.

In response Carter and his advisers sought a peaceful solution, playing by the rules of international diplomacy, contacting known moderates in Iran, calling on the United Nations for support or for economic sanctions, but all to no avail. Moderation was clearly not working, but would a more forceful reaction prove any more successful? Was war an option?

President Carter faced enormous problems in considering a military response. As commander-in-chief he had a responsibility to the nation to protect national interests and to uphold America's standing in the world. However, as a democratic president, he had an obligation to try to bring out the hostages alive. In Carter's own words: "The hostages sometimes seemed like a part of my own family." A military response, however successful, was unlikely to result in rescuing all of the hostages alive. And a military response that was no more than a reaction to the deaths of the diplomats would be nothing more than retribution, without even the humanitarian aim of liberating hostages. To enter a country as large—and as far away—as Iran to rescue hostages from the middle of a city with a population uniformly hostile to the United States and everything she stood for was a pretty tall order. And failure would bring with it not just the death of the hostages but virtual political suicide for Carter as president.

A second objection to the military option was that Carter had been given reason to believe that the hostage crisis—

intractable as it seemed—would not last long enough to necessitate military planning. Some Americans believed that Khomeini was demonstrating his power to humble the "Great Satan" and that the release of the women and black men was the first sign of a softening in his stance. Quite misjudging the strength and sincerity of Khomeini—whom many Americans unwisely considered mad—it was thought by the president's advisers that the fear of an American military reaction would eventually persuade the militants to release the hostages.

But there was a third factor, one that made war an unacceptable option. The Soviet Union's invasion of Afghanistan in 1979 had plunged Soviet-American relations to a new low point and it was unlikely that the Soviets would take a disinterested view of American military action on the Iran-Afghan border. Nor was it certain that the American people as a whole would back the president's strong stand, particularly so soon after the Vietnam debacle. As Carter was told by his national security adviser: "A declaration of war would be met with a burst of initial enthusiasm, followed by severe second doubts and internal debate, which would not only fail to strengthen the President's hand but conceivably could even splinter the spirit of national unity that had prevailed throughout the ordeal."

President Carter also faced a fourth problem, a direct outgrowth of the poor relations that existed with the Soviet Union. Strategically, Iran—at least until the shah's overthrow—had been an American client and a buffer against Soviet expansion toward the oil-rich Persian Gulf and the vital Middle East. European and Japanese economies depended on Middle Eastern oil, and the United States could expect no support from her NATO allies if she became drawn into a regional struggle that could be exploited by the Ayatollah in terms of a Western attack on Islam. His brand of Shi'ite fundamentalism might have aroused the hatred of states like Egypt, but if it was Islam itself that was in peril then he would have the support of the Arab world.

So, if war was not an option, what was available to Carter once diplomacy had failed? As one of the president's aides made clear, "President Carter has never lost sight of the fundamental truth that, painful as it was to have American diplomats held prisoner in Teheran, there were other possible outcomes that were even worse." This is an intriguing comment, and one would like to know what Carter thought could be worse. Presumably threatening war and having one's bluff called would have damaged America's standing in the world more than the sight of her impotently watching from the sidelines as her diplomats were manhandled in the streets of Teheran. So would going to war, destroying an important anti-Soviet buffer, suffering and inflicting heavy casualties and still seeing the hostages slaughtered in cold blood before the television cameras. Both of these scenarios would have been far worse. But what about an undercover rescue mission, carried out with such precision that the Iranians suffered no casualties themselves and hardly knew how their hostages had been ghosted away? Attractive, maybe, but was this "Mission Impossible"? Was the United States moving into the realm of cinema fantasy, inspired by directors like Steven Spielberg? The answer is definitely in the negative. From the outset of the hostage crisis plans had been afoot to stage just such a snatch to rescue the diplomats with the fewest possible civilian casualties and damage to relations with Iran and other Muslim states in the Middle East and the Persian Gulf. National security adviser Zbigniew Brzezinski believed that such a raid was possible but Carter was adamant that if carried out it should be "quick, incisive, surgical" with "no loss of American lives . . . [and] minimal suffering to the Iranian people themselves." Carter was setting tight parameters—perhaps too tight to allow for success.

Planning for the military option went on, although the hope was still for a diplomatic solution. But by March 22, 1980, the Americans faced the fact that they were no closer to rescuing the hostages than they had been at the outset of the crisis. On that day Carter assembled his senior advisers at Camp David to investigate the options that were still available. Depressingly, they had not changed. Diplomacy seemed to have failed, and bombing—or war—seemed even more farfetched now that the temperature of the crisis had been allowed to drop. In this situation the "surgical operation" began to seem the only hope. But Carter was setting his military men an impossible task. So strong was the president's insistence on the need to avoid bloodshed that he was asking his own men to risk life and limb to avoid harming the enemy in what was, after all, virtually a war situation. It was against this background that Operation Eagle Claw first saw the light of day.

On April 10 President Carter recorded in his diary: "The Iranian terrorists are making all kinds of crazy threats to kill the American hostages if they are invaded by Iraq—whom they identify as an American puppet."

This galvanized Carter into action and he called another meeting of his top advisers. Cyrus Vance was strongly opposed to the military option and cautioned Carter to wait. But Carter was already sold on the "surgical operation" and met the mission commanders, including General James Vaught and Colonel Charles Beckwith, who would lead the ground operation to rescue the hostages from within Teheran. Carter found their detailed description of the operation reassuring and told them that they had his complete confidence. The operation was now set to commence on April 24.

On D day aboard the U.S. carrier *Nimitz* eight twin-engined Sea-Stallion helicopters led by Lieutenant Colonel Edward R. Seiffert took off at 1905. Their task was to fly to a rendezvous at Desert Base One in the Iranian desert, where they would land. refuel and then lift the Delta force—the troops who would carry out the rescue mission in Teheran—toward the Iranian capital. Just an hour earlier but far to the west of the *Nimitz*, at Masirah Island, off the coast of Oman, six four-engined C-130 transport planes were taking to the air. Three of the transports—combat MC-130Es—were carrying troops and equipment, while the other three—EC-130Es—were each carrying three thousand-gallon fuel reservoirs. In the lead transport was transport commander Colonel James H. Kyle and ground force commander Colonel "Charging Charlie" Beckwith. The transports encountered little difficulty and arrived safely at Desert Base One. However, their problems were just about to begin.

Desert Base One—on the Dasht-e-Kavir salt flats—had been selected because it was far enough away from habitation to avoid the risk that the American preparations could be disturbed. Although the Yazd-Tabas highway ran by the base, it was rarely used. But as fate would have it the road proceeded to see as much traffic in a few minutes as it generally saw in a day. No sooner had the American transports landed that an old Mercedes bus, carrying some

forty-four Iranian peasants—mostly women and children—
came bumping along the road. Whether the driver noticed
anything unusual in the transformation of the desert into
an American airfield, complete with security guards and
motorcycle cops, we cannot be sure, but he certainly declined to stop when signaled to slow down by the U.S. road
watch team. There was no alternative but to bring the bus
to a halt by blowing out its tires and radiator. The bus
passengers were next evacuated at gunpoint but seemed
to show little concern as they were herded to one side of
the landing field. Colonel Beckwith was still in good humor,
quipping that he "wasn't going to worry until we stopped
ten buses. Then we'd have a parking problem." But matters
took a more serious turn a few minutes later when a fuel
tanker, driven at near-suicidal speed, came thundering
along the lonely road. The American checkpoints were
knocked sideways by the tanker and it was only brought
to a standstill by an anti-tank weapon that ignited the fuel,
so that the sky was illuminated by a fireball, visible for
many miles. The driver leaped free of the inferno but instead of seeking medical aid he sprinted back down the
road to where a small truck had appeared, apparently driven by his partner in crime. Before the Americans could
react the truck had left the road and set off across the
desert. In fact, as Beckwith suspected, the men were gas-
oline smugglers who thought they had been stopped by
Iranian police. Not surprisingly, these men would not be
in a hurry to report the incident.

Beckwith, meanwhile, awaited the arrival of the eight
Sea-Stallion helicopters from the *Nimitz*, little expecting
the problems their arrival would bring. Great reliance was
being placed on the helicopters in this operation and it is
clear that insufficient allowance was made for mechanical
failure or instrument malfunction. The choppers and their
crews were going to be pushed to and beyond their limits
with disastrous consequences for all concerned. From
the outset everything seemed to go wrong and this was
heightened by the insistence on keeping radio silence that
governed the mission. No sooner had the choppers, in dia-
mond formation, crossed the Iranian coastline than mechanical problems began to surface. The pilot of chopper
number eight experienced problems with his rotor gearbox
but was unable to report to any of his colleagues and just

had to grin and hope that his luck held. One problem that all the choppers faced was the fact that the Americans had an exaggerated respect for the Iranian radar and had ordered all of them to fly under its imagined umbrella by skimming the desert floor at not much more than one hundred feet. This was a nightmare for the pilots, who knew that a moment's loss of concentration could result in a fatal crash. The next emergency occurred when chopper number six was forced to land because of a damaged rotor blade. There was no alternative but to abandon the helicopter, and with radio silence in operation, the crew members were fortunate to have been spotted by chopper number eight, which landed to pick them up.

As if the problem of mechanical failure and the threat from low flying were not enough, the choppers now encountered something for which they had not been prepared. Clouds of sand and dust—known as haboobs—thousands of feet high and miles in width, lay in their path. With the sand clouds thickest nearest to the ground, where the choppers were forced to fly to avoid radar, one pilot commented that it was like "flying in a bowl of milk." Not only was visibility obscured but the temperature inside the helicopters rose dramatically, adding to the discomfort of the journey and making breathing difficult. And beyond the first haboob was a second even larger one. It was now that chopper number five hit trouble. With its navigation instruments malfunctioning there was no point at all in continuing with the flight. Even if it succeeded in arriving at Desert Base One it would have been the height of folly to risk the lives of troops and possibly hostages in a chopper with faulty navigation. Chopper five turned away and limped back to the *Nimitz*, reducing the helicopter force to just six, the bare minimum for the mission to be given the go-ahead.

The arrival of the choppers at Desert Base One was an anti-climax for Colonel Beckwith, whose heart must have leaped as he heard the throaty sound of the rotor blades emerging from the dark sky overhead. His first meeting was with the pilot of chopper number three, Major James Schaeffer, and Schaeffer was in no mood to exchange pleasantries. His flight had been a nightmare. Beckwith was disappointed, even more so when number four arrived and the pilot told him, "You have no idea what I've been through.

The damndest sandstorm I've ever seen hit us. I'm not really sure we can make it." These pilots were experienced men, the best there were, and yet their nerves had been drained by the journey through the haboobs. After such an experience were they up to the next demanding stage of the mission? The choice rested with Beckwith, but his decision was made slightly easier when he was brought news that chopper number two was experiencing hydraulic problems and could not be relied on.

Should Beckwith abort the mission? He and Colonel Kyle now used the satellite transmitter to contact the operation commander, General Vaught, in Egypt. Beckwith explained the difficulties—and dangers—of going ahead with the mission with just five helicopters. Men and equipment would have to be discarded. Vaught responded by asking him to consider going ahead with just the five choppers rather than aborting the mission, but Beckwith was resolute. It had been agreed before the mission started that six choppers was the minimum number needed to carry out the mission in safety, and that was now Beckwith's prime consideration. To the tough army colonel it would be better to get out cleanly with nothing lost and "come back in a few days" for another attempt. And so the decision was taken to abort the mission.

To the north of the highway two of the C-130s had been parked with four of the helicopters behind them, while to the south were positioned the other transport and the remaining choppers. Colonel Kyle ordered the helicopters to return to the *Nimitz*, but before they could do so number four needed to refuel. Major Schaeffer in number three moved his chopper aside to let number four pass, but as he did so the helicopter was lifted by a sudden blast of wind and dropped on top of the nearest transport. Its rotor blades cut through the C-130's cockpit and there was a sudden fireball as both planes burst into flames. The transport had only just been boarded by members of Delta Blue, who imagined that they were under attack. One officer aboard the transport described the horror of that moment:

A spray of sparks lit up the entrance to the cockpit and the bulkhead, where most of the avionics were stored. The electrical fire, combined with one fed by aviation fuel, was turning the front of the plane into a murderous oven. We were obviously under attack.[1]

In the inferno that now engulfed the two planes eight American servicemen died and five more were seriously injured. Many soldiers abandoned their equipment in their panic and all the helicopters were abandoned in the desert, leaving their secret maps and equipment for the Iranians to collect the following day. As the Americans left their desert base, now littered with debris, the puzzled occupants of the Iranian bus must have wondered at the mysterious ways of Allah.

In Washington, President Carter received the news he had least wanted to hear at 5:58 P.M. The surgical operation had failed and there were casualties—American ones.

What had gone wrong? The Holloway Special Operations Review Group later noted twenty-three different factors that had contributed to the failure of the mission, ranging from inadequate weather reconnaissance to mechanical deficiencies in the helicopters. Yet, in a sense, the overriding problem was the mission itself. Within the constraints imposed by President Carter—the surgical nature of the operation and the unwillingness to accept or impose casualties—the question had to be raised as to whether the operation was feasible or indeed worthwhile. The consequences of failure were so serious that one is tempted to consider Carter's decision to give it the go-ahead irresponsible. As one of the hostages said, on hearing of the failure of Eagle Claw, "Thank God for the sandstorm." The losses in American lives—both military and civilian hostage—not to mention Iranian casualties, if the plan had backfired in Teheran rather than at Desert Base One, should have been part of the military equation and as such sufficient to consign the plan to the trash can. And the consequences to relations with Iran, the Soviet Union and the Muslim world of a shootout in downtown Teheran are almost too serious to contemplate.

President Carter's secretary of state, Cyrus Vance, offered the president his resignation before the hostage rescue was attempted. Vance believed that even a successful mission would create a diplomatic upheaval, while failure was bound to be political dynamite. Vance had no confidence in Carter's concept of a "surgical strike." He simply

could not accept that such a complex operation as Eagle
Claw should finally rest upon chance encounters within a
hostile city. There was bound to be shooting and once this
started casualties were inevitable. What were acceptable
casualties in a "surgical strike"? The American military
had no real faith in Carter's belief that the hostages could
be spirited away as if by magic. They were expecting up to
fifteen hostage casualties, along with perhaps twice as
many servicemen killed and wounded. And what of Iranian
losses? Fanatics convinced that all Americans were
spawned by the "Great Satan" were unlikely to surrender
their hostages without a stern resistance. And if the mission was successful what then could be expected from
these same fanatics? As Cyrus Vance tried to point out to
Carter, there were still as many as two hundred American
nationals in Teheran—press and media in the main—and
in the backlash caused by Eagle Claw there was every likelihood that their lives, or certainly their liberty, would be
in danger.

In the final analysis, Operation Eagle Claw was a flawed
concept, far too inflexible to accommodate chance occur-
rences and mechanical breakdowns, but also based on a
faulty rationale. Even in success it might have failed. Some
lives saved, others lost—and no guarantee that it would do
other than increase the spiraling hostility between America and the Muslim world. Eight months were to pass before
the hostages were released, during which time Jimmy
Carter lost the presidency to Ronald Reagan. But at the end
of those eight months the hostages came home safely—all
of them.

The Gulf War, 1991

THE EASE WITH WHICH THE AMERICAN-LED COALITION DEFEATED
Saddam Hussein's much-vaunted Iraqi army in January
and February of 1991 has been allowed to overshadow consideration of whether the war against Iraq could have been
avoided by more skillful diplomacy. Minimal coalition
losses and recently scaled-down Iraqi military and civilian
casualties have given Operation Desert Storm an air of almost surgical precision, exceeding by far the most optimistic hopes of the Bush administration. Yet some
commentators have called the Gulf War the apotheosis of
the "Great American screwup." According to them, American diplomacy had made war with Saddam Hussein more
rather than less likely, and failures of intelligence and
warning at the last moment brought about a wholly unnecessary conflict. Rather than the war being a triumph for
President Bush it was in fact a diplomatic defeat that no
amount of television pictures of wrecked Soviet hardware
could turn into a meaningful victory.

American strategist Gerald W. Hopple has clearly shown
that when wars begin with a surprise attack—as with the
Japanese attack on Pearl Harbor in 1941, or the North Korean attack on South Korea in 1950, or most recently the
Argentinian occupation of the Falkland Islands in 1982—
the surprise factor is always more apparent than real. In
fact, such surprises are not really surprises at all, but arise
from periods of unrelieved tension that are seriously misjudged by those responsible for political decisions. In every
case of such surprise attacks sufficient warnings have
been received but inadequate responses have been made.

Enemy intentions are incorrectly assessed because the victim—the state that will suffer the attack or its friends and
protectors—makes false strategical assumptions. The failure of Britain to anticipate the Argentinian invasion of the
Falklands in 1982 provides a prime example of this problem
in intelligence and warning, and should have provided a
lesson for the United States in its handling of data that
suggested that Iraq was about to attack Kuwait on August
2, 1991.

The roots of the Gulf War of 1991 are to be found in
American reactions to the Iranian revolution of 1979. The
overthrow of the Shah of Iran, America's strongest ally in
the Middle East, and his replacement by the fundamentalist Shi'ite regime of the Ayatollah Khomeini, were great
blows to traditional American policy in the region. The
hostility of the Khomeini regime was quickly demonstrated
when the American embassy was overrun by militants and
American diplomatic hostages were taken. From that time
onward relations between the United States and Iran continued at a very low ebb, with the Ayatollah Khomeini condemning the United States as the "Great Satan" and
preaching hostility against her every move. When, in 1981,
the Iraqi leader, Saddam Hussein, made an opportunist
strike against what he believed to be a weakened Iran he
found himself enjoying the support of the United States.
However, America was backing a dangerous regime in Saddam Hussein's Iraq. The Israelis had demonstrated in 1981
just how dangerous Saddam might be when they felt
obliged to make a preemptive strike against Iraq's nuclear
research facility at Osirak. Yet the Americans continued
to be so blinkered by their hostility to the religious fundamentalism of Khomeini that they saw Iraq as less of a
threat to the stability of the Middle East than Iran.

As the Iran-Iraq War limped on from year to year, the
Americans increasingly favored Saddam Hussein, in spite
of well-publicized accounts of the atrocities the Iraqi leader
perpetrated on his own people, notably the Kurds. But it
was the Iranian seizure of the Faw Peninsula in 1986 that
really alarmed the Western powers. Faw was just twenty-
five miles from Kuwait and its occupation by Iranian troops
seemed to presage a general uprising among the Shia pop-
ulations of the Gulf states. Both Britain and the United
States were determined to prevent any further Iranian ad-

vance in the Gulf region and saw Saddam's Iraq as the best way of achieving their aim. From this point Saddam began to benefit from American aid, from European expertise, and—through his substantial oil wealth—from the latest Soviet and French military equipment. The United States now became Saddam's secret ally, allowing him to benefit from American satellite surveillance of Iran while American advisers plotted Iranian troop movements for the Iraqis. Relations between Reagan's America and Saddam's Iraq became so close that even an accidental attack by Iraqi MIGs armed with Exocets on the U.S.S. *Stark* caused no more than a slight ripple on an otherwise smooth relationship. The Iranians were not slow in condemning American involvement with Iraq, but they had accused the "Great Satan" of threatening the Iranian state so often before that no one took much notice.

It was not really until 1988 that America began to realize that she was backing the wrong horse. Iran, having suffered heavily from its war with Iraq, was no longer likely to upset the balance in the Middle East. On the other hand, Iraq had emerged from the war with the world's fourth largest army, with massive numbers of tanks and with ground-to-ground Scud missiles capable of carrying conventional and perhaps even nuclear payloads against Israeli cities. The balance in the region was changing, and it was Saddam who was changing it. Israel was first in bringing this to the attention of the American government. Non-Arab Iran had been Israel's natural ally in the region against the radical, pro-Soviet Iraq, but now she was temporarily off the board. The West had misread Iran's occupation of the Faw Peninsula in 1986, assuming it to be a first step in the expansion of Iranian fundamentalism, rather than the defensive measure it undoubtedly was. In the view of Israeli diplomats the United States had blundered in helping Saddam to victory over Iran, in that it had disrupted the balance in the region and created in Saddam a new and very dangerous threat to Israel's survival.

A belief in balance-of-power diplomacy should have suggested that the United States seek to improve relations with Iran as a counterbalance to Iraq, but this was never seriously considered, so alien did the fundamentalist nature of the Iranian state seem to the president's advisers in Washington. It was only when Saddam Hussein began to speak of using nuclear or chemical weapons against America's client-state Israel that the United States woke up to the monster she had created in Iraq. Yet even now President Bush never considered raising the stakes with Iraq, and the policy followed was to placate and contain Iraq rather than seek to influence or change its governmental policy.

The Saddam Hussein who had emerged triumphantly from the war he had come close to losing three years before was a dangerous ally, as Kuwait and Saudi Arabia were soon to discover. He had been forced to use some 70 percent of his national oil revenue to maintain the war against Iran and now that the war was over he felt able to put this oil revenue to better uses. Ending the war with a million men under arms, with Soviet Scud missiles and with five thousand tanks, he saw himself as the successor to Sultan Saladin as the leader of the Arab world. He would use his money to buy state-of-the-art defenses that could defy even the power of the Western democracies, and he would build superguns to deliver nuclear shells onto Israel. The West had produced a Frankenstein monster and now they were going to have to find a way of destroying him.

During the Iran-Iraq War most Arab states had seen Saddam as a champion of the Arab world fighting against their ancient enemies—the Persians. Saudi Arabia and Kuwait had both financed the vast cost of Iraq's war effort—Saudi Arabia paying Saddam the enormous sum of $80 billion and the Kuwaitis $40 billion. Neither of the two southern Arab states had asked Saddam to repay these huge loans, but with the end of the fighting both felt much relieved of the burden of supporting the Iraqi economy. In order to recoup some of her losses, Kuwait informed OPEC, she wished to increase her output by more than 50 percent.

Iraq's economy had suffered severely from the eight years of the Iran-Iraq War, and her annual expenditure was twice her oil revenue, leaving her with accumulated overseas debts of $80 billion. Western experts said it would take twenty years to reconstruct the country, even if the whole of the nation's oil revenue was used for that purpose. Saddam—and Iraq—faced a stark future and so he pressed Kuwait for further help. But Kuwait—confident in the backing of Saudi Arabia and the United States—was no longer willing to help him and was more concerned about repairing her own relations with Iran. To make matters worse Kuwait's increased production of oil was lowering the world price, severely hitting Iraq's national earnings, which were almost entirely in the form of oil revenue. Saddam therefore increased the pressure on Kuwait. He asked for the entire income earned from the Ratga oil well, situated on the border between Iraq and Kuwait. When the Kuwaitis refused, Saddam declared that the oil was his anyway because the entire area belonged to Iraq. Convinced that he would not be able to get satisfaction from the Kuwaitis, Saddam had two alternatives: either to back down or to press on and occupy Kuwait. The first was not really an option if he hoped to retain his position of supremacy in Iraq and the Arab world. As a gambler he had little choice but to go ahead with his aggression.

It was against this background that the meeting between America's ambassador April Glaspie and the Iraqi dictator took place on July 25, 1990—just a week before Iraq invaded Kuwait. At this meeting, it has been claimed—in an Iraqi transcript of the conversation that took place between Saddam and Glaspie—that the American ambassador told Saddam that America had "no opinion on the Arab-Arab conflict, like your border dispute with Kuwait." If this was true it was all Saddam needed for him to give the green light to his generals to occupy Kuwait. For her part, Glaspie found herself in an unenviable—perhaps an impossible—position, needing to convey a double message to the dictator: that the United States was alarmed by his threats toward Kuwait and yet still wished to maintain good relations with him. This dual message was the result of apparently conflicting signals that Saddam had been sending to Washington. On the one hand, he liked to portray himself in the image of the ravening wolf of the Arab world, always ready to snatch any tidbit that might fall his way, even if that meant one of America's friends in the Gulf, like Kuwait. On the other hand, he valued America's friendship, particularly as he had received such nice presents in the past, like military and intelligence equipment. Moreover, Iraq would always be a receptive export market for the United States and the Bush administration knew it could rely on Saddam to resist any expansion by Iran. It had been a comfortable arrangement as long as American politicians did not look too closely into their consciences, but now questions were being asked in Congress about Saddam's violations of human rights.

On July 25 Ms. Glaspie found Saddam in a dangerous mood. He had been angered by news that America was planning joint maneuvers with the tiny navy of the United Arab Emirates, another of the juicy morsels that might have fallen Iraq's way. Was Washington now joining with the oil-rich sheikhs of the Emirates to balk him? Encouraged when Saddam returned from a telephone conversation with President Mubarak of Egypt saying that he would not "solve the problems of Kuwait by violence" Glaspie spoke to him as follows:

I admire your extraordinary efforts to rebuild your country. I know you need funds. We understand that and our opinion is that you should have the opportunity to rebuild your country. But we have no opinion of the Arab-Arab conflicts, like your border disagreement with Kuwait.

I was in the American embassy in Kuwait during the late sixties. The instruction we had during this period was that we should express no opinion on this issue and that the issue is not associated with America. James Baker has directed our official spokesmen to emphasize this instruction. We hope you can solve this problem using any suitable methods via Klibi or via President Mubarak. All that we hope is that these issues are solved quickly. With regard to all of this, can I ask you to see how the issue appears to us?

My assessment after 25 years service in this area is that your objective must have strong backing from your Arab brothers. I now speak of oil. But you, Mr. President, have fought through a horrific and painful war. Frankly, we can only see that you have deployed massive troops in the south. Normally that would not be any of our business. But when this happens in the context of what you said on your national day, then when we read the details in the two letters of the foreign minister, then when we see the Iraqi point of view that the measures taken by the UAE and Kuwait is, in the final analysis, parallel to military aggression against Iraq, then it would be reasonable for me to be concerned. And for this reason, I received an instruction to ask you, in the spirit of friendship—not in the spirit of confrontation—regarding your intentions.[1]

In her efforts to conciliate Saddam as well as warn him Glaspie was undoubtedly giving him the wrong impression. In later evidence to Congress after the war she insisted that she had added a sentence, left out in the Iraqi version of the interview, to the effect that "We [the United States] insist you settle your disputes with Kuwait nonviolently." Whether she did say this or not we will never know. In its definite—almost curtly aggressive—form the sentence seems very much out of sympathy with the rest of her words to him. In any case, whatever she said, she failed to convince Saddam that the United States wanted him to act peacefully. There was nothing in the American attitude— or indeed in the previous decade's policy—that hinted that the United States was being prepared to oppose Iraqi expansion. At this crucial moment Glaspie—and through her, President Bush—failed to give Iraq the sort of incontestable signal that America would resist with force Iraq's occupation of Kuwait. This was a serious diplomatic blunder that made military confrontation unavoidable.

Yet everything could have been different—and this is not merely a pointless exercise in the use of hindsight. The evidence was there for those who wished to see it and for those who were not blinded by hostility to Iran. While America still saw Iran as the fundamental threat to the region there was a tendency to overlook data that appeared to contradict established policy assumptions. Thus satellite photographs that revealed the massive buildup of Iraqi troops and armor on the Kuwait border were not taken seriously. Western defense attachés had even left their offices in Baghdad at the end of July to watch the massive troop convoys leaving the city and blocking the highways leading south. Yet Saddam Hussein was thought to be bluffing or—if serious—only concerned with seizing the oil-rich islands off the coast of Kuwait. This was an incredible conclusion, particularly because the Pentagon's leading Middle Eastern expert, Pat Lang, decided the day before the invasion of Kuwait that all this activity was more than a bluff. Saddam must mean it this time. The UN Security Council certainly did not see it this way. On the same day a meeting of the five permanent members took place and concluded, in the words of British ambassador Sir Crispin Tickell, that "the heat appeared to have gone out of the immediate crisis"!

For years American diplomats had overlooked the human rights abuses of Saddam's regime and his many threats to Israel because they believed that he was far less of a threat than Shi'ite Iran. And this narrow interpretation of Gulf politics had even encouraged successive American administrations to see Saddam as a friend—on the basis that any enemy of an enemy is a friend. This resulted in America trading grain and military hardware for oil. During Iraq's struggle with Iran, the United States even went so far as to share intelligence and instruct Iraqi personnel in the use of American systems. In view of Saddam's known hostility to Israel, this was a dangerously shortsighted policy.

American Middle East experts had encouraged President Bush to believe that Saddam's extreme behavior could be moderated and that he was always susceptible to bribery based on the military hardware he liked to parade in public like the Prussian kings of old—almost like toy soldiers. But again their judgment of Saddam was a false one, and it paid little heed to his ruthless record in coming to power and maintaining power. Saddam was an opportunist and a man who regarded moderation as a weakness to be exploited. What the Americans saw as saber-rattling toward Kuwait and Israel was nothing of the sort. Once he felt strong enough Saddam would certainly use his army against weaker neighbors. He had little fear of the United States because he felt that in spite of her enormous technological power she did not have the spirit to fight a war. The example of Vietnam, as well as more recent examples in Iran, Lebanon and Grenada, had shown that the Americans did not have the stomach to take casualties, something he was quite prepared for his own people to accept on his behalf. As he told April Glaspie:

> I do not belittle you. But I hold this view by looking at the geography and nature of American society into account. Yours is a society which cannot accept 10,000 dead in one battle.[2]

With Bush's administration viewing Saddam's hostile moves toward Kuwait as merely part of a bluff, they never

gave the Iraqi leader any reason to believe that they cared
enough about Kuwait to use force to evict him. He was
prepared to face any amount of diplomatic pressure—he
thrived on it—but he did not believe that America would
consider Kuwait worth the bones of a single U.S. Marine.

Even after the American-led coalition of states had been
created against him, Saddam did not believe that America
meant to fight. As he told Secretary Baker, "Your Arab
allies will desert you. They will not kill other Arabs. Your
alliance will crumble and you will be left lost in the desert.
You don't know the desert because you have never ridden
on a horse or a camel." Saddam's confidence seemed complete. But why was this so? If the United States had made
it clear that she was prepared to fight and to bring virtually
the full weight of her military potential to bear on Iraq, how
could Saddam not have believed her? In the final analysis,
of course, the Americans were unable to accept that in
dealing with an Islamic dictator they were facing the problem—as they always did with Libya's Colonel Qaddafi—of
the closed mind. Saddam Hussein did not surround himself with ministers who challenged his perceptions. Instead he was constantly fed with intelligence that fueled
his own beliefs. No minister would survive long who told
Saddam too much of the truth. And in the absence of internal dissent to suggest alternatives, Saddam was not prepared to listen to foreign diplomats who challenged his own
views. Gerald Hopple has used the term "egomaniacal, al-
beit pragmatic" about Saddam Hussein, and too many experienced American diplomats lacked the capacity to
advise President Bush on how to deal with this kind of
Messianic figure. In the end he chose to fight. But as the
allied forces swept through the Iraqi positions they found
that they were fighting phantoms—figments of Saddam
Hussein's capacity to bluff a gullible American president.
The "Mother of all battles" was little more than a demonstration—at enormous cost—of how to crush a walnut with
a sledgehammer.

Postscript: A Rogues' Gallery?

As the world stumbles from one crisis to another, incompetence remains an ever present feature of human activity. Its manifestation in military affairs may be inevitable, since the military profession imposes stresses of an intensity and nature that far exceed those of any other. Yet while it may be possible to understand why our service and political leaders mismanage military affairs it is no easier to forgive them. Admittedly generals who fail are no longer crucified as in ancient Carthage or guillotined as in revolutionary France. Yet is it right for such men to return home to write their memoirs, publish them more or less successfully, and fight and refight their old battles in the correspondence columns of newspapers or with salt and pepper pots on the dining tables of their clubs? Is their incompetence any more acceptable now than it was in the past? It has been my contention—and the thesis of this book—that we can only hope to avoid the mistakes of the future by a thorough knowledge of the mistakes of the past. There is no more reason now for the public to accept the frivolous wasting of human life in unnecessary, preventable military disasters than there is for incompetence in the accounting methods of large companies or safety methods in the food industry to pass by without a public outcry. And though for most people the military world is a closed one, hedged around by an unscalable wall of secrecy, the public has a voice and should be prepared to use it. The mere fact that the military profession is so adept at concealing its incompetence is no reason for it to remain unchallenged. In this book I set out to study aspects of military incompetence, notably within the armed services of the United States. At no point have I suggested that the military history of the United States is more scarred with such failings than that of any other country, merely that it does provide striking examples that may help us to understand the problem of incompetence in high places.

Even as young a nation as the U.S.A. has stored up for itself a deep fund of military failure, much of it hidden from the general public by the apparent successes enjoyed by America's armed forces. The 1812 war against Britain, for example, has been remembered most often for Andrew Jackson's victory at New Orleans in 1815 and the heroic victories over the Royal Navy by American frigates in single ship actions. Yet, as I have shown, a triumvirate of generals—Hull, Dearborn and von Rensselaer—so mismanaged the invasion of Canada that they heaped humiliation on the young nation. And the costly hit-and-miss method of officer selection used by President Lincoln in the Civil War can only be read with great pain. Although he finally got the man he wanted in Ulysses S. Grant, it was only after he had given John Pope, Ambrose Burnside and Joseph Hooker free rein to squander lives in proving their own incapacity. The dead at Second Manassas, Fredericksburg and Chancellorsville would have applauded Lincoln's final choice if they had lived to see it. Nor, as I have shown, was Grant himself immune from failure. His loss of self-control at Cold Harbor was as destructive in terms of his own men as Burnside's at Fredericksburg.

In recent times incompetence has undergone a period of evolution so that its manifestation at the highest level now forms part of a grand strategy in which politicians play an ever greater role. Examples of this kind are very common in the Second World War and in more recent encounters, such as Vietnam, Korea and the Gulf War. Yet the mistakes are the same—only perhaps larger—and the victims suffer the same agonies, whether wasted in the forests of the American Northwest, on Cemetery Ridge or in the freezing waters of the English Channel. What is different now is the public realization that military and political leaders are not free from error. Even the greatest figures—Lincoln, Grant, Lee, Roosevelt, MacArthur—sometimes had clay on their boots.

In Europe the First World War marked a watershed in

the public appreciation of military competence and otherwise. Developments in the media exposed people to the true horrors of modern warfare as well as to the consequences of military and political incompetence. After 1918 the idea that the generals had been mere butchers, wasting a whole generation of young men through a failure to master the complexities of modern warfare, became prevalent. Even the United States, whose late commitment of troops on a massive scale saved her from the obscene bloodletting of 1915–17, had generals unwilling to learn from the mistakes of their British and French allies and who tried to make up for lost time, squandering troops in gung-ho assaults, as at Belleau Wood in 1918. Only the end of the fighting in November 1918 prevented the Americans from adding even more names to the already overloaded ossuaries of northern France.

Meanwhile, the politicians and strategists—shielded from the front-line fighting by distance, or telephone lines, or radar screens, or simply concrete bunkers—rarely saw the blood on their own hands. Seated in leather chairs, behind oak desks and in wood-paneled offices, they called on the military to make their sacrifices. In the name of the people they lay waste those who voted for them. Distanced from the fighting by the filtering presence of staff officers and commanders desperate to impress, the politicians are able to deal in concepts and statistics, far removed from the individual dead of the battlefield. A crime is more easily accepted if it is too large to be defined in individual terms. The mistakes of the politician are more costly than the blunders of his generals or the mistakes of junior officers. The politician deals in death but it has not got a human face. In the final analysis it is for you to decide whether the military commanders of whom I have written were culpable and thoughtless, or merely pawns in a system they were helpless to control—rogues, in fact, or victims.

There are few more poignant scenes in American history than the one of the Union troops, the night before the attack on Marye's Heights at Fredericksburg in 1862, writing their names and addresses on their handkerchiefs and sewing them on the backs of their uniforms so that their bodies could be identified after the battle. Any general who saw this would have done well to rethink his tactics for the next day. Yet Ambrose Burnside went ahead with a plan

as foolish and as deadly as any in military history. In just
one small part of the battlefield six thousand of his men
were to fall—as they knew they would. Why was Burnside
alone—apparently—in not understanding what would happen? Was he so distant from the battlefield that he could
not see, or so stupid that he could not understand, or so
desperate that he did not care anymore? Was the Burnside
of Fredericksburg a butcher, then, and a worthy member
of any military rogues' gallery? Or was he merely the likable
"bewhiskered buffoon" that is often depicted, an Oliver
Hardy with a line in the darkest of black comedies? Rogue
or buffoon, Burnside should have the right of reply in the
Court of History. With John Pope at one shoulder and Joe
Hooker at the other, and with Nathaniel Banks, Benjamin
Butler, John McClernand, Franz Sigel and a host of other
failed commanders around him, why should Burnside not
point the finger of accusation at the men who did well out
of the war, the successful generals whose details fill the
pages of books of great commanders? Were the men Grant
sent to unnecessary slaughter at Cold Harbor any less dead
than those Burnside squandered at Marye's Heights? And
had Grant's reasons been any sounder than Burnside's?
Was it not true that Grant had lost his patience—an eminently human failing in a lesser man but unforgivable in a
man upon whose self-control the lives of thousands depended? And why should Lee sleep soundly when the cries
of the slaughtered Virginians squandered in Pickett's
charge on Cemetery Ridge are heard as echoes in the night?
Lee had been guilty of hubris and had felt his men—and
presumably himself—unbeatable. Why was it any worse for
poor William Hull to believe himself eminently beatable at
Detroit in 1812? At least his men lived to tell the tale, even
if his country felt the shame. And as Burnside stands before the Court of History what does he think as the shades
from this book—Wentworth, Burgoyne, St. Clair, Whitelocke, Kearney, Rosecrans, Fredendall and so many others—pass by, men condemned by history as incompetents
yet few guilty of more than being promoted beyond their
capacity? In other walks of life their failures would have
been personal tragedies but no more. Only in their role as
military leaders did they have the capacity to inflict death
and suffering on thousands of their fellow men and shame
and disaster on their countries. Few if any of them had

more than the average human failings. In a sense, therefore, military incompetence is frequently no more than a problem in personnel selection—Burgoyne, after all, was a more than adequate playwright. As he surrendered to his onetime subordinate, Horatio Gates, he should have appreciated the irony of the situation. And so should we.

Military promotion seems to involve a law of diminishing returns, by which able junior officers become less able to cope with their duties the more they are promoted. This— the Peter Principle—is at the root of most cases of incompetence. An ability to follow orders—a prerequisite for promotion in the armed forces—does not guarantee a similar capacity to give them. And each blunderer in this book had his accomplice—often a faceless bureaucrat or distant politician—who made the choice that he should enjoy high military command with all that that entails: perhaps not a Carthaginian crucifixion, but instead trial and punishment by the writers of military history.

Sources

The Siege of Cartagena, 1741
1 Smollett, Tobias. *Roderick Random.* New York: Fawcett Publications Inc., 1962, p. 198.
2 Smollett, p. 199.
3 Smollett, p. 200.

The Campaign of Saratoga, 1977
1 Lunt, James. *John Burgoyne of Saratoga.* London: Macdonald and Janes', 1976, p. 127.
2 Willett, William M. *A Narrative of the Military Actions of Colonel Marinus Willett, taken chiefly from his own manuscripts.* New York: Carvill, 1831, pp. 131–33.
3 von Riedesel, Baron Friedrich. *Memoirs and Letters and Journals of Major-Gen. Riedesel During His Residence in America.* Edited by Max von Eelking. Translated by W. L. Stone. New York, 1868.
4 Commager, H. S., and R. B. Morris, eds. *The Spirit of 'Seventy-Six.* Indianapolis: Bobbs-Merrill, 1958, p. 579.
5 Trevelyan, Sir George Otto. *The American Revolution.* Vol. 3. London, 1907, p. 184.

The Expedition to Buenos Aires, 1806–1807
1 Fortescue, Hon. J. W. *A History of the British Army.* Volume 5, 1803–1807. London: Macmillan, 1910, p. 416.
2 Fortescue, pp. 430–35.

The Loss of Detroit, 1812
1 *The Historical Register of the United States.* Part 2 (1812–13). Edited by T. H. Palmer, Vol. 2 (Official Documents), p. 50.

The Battle of San Pasqual, 1846
1 Clarke, Dwight L. *Stephen Watts Kearney: Soldier of the West.* Norman: University of Oklahoma Press, 1961, p. 203.

The Battle of Gettysburg, 1863
1 Commager, H. S., ed. *The Blue and the Gray.* Vol. 2. Indianapolis: Bobbs-Merrill, 1950, p. 591.
2 Commager, *The Blue and the Gray,* p. 637.

The Battle of Chickamauga, 1863

1 McPherson, James M. *Battle Cry of Freedom*. Oxford University Press, 1988, p. 665.
2 Buel, C. C. and R. U. Johnson, eds. *Battles and Leaders of the Civil War*. Vol. 3. New York: The Century Co., 1888, pp. 641–42.
3 Buel, pp. 641–42.
4 Buel, p. 644.
5 Buel, p. 644.
6 Buel, p. 644.
7 Buel, p. 644.
8 Buel, p. 663.
9 Buel, p. 663.

The Battle of Cold Harbor, 1864

1 McPherson, p. 735.
2 Porter, Horace. *Campaigning with Grant*. New York, 1897, pp. 69–70.
3 Catton, Bruce. *A Stillness at Appomattox*. New York: Doubleday, 1953, p. 157.
4 Catton, p. 162.
5 Catton, pp. 170–71.

The Battle of Manila Bay, 1898

1 Dewey, George. *Autobiography*. London, 1913, p. 192.
2 Mitchell, D. W. *History of the Modern American Navy*. New York: Knopf, 1946, p. 66.
3 Ellicott, John M. *The Defense of Manila*. Proceedings of the United States Naval Institute, 1900, pp. 279–85.
4 Dewey, p. 225.
5 Dewey, p. 225.

France: The Problem of Armored Warfare, 1940

1 Horne, Alistair. *To Lose a Battle*. New York: Little, Brown & Co., 1969, p. 140.
2 Horne, p. 165.
3 Horne, p. 159.
4 Horne, p. 222.
5 Horne, p. 177.
6 Horne, p. 385.
7 Horne, pp. 385–86.
8 Horne, pp. 416–17.

The Battles of Sidi Bou Zid and the Kasserine Pass, 1943

1 Truscott, L. K. *Command Missions*. New York, 1954, p. 124.
2 Messenger, Charles. *The Tunisian Campaign*. London: Ian Allen, 1982, p. 40.

3 Macksey, Kenneth. *Crucible of Power*. London: Hutchinson, 1969, pp. 129–30.
4 Eisenhower, Dwight D. *Crusade in Europe*. New York, 1948, p. 157.
5 Messenger, p. 41.
6 Jackson, W. G. F. *The North African Campaign*. London: Batsford, 1975, pp. 340–41.
7 Messenger, p. 48.
8 Messenger, p. 51.
9 Jackson, p. 345.

Exercise Tiger, 1944

1 Small, K. *The Forgotten Dead*. London: Bloomsbury, 1988, pp. 13–14.
2 Small, pp. 15–16.
3 Small, p. 27.
4 Small, pp. 68–69.

The Battle of Leyte Gulf, 1944

1 Jackson, p. 347.
2 Woodward, C. Vann. *The Battle for Leyte Gulf*. New York: Macmillan, 1947, p. 107.
3 Humble, Richard. *The Japanese High Seas Fleet*. New York: Ballantine, 1973, p. 136.

Korea, 1950

1 Hastings, Max. *The Korean War*. New York: Simon and Schuster, 1987, p. 111.
2 Alexander, Bevin. *Korea: The Lost War*. New York: Hippocrene, 1986, p. 247.
3 Hastings, p. 213.
4 Hastings, p. 242.
5 Hastings, p. 243.

Vietnam: The Media War, 1968

1 Arnold, James. *Tet Offensive 1968*. London: Osprey, 1990, p. 88.
2 Karnow, Stanley. *Vietnam: A History*. New York: Viking Press, 1983, p. 523.
3 Karnow, p. 523.
4 Karnow, p. 548.

The Iranian Hostages, 1980

1 Bolger, Daniel P. *Americans at War*. New York: Presidio, 1988, p. 119.

The Gulf War, 1991
1 Bennis, Phyllis and Michael Moushabeck, eds. *Beyond the Storm: A Gulf Crisis Reader*. Glaspie-Hussein Transcript, Appendix B. New York: Olive Branch Press, 1991, pp. 391–96.
2 Bennis, pp. 391–96.

Index